The Dickinson Sublime

The Dickinson Sublime

Gary Lee Stonum

THE UNIVERSITY OF WISCONSIN PRESS

The University of Wisconsin Press
114 North Murray Street
Madison, Wisconsin 53715

3 Henrietta Street
London WC2E 8LU, England

Library of Congress Cataloging-in-Publication Data
Stonum, Gary Lee.
The Dickinson sublime / Gary Lee Stonum.
232 pp.   cm. — (The Wisconsin project on American writers)
Includes bibliographical references.
1. Dickinson, Emily, 1830–1886—Criticism and interpretation.
2. Dickinson, Emily, 1830–1886—Aesthetics. 3. Sublime, The, in
literature. 4. Romanticism—United States. I. Title. II. Series.
PS1541.Z5S88   1990
811'.4—dc20   89-38996
ISBN 0-299-12460-6   CIP

To Marilyn and Lee,
without whom nothing

Contents

Preface

Because this book was written expressly for a series designed to re-examine American literature from new and theoretically informed perspectives, I had better forewarn any readers expecting poststructuralist fireworks. Although I would happily claim allegiance to much such thinking, the goals of the present study are more primitive. Contemporary textual and cultural theory shines brightest when challenging hegemonic ideas and canonical interpretations. With respect to Dickinson's poetry, however, we do not yet have such things. Although her poetry has long been highly regarded, as a body of work it has so far resisted critical appropriation.

A different warning may be in order for those who get annoyed by polemics over the so-called secondary literature, regarding such matters as a distraction from the main tasks of interpretation and understanding. Dickinson's elusiveness stems largely from the challenge her poetry offers to some widespread critical preconceptions, I maintain. As a result, I take quite seriously the assumptions and the consequences of certain critical views, particularly ones bold enough to measure Dickinson's work and find it lacking.

The aim of this study, warnings aside, is to identify the conception of poetry motivating Dickinson's literary enterprise and binding her writings into what I argue is a coherent body of work. That conception is a version of the romantic sublime, the most important and distinctive features of which are an affective understanding of poetry, a complexly motivated practice of postponing the normally climactic moment of the sublime, and an orientation both ethical and rhetorical toward provoking the reader's imagination without dictating to it.

The first chapter briefly surveys the unsettled state of Dickinson scholarship in order to identify its tacit commitment to an author-centered esthetics, which I argue is contrary to Dickinson's own assumptions. By means of an inquiry into the motives for her conspicuously idiosyncratic style, the second chapter then locates the origin of these assumptions in Dickinson's allegiance to Elizabeth Barrett Browning and the English poetic tradition she represented.

In Chapter 3 both the rationale for Dickinson's style and the appeal of the sublime are derived from her endorsement of cherishing power. The chapter thus introduces the argument that Dickinson is preeminently a poet of the romantic sublime. The argument is then extended in the following chapters. In Chapter 4 I examine Dickinson's beliefs about language, art, and authorship, proposing that they can collectively be subsumed under her commitment to a rhetoric of stimulus. Chapter 5 examines what is distinctive about Dickinson's version of the sublime, finding it mainly in her strategic postponement of finality or closure. Chapter 6 examines some of the main thematic implications of the Dickinson sublime, chiefly those having to do with mastery. A brief conclusion then summarizes the main points of the argument and suggests some implications for Dickinson's place in American literary history.

This book has been a long time in the making, probably too long, and over the period I have been helped by more persons than I can name. Frank Lentricchia deserves particular recognition for a service he may not even have known that he rendered. It was only at his invitation to contribute to the Wisconsin Project that I first gave thought to a full-scale study of Emily Dickinson. Years later William Cain and Martha Woodmansee each read the manuscript with the kind of generously scrupulous attention every writer hopes to receive, and each made a number of contributions to the final form of the book. I owe thanks as well to Robert S. Baker and Frank Lentricchia for their comments on the manuscript. Allen Fitchen has been a model of patience and encouragement.

For financial support of my research, I thank Case Western Reserve University, which twice granted me leave from teaching and administrative duties.

Many friends and colleagues have cheered the work on in one way or another, and one group of them has especially fortified the ideals of a scholarly community. I refer to the band of critics responsible for founding the new Emily Dickinson International Society, particularly Jane Eberwein, Margaret Freeman, Suzanne Juhasz, Cristanne Miller, Barbara Mossberg, Vivian Pollak, and Martha Nell Smith.

Earlier versions of material in Chapters 3 and 5 appeared in *The American Sublime*, ed. Mary Arensberg (SUNY Press, 1986) and in the *Dayton Review* 19 (Winter 1987–88).

The Dickinson Sublime

I

A Poet without a Project?
A Poetry without Scope or Structure?

By now one would expect Emily Dickinson's poetry to have been fully appropriated by academic criticism. For better or worse, a triumph of modern literary studies has been the thoroughness with which it has interpreted, classified, and theorized all those authors deemed to be major artists. Such assimilation into a critical discourse may have shortcomings, even confessed ones, but it almost always succeeds in establishing the general terms and categories within which a writer's work is understood. The appropriation of a writer leaves considerable room for discussion within the established categories, and it never wholly rules out the emergence of sharply new perspectives. Yet once a writer has achieved sufficient stature, some broad framework for understanding has almost always been put in place.

Emily Dickinson is the conspicuous exception. An astonishing and apparently unprecedented gap exists between the certainty that she is a major poet and the uncertainty about what her business as a poet might be. Although her work continues to delight readers and critics, it also eludes the usual forms of critical domestication. We remain particularly unable to define Dickinson's general literary enterprise or even to be certain that her poetry manifests any coherent set of aims and accomplishments.

One measure of the gap between acclaim and uncertainty is supplied by the major anthologies of American literature. All agree that she is one of the nation's handful of essential authors and accordingly provide generous space for her writings, 66 poems in the Norton, 68 in the Macmillan, and 62 in the Harper.[1] On the other hand, the editors of these volumes are perforce obliged to select which sixty or so

3

of her 1,775 extant poems are the best, the most important, or the most representative. They disagree substantially. Of the 105 poems included in at least one anthology, fewer than a quarter (25 poems) are common to all three, and fully 43 poems appear in only one. By comparison more than three quarters of the space each anthology devotes to Whitman consists of poems the other two also print. In other words, all three anthologies depict in their samples of his work roughly the same, presumably essential, significant, or representative Whitman, reflecting the cultural consensus such anthologies are obliged to respect. Likewise, they give us largely the same Emerson, Melville, Frost, and so on, for these are all writers whose aims, achievements, and literary identities we have been able to recognize satisfactorily. Yet the anthologies are unable to identify an essential Dickinson. The divergent selections do not even represent distinct but contested views of Dickinson, for although such views exist none has been commanding or comprehensive enough to bring her poetry sharply into focus. As the editors of the Harper anthology admit,

The almost two thousand poems in the Dickinson canon can scarcely be fully present even to Dickinson critics, let alone to the common reader. A search through Dickinson's complete poems never fails to turn up poems of great value.[2]

Why is this so? Why is it that, unlike every other classic American writer, Emily Dickinson has eluded all attempts to define her achievements or to diagram their general shape and structure? It is not that she has escaped critical attention, of course, or that such scholarship has been in vain. The continuing flood of thematic and stylistic criticism has markedly enhanced our ability to read her often challenging poems and to appreciate them one by one. It has often also been able to make good sense out of themes, images, and techniques to be found in various ad hoc groupings of poems. Only in very limited ways, however, has this criticism supplied us with a vantage point on Dickinson's entire career or on whatever designs and accomplishments might be central to it. Consider, for instance, the genteel categories in which Dickinson's poems were grouped in early editions: love, God, nature, and so on. We may smile condescendingly at such topical headings now, yet we have certainly failed to identify any more satisfactory principle of selection and arrangement.

What we lack is a sufficiently comprehensive and credible vantage point on Dickinson's poetry as a whole. It has not been at all obvious to readers and critics that her work has any discernible overall shape. We have been similarly unable to agree that her writing adheres to any set of consistent literary principles, let alone what those principles might be, or that her poetry is finally coherent enough to be regarded as a unitary enterprise. Indeed, so conspicuously resistant has Dickinson seemed to the norms of literary vocation that her poetry can be cited without comment or need for explanation as the paradigmatic example of an anticareer.[3]

The only comparable situation I can cite is William Blake's reputation before 1947, the year Northrop Frye's *Fearful Symmetry* first persuaded readers that, contrary to the opinion of all but cultists, Blake's poetry was not only coherent but unusually systematic. A difference is that Blake gained a secure poetic reputation only in the wake of Frye. Dickinson, by contrast, has been widely acclaimed as a great poet even though the coherence of her poetry remains an unsettled question.

Dickinson's poetry certainly could not be called systematic or programmatic, but it does have a more coherent design than has been generally recognized. We have been slow to grasp this design not because Dickinson's critics have not done their job or because they have failed to take her work seriously enough (this was arguably often the case with Blake) but because the coherence of Dickinson's literary enterprise is of an unusual kind. Indeed, it is best approached by examining how and why the poetry has so resisted our efforts to define its aims and achievements.

One obstacle is certainly the sheer number of poems she wrote. To read through them all is always to risk the vertigo characterizing the reader's sublime, a bewilderment in the face of some vast surfeit of meaning. On the other hand, among Dickinson's coevals both Tennyson and Hardy wrote more separate poems than she did, and their collected works do not present quite the same challenge to our faculties. A second and equally apparent obstacle stems from Dickinson's reluctance to publish her poems. We accordingly lack some of the social, rhetorical, and institutional contexts that can frame a body of writing and guide our understanding of it. Here too, however, Dickinson's case is not unique. Both Hopkins and Kafka left the majority of their writings unpublished during their lifetimes, and in neither case did the circumstance create such an uncertainty about their purposes and accomplishments.

A more fundamental barrier can be observed in the complaints most frequently leveled against Dickinson's poetry by unsympathetic critics. Half a century ago, for instance, R. P. Blackmur charged that her "relation to the business of poetry" was helplessly "private and eccentric."[4] The adjectives are familiar ones in the literature on Dickinson, but whereas others have attached them mainly to the idiosyncrasies of her life in Amherst, Blackmur deploys them to characterize the waywardness of her literary practices.

The first person to make such a charge was Thomas Wentworth Higginson, also the first person outside Dickinson's immediate circle to read any number of her poems. In his second letter to Dickinson Higginson apparently called her poetry spasmodic. (Or so she quotes him; his letter has not survived.) The epithet is not quite a denunciation of Dickinson's irregular prosody, grammar, and diction, as it has sometimes later been taken to be. Higginson refers to a then recently voguish group of English poets, derisively called the Spasmodics by their detractors. Alexander Smith, Sidney Dobell, and others (including the Tennyson of *Maud*) had attracted considerable attention at midcentury for their extravagant, naturalistic, and metrically irregular style of verse, as well as for the social protest frequently evident in their poems. The reviewers were generally hostile, however, and the Spasmodic School quickly became a byword for literary sensationalism. Arthur Hugh Clough, reviewing Smith's *Life-Drama* in the June 1853 number of the *North American Review*, is typical in his judgment if more tempered than many in his tone. "He writes, it would almost seem, under the impression that the one business of the poet is to coin metaphors and similes." Although granting Smith a real "continuity of poetic purpose," Clough points out that the coherence of his poetry is vitiated because the reader is "incessantly called off to look at this and look at that."[5]

By calling Dickinson's poetry spasmodic then, Higginson diagnoses it as suffering from an amply precedented tendency to sacrifice coherent artistic design to extravagant local effects. Dickinson would have understood the diagnosis thoroughly. She had read *Life-Drama* the same month Clough's review appeared in the United States, and her first reaction was similar to his. She wrote to her brother Austin that the volume contained "some wonderful figures, as ever I met in my life" but that the poems "are not very coherent" (*Letters*, 256).[6] The contrast would seem to be between the poetry's impressive tropes and its suspect unity (although "figures" could refer to Smith's characters as well as to his figures of speech or thought). Two weeks later, revising her initial doubts, she wrote again to say, "I admire the Poems very much" (*Letters*, 260). Her responses to Higginson similarly acknowledge a disjunction between local intensity and overall coherence, and they similarly waver over the respective merits of the two. At first she replied with elaborate mock deference: "You think my gait 'spasmodic'—I am in danger—sir—You think me 'uncontrolled'—I have no tribunal" (*Letters*, 409). Two months later, however, she softened, forwarding additional poems in the hope that Higginson would find them "more orderly" and seeking to justify her having sought him out as a preceptor: "I had no Monarch in my life, and cannot rule myself, and when I try to organize—my little Force explodes" (*Letters*, 414).

Higginson and Dickinson both recognize a split between force or intensity on the one side and design or coherence on the other. They agree further in that he implicitly and she more explicitly link force to figurative language.[7] Their agreement reverberates throughout the subsequent history of responses to Dickinson's poetry. On one hand, we find widespread acknowledgment of the singular intensity and power of Dickinson's language, even among unfavorable reactions to her poetry. On the other hand, we find equally widespread puzzlement and sometimes also exasperation about the poetry's shape and coherence. "It is easier to hold in mind and sort out the plays of Shakespeare or the novels of George Eliot, for they have scope and structure," J. V. Cunningham has grumbled.[8] David Porter, who has devoted much of his career to holding Dickinson's poems in mind, goes considerably further. "The special experience of reading Dickinson is that there is an unprecedented lack of leading, or organizing, of general direction. It is like driving in a shopping-plaza parking lot."[9]

As these frustrated remarks suggest, Dickinson conspicuously neglects much of the cuing we expect every poet's work ultimately to provide. The neglect challenges some of our most persistent assumptions about literary coherence, integrity, and design. It is not clear whether Dickinson challenges these assumptions deliberately, but a challenge nevertheless does arise as an immediate consequence of how she understands the value and function of poetry. As should be evident from her response to Higginson's diagnosis, Dickinson does not repudiate the value of coherence. Yet throughout her work and in a variety of ways she persistently questions several common assumptions about the poet's enterprise.[10]

Porter supplies the most exhaustive litany of Dickinson's negligence, and in so doing he also voices with unusual boldness several key expectations about what a major poet's business ought to be. One of our most distinguished interpreters of Dickinson's poetry and probably the single most thorough student of her compositional practices, Porter attempts in his second book on the poet to derive from those practices a comprehensive view of her poetics and then use that view to locate her place in American literary history. The poet fails him in almost every way. Reluctantly but inexorably Porter accuses Dickinson of artistic irresponsibility for neglecting to publish, for neglecting to delete the chaff from the wheat in her work, for neglecting to title her poems and thus signal even the nominal finality and the minimal impress of authorial control that titles can supply, for neglecting to define or even broach an *ars poetica*, for neglecting to attempt the magnitude of a sustained poem (much less a deliberate chef d'oeuvre), for neglecting in any other way to rank her poems according to centrality or importance, for neglecting to develop or advance during the course of her career, and most of all for neglecting to provide any cumulative wholeness to the body of her work. All these departures from the customary business of literature make Dickinson "the only major American poet without a project." Dickinson's amorphous body of work lacks even the unbidden coherence that a unified sensibility would supply. Presiding over Dickinson's "canon of odds and ends," Porter can discover only "hyperconsciousness without system or order."[11]

Dickinson disappoints Porter in two related ways. First, in identifying a version of the gap between force and design Porter tendentiously charges that Dickinson possesses a hopelessly inconclusive, finless mind. The verbal brilliance of her poetry is finally an "idiolect of confusion" betraying the "instinctive formlessness of her thought."[12] Relatively few other readers and critics would go this far, but most would agree that Porter's standard is appropriate. Indecisiveness, evasion, and an inability to engage reality do not greatly recommend an author, we can probably agree. We ask of poetry that it give us some achieved wealth of meaning or at least a reasonably finished vision of what the poems set out to examine. A poetry "Without Order / Or Design, or Apparent Action" will not suffice (742).[13]

The more credible charge Porter brings against Dickinson is that she fails to fulfill the vocational responsibilities of a serious author. His litany of neglect reveals a clear and plainly factual difference between Dickinson's authorial practice and that of virtually all her peers and contemporaries. Other writers exert considerably more control over how their works are to be read and over what aims and standards they are to be judged against. More important, they presume they have the authority thus to direct our responses, an authority so basic to our assumptions about literary communication as to be usually almost invisible. Like Porter, we expect such guidance from authors; it is part of their obligation to us. Moreover, fulfilling that obligation well is one mark of a major author's achievement.

Porter's assumptions about normal and desirable literary practice indicate an overwhelmingly author-centered esthetics, one which in his and various other forms has long been central to our understanding of literature and which has especially dominated romantic and postromantic values. A major poet should have some more or less deliberate project that binds the writings into a coherent whole. Failing that, a major poet ought to construct or be blessed with a distinct literary identity that will underwrite the integrity of her endeavors. Failing even that, she ought to embrace some external principle that will allow her to establish the needed control over her work. Possibly, as Blackmur primly supposes, she should submit herself to the discipline entailed by the established business of poetry. Such various means of organizing a literary career will not dominate each and every text or answer every question her readers may have, but they will at least give some shape and direction to the poet's work.

In other words, the author is the indispensable source of coherence and integrity. Literary masterpieces presuppose the idea of the author as master. Even with lesser works we readers expect to take our cues from an authorial figure, whether we understand this being as the writer's everyday self, as an imaginative construct in its own right, or merely as the ghostly principle of intentionality activating and ordering a text. Furthermore, our expectations about the author's directive role lend themselves to specifically heroic conceptions of the literary vocation. With the advent of romanticism and of the poet's subjectivity as a central topic for poetry, the author's role expands to include spiritual, epistemological, and artistic risk. The vocation of literature becomes itself potentially an adventure, one consequence being a new emphasis on pursuing an original, sustained, and coherent enterprise. A strong animating project such as Whitman's thus confirms cherished romantic ideals about the artist as hero of his or her own spiritual quest.

Rival assumptions can be imagined or cited, to be sure, but the author has had such a strong hold on our imaginations that even the alternatives tend to reinforce its primacy. For instance, one could in allegiance to neoclassical principles demand that literature primarily keep faith with established genres or other manifestations of traditional authority. One could from a formalist perspective expect of each work its own internal, hence impersonal and theoretically anonymous, formal integrity. Of one could look with the cultural historians to the fate and function of the writings in society, expecting a work's value to be manifested in its impact. Yet at least since the romantics tradition has mainly been seen as a backdrop for the individual talent, formal autonomy as a product of authorial genius, and cultural reception as a measure of the major author's influence.

Dickinson may fail to meet the standards Porter assumes, but judging her against romantic and even heroic notions of the poet's business is hardly impertinent. Poets and poetry constitute the only topic Dickinson persistently idealizes, and she regularly attributes to the figure of the poet a typically high romantic majesty. A large number of Dickinson's poems present the self as a romantic quester, searching the secrets of her own mind or of nature and hoping to return triumphantly with what she has found.[14] In addition, Dickinson at least claimed a sustained, even inviolable commitment to lofty poetic and spiritual aims, this being one of the authorial virtues Porter finds lacking. "Perhaps you smile at me. I could not stop for that — My Business is Circumference," she famously told Higginson (*Letters*, 412). A similar declaration to the Hollands even more defiantly asserts her solitary claims against the world's opinion: "Perhaps you laugh at me! Perhaps the whole United States are laughing at me too! *I* can't stop for that! *My* business is to love" (*Letters*, 413).

On the other hand, Dickinson parts company with at least some romantic values in focusing more on readers than on authors. Nearly all of her remarks about poetry in letters, poems, or recorded conversation imagine literature from the point of view of the audience. By contrast, she shows no interest whatsoever in the nature of the poetic imagination, that staple topic of esthetic speculation from the eighteenth century until the present day. Furthermore, in these same remarks she almost never attends to the objective features of a text (word choice, for instance, or stanza form), even though the originality of her own poems is unthinkable without considerable self-consciousness about such features. If such interests exhausted the possiblities of an *ars poetica*, David Porter would be quite right in saying she had none. Yet time and again Dickinson dwells on the effects that words, poems, and other forms of expression can have on an audience. She wholeheartedly and even one-sidedly defines poetry by its affective consequences. To Higginson, for example, she famously declared:

If I read a book [and] it makes my whole body so cold no fire can warm me I know *that* is poetry. If I feel physically as if the top of my head were taken off, I know *that* is poetry. These are the only way I know it. Is there any other way? (*Letters*, 473–74)

Even poems that explicitly take poets as their subject understand the subject from the audience's point of view. Dickinson regularly idealizes the poets she writes about but always from the perspective of a reader and in terms of the bounty poets can provide to readers.

> I reckon—when I count at all—
> First—Poets—Then the Sun—
> Then Summer—Then the Heaven of God—
> And then—the List is done—
>
> But, looking back—the First so seems
> To Comprehend the Whole—
> The Others look a needless Show—
> So I write—Poets—All—
>
> (569)

Poets are obviously the subject of this poem, but its minimal action concerns reckoning by a reader, who views poets mainly as the agents who provide experiences to be reckoned. This is especially true of the first half of the poem, the two stanzas just quoted, which I would like to examine in isolation for a moment.

The poets here are estimable figures because, as the speaker comes to realize in the second stanza, they are categorically distinct from sun, summer, and heaven. Each of the lesser objects is a "Show," a fine but finite spectacle that the connoisseur-speaker may experience, appreciate, and reckon. Poets, however, are the showmen, producers of spectacles that can then be experienced. They accordingly comprehend the whole in the sense of preempting it or rendering it superfluous. As long as poets produce new shows, the speaker needs no others.

Such productivity would certainly not be formless or uncontrolled, but it also does not appear to determine the reader's understanding in any very specific way. Even the speaker's reckoning is more occasioned by the poems than directed by them. It happens "when I count at all," that is to say, casually and at the speaker's leisure.

As a spectator and possibly also as a reckoner, the speaker is clearly a reader of what poets create. However, the explicitly named outcome of her reading is an act of writing. The distinctive glory of the poets is their productivity and hence the bounty they provide for readers. Here that glory occasions or stimulates further production on the part of a reader who becomes a writer—part poet, part recording auditor— in her turn. Dimly visible here is an ethic of productivity that would measure poetry by its catalysis of further writing. Part of the ultimate business of Dickinson's poetry, in addition to and sometimes in lieu of creating finished spectacles, is producing poems that may then beget from her audience new poems and other forms of free, active response.

"I reckon when I count at all" goes on for two more stanzas, however, and in those the possibility of beneficent productivity is overshadowed by the brilliance of the initially produced spectacles.

> Their Summer—lasts a Solid Year—
> They can afford a Sun
> The East—would deem extravagant—
> And if the Further Heaven—
>
> Be Beautiful as they prepare
> For Those who worship Them—
> It is too difficult a Grace—
> To justify the Dream—
>
> (569)

The spectacles become too bountiful once the speaker wonders about the representational adequacy of the poet's heaven. Earlier the heaven of God had come in a poor fourth in the reckoning, but now the speaker considers that God's further heaven might indeed be as beautiful as the poet's representations. More important, it might be the destiny from which they derive and for which they prepare us. If so, the bounty becomes a threat or at least an occasion for unwelcome, discomforting humility, as at the terrible or awestruck moment when a person is offered the chance to accept God's grace. Such a gift requires absolute acceptance of the giver's absolutely superior authority. Rather than catalysts, inspirations, or potentially even peers, the poets thus become demanding masters, who require worshipful submission to their now definitive spectacles.

Each half of the poem diagrams some invidious comparison among the agents present in the verse: God, poets, and the speaker. In the first half, to the speaker's evident delight, the poets best God. In the second half, however, God and the poets line up against the speaker, at least within the conditional grammar of the poem's ending. If the poet's spectacles represent truth rather than just imaginative fecundity, that is, if they take on the authority of God and hence of God's proper claims on the speaker, then the poets threaten to triumph over the speaker. The difference is that their spectacles would acquire ontological validity and also finality or conclusiveness, thereby directing us to a truth that obviates any response but acceptance.

An otherwise even more hyperbolic celebration of the figure of the poet also turns on his potentially rivalrous relation with the reader and on the humbling authority of what he masterfully creates. This poet definitely controls the reader's response, much as Porter would have him do, but such control is a mixed blessing.

> This was a Poet—It is That
> Distills amazing sense
> From ordinary Meanings—
> And Attar so immense
>
> From the familiar species
> That perished by the Door—
> We wonder it was not Ourselves
> Arrested it—before—
>
> Of Pictures—the Discloser
> The Poet—it is He—
> Entitles Us—by Contrast—
> To ceaseless Poverty—
>
> Of Portion—so unconscious—
> The Robbing—could not harm—
> Himself—to Him—a Fortune—
> Exterior—to Time—
>
> (448)

The poet celebrated here is clearly a mighty and heroic figure, whom Dickinson nearly apotheosizes in describing as "Exterior—to Time." Her conception of his superiority and even some of the poem's language may owe a debt to Carlyle's "The Hero as Poet."

It is in what I called Portrait-Painting. . . . that Shakespeare is so great. . . . The seeing eye! It is this that discloses the inner harmony of things; what Nature meant . . . Something she did mean. To the seeing eye that something were discernible.[15]

Yet whether Carlyle is her specific source or merely one instance of the widespread nineteenth-century glorification of the artist, Dickinson shifts the emphasis slightly but decisively in registering discomfort about the heroic poet's mastery. Both Carlyle and Dickinson imagine poetic greatness as the pictorial disclosure of the authentic and harmonious meanings otherwise hidden in nature. But whereas Carlyle stresses the poet's eye as a synecdoche of his rare and grand powers, Dickinson's concern is with the effect of poetry, not its production. And although she unmistakably celebrates the poet's grandeur, the outstanding thing about him is that he devastates the reader. His wealth "Entitles Us—by Contrast— / To ceaseless Poverty." His indisputable ascendancy does not enrich us; it makes us more aware of our poverty. And the only way the poem imagines access to his riches is by petty theft. One can look at his pictures freely, but gaining their wealth requires taking it from him.

The poet's relation to the speaker-reader is strikingly different from the initial relation in "I reckon when I count at all," and also somewhat different from the relation in the second half of that poem. Whereas the poets of "I reckon" create spectacles for the speaker to observe, this one not only makes pictures but discloses them. Whereas they produce marvels that make sun, summer, and heaven a needless show, this one distills amazing sense from humble or ordinary scenes. In other words, the Carlylean poet produces verbal and visual experiences for the reader, and he also determines their meaning. Even in the darker second half of "I reckon," control of meaning derives mainly from God, the poets approaching such authority only to the extent that their heaven approximates His. But here it is the poet who actively distills immense attar and arrests amazing sense. Moreover, he exerts this power over meaning in such a way as to foreclose the reader's activity. Once it has been revealed, the meaning of the picture is apparently fixed and final, leaving us no particular opportunity for the sort of further productivity possible in "I reckon when I count at all."

Carlylean poetry seems further to demand that we acknowledge the heroic poet's superiority. Whereas the speaker's comparative judgments in "I reckon when I count at all" are voluntary and the act of judging is almost capriciously casual, here the speaker apparently cannot help but compare the author's powers and her own. Although the poet is "unconscious" of his "Portion," the speaker is obsessed with it, for his wealth is a kind of affront to her. Rather than an undemanding bestower of benefits, the poet is thus startlingly like the figure Dickinson first described in "I never lost as much but twice" as a "Burglar! Banker—Father!"(49). The heroic or Carlylean poet is one of the series of domineering Masters so prominent throughout Dickinson's writings. He is this not because he deliberately plays the bully or even takes note of the reader's impoverished existence, but because the reader cannot help reading back through the brilliantly disclosed pictures to their masterly creator. The poet does not demand the reader's idolatry, that is, but his poems effectively do and they demand that its object be not themselves but their author.

In the resemblance of the Carlylean poet to a patriarchal Nobodaddy and in the personalization of reading accomplished by this poem and by "I reckon when I count at all," we glimpse the source of the resistance to coherence, integrity, and design in Dickinson's poetry, at least in their conventional, author-centered forms. Reading and writing, like most other acts in Dickinson's world, are always vulnerable to some form of a master-slave relation. More specifically, authorial control is usually for Dickinson a mark of the author as Master. For her to direct a reader by means of the activities Porter expects would be to cast the reader in the role of humbly submissive liege.

Put another way, Porter imagines that reading and writing are neutral or benign and that poems ideally transmit to the audience finished meanings the author has fashioned, devised, or determined. For Dickinson, however, the circuit of author and audience is never simply a neutral channel; it is always a power relation and hence always potentially charged with the affects of power: anxiety, resentment, exultation, and so on. "This was a poet" even hints that definitive meaning necessarily humbles a reader. The Carlylean poet unmistakably produces a coherent discourse, but for Dickinson the cost of his success — or the temptation it entails — is dominion over the reader.

Can there be a literary integrity without the authorial control that Dickinson here reads as humbling mastery? The greatest obstacle to conventional forms of coherence in Dickinson's literary career is her ambivalence about authorial mastery. She by no means always rejects mastery, but she also never remains comfortable with that role for long. A major challenge for her poetics then is to fashion some alternative coherence or design, something which might circumvent the temptation to be ruled by a "Monarch" or to be the monarch herself.

Other notions of literary design are visible in Dickinson's work. "I reckon when I count at all" imagines in its first half an almost entirely benign form of authorship, and even "This was a poet" distinguishes somewhat between the pictures and what the masterly poet discloses in them. A similar distinction appears more emphatically in the following poem, between the spectacle Dickinson encounters and the meaning she is able to disclose about it.

> Four Trees — upon a solitary Acre —
> Without Design
> Or Order, or Apparent Action —
> Maintain —

The Sun—upon a Morning meets them—
The Wind—
No nearer Neighbor—have they—
But God—

The Acre gives them—Place—
They—Him—Attention of Passer by—
Of Shadow, or of Squirrel, haply—
Or Boy—

What Deed is Their's unto the General Nature
What Plan
They severally—retard—or further—
Unknown—

(742)

The design, order, and plan missing from this nonetheless haunting scene are precisely the qualities Porter finds lacking in Dickinson's poetry. Indeed, he singles the poem out as a cardinal instance
of her baffled consciousness.[16] As it happens, however, the kind of
control that he advocates has a phantom presence in the poem. An
abandoned variant for the key term "maintain" is "do reign." The variant, in other words, attributes to the trees a monarchical dominion
over the scene, albeit one that is still without design or order. "Maintain," on the other hand, suggests a different notion of control and
coherence.

The barren starkness of both scene and langauge in the poem is
apparent, but it is less obvious how or even whether we are cued to
respond. If one supposes, as may be true of most landscape poems
and more than a few by Dickinson, that the scene is to be taken as
a synecdoche of the universe and its significance, then the poem shows
us randomness. If one further supposes that a scene's meaningfulness
requires teleological or theological sanction and that the nature poet's
role is to seek after such guarantees, reading them out of the design
that inheres in a landscape or imposing them upon a nature that lacks
evident purpose, then the case is even worse.

These suppositions belong, however, to an esthetics the poem
ultimately evades. They belong in the first place to a heroic conception of the artist that openly values mastery over acquiescence. As
Childe of the Meaningful Landscape, the poet discovers or constructs
significance that would otherwise have eluded us. More accurately,
for the poem allows no place for such questing and gives about as
little voice to the poetic self as possible, the suppositions belong to
an esthetics of beauty. However derived or discerned, qualities such

as order, design, harmony, and wholeness are inherently pleasing to our taste; they constitute essential attributes of beauty as it is found in nature and in artistic representations of nature. What the poem offers, by contrast, in carefully but as it were jarringly ordered lines and stanzas, is a scene flagrantly without beauty, one whose essential randomness belies the obvious care Dickinson has taken with the poem's form. No pleasurable order or intelligible purpose exists in the scene, nothing the human mind might attach itself to and find comfort in.

Yet the negative conclusions the poem records (no order, no design, no revelation or meaning) are hardly anguished, as one might expect, or even conspicuously portentous. The poem is one of the quietest in Dickinson's corpus. Revealingly, it omits all reference to the speaker and articulates no difference between inanimate objects (trees, field, sun, wind, or shadow) and things ordinarily characterized by subjectivity (God, passerby, and boy). All seem comparably if minimally endowed with sentience, and all seem equally capable of the forms of agency affirmed in the poem (maintaining, meeting, giving place, neighboring, attending, and passing by). These deeds are quiet in comparison to the forceful kinds of "Action" that are not "Apparent" or that get specifically disaffirmed (ordering, designing, acting, performing deeds, planning, retarding, furthering, and knowing), but they are also the occasion of a quiet wonder. Without teleology or any other metaphysical support, what the poem and scene both do here is to *hold,* that being the root action in both "maintain" and "attention." What each holds is itself and the others, the indeterminacy of direction, object, and transitivity nicely rendered by the grammatical suspension of "maintain." This holding is both reciprocal, in that the giving place exactly matches the giving attention, and peculiarly indiscriminate or egalitarian. A shadow pays as much attention as a boy or a squirrel, and sun, wind, and God all equally and with equanimity neighbor the trees.

The force of this unordered framing is primarily attributed to the four trees, which hold the landscape together without exactly dominating it. If the trees are held to the normal standards of monarchical control, the scene must be judged amorphous and incoherent. "Do reign" would be ironic, even mocking, for trees that reign over an acre and its neighbors fail if they do so without design or order. The resulting scene would then be properly lamentable as an emblem of senselessness or inscrutability. Trees that maintain, however, continue to present a mystery, one whose entirely self-sufficient and unenclosed immanence precludes the usual allegorization of landscape as a *pay-*

sage moralisé. Instead of senselessness and disorder, we have a curiously affecting presence that does without sense and order and even does much of its work by means of their absence. If we are drawn to the scene, it is not by its beauty but by its strangely haunting presence and its incompatibility with our epistemological and teleological hopes. This is a domain of the sublime, an affective and effective power that draws attention but also eludes or even disrupts pleasing harmonies and intelligible schemes.

"Four trees" is an unusual poem among Dickinson's works because it almost entirely dispenses with questions of conflict, domination, and submission. The force it invokes is thus not typical of what I shall call the Dickinson sublime, but it is also quite far from the mastery she regards in "This was a poet."

This is not the place to examine the complex thematics of mastery in Dickinson, but a few points are essential to understanding her theory of poetry. First and most obvious, Dickinson is acutely sensitive to relations of domination and submission, so much so that she tends to measure all conceivably bipolar phenomena for their resemblance to the structure of mastery. Second and nearly as evident, over the course of her career Dickinson speaks from every position within the hierarchy of master and minion, and she adopts every possible attitude toward the relation. "This was a poet" betrays both resentment and awe of the idolized poet, and elsewhere Dickinson is as likely to speak in tones of haughty imperiousness ("The soul selects her own society" [303] and "I make his crescent fill or lack" [909]) as of baffled, meek, or resentful submission ("My worthiness is all my doubt" [751], "I got so I could take his name" [293], or "'Heavenly Father' take to thee" [1461]).

A central instance of mastery is idolatry, the situation in which one person invests another with an utterly superior glory. "Oh, my too beloved, save me from the idolatry which would crush us both," she wrote to Judge Otis Lord, the only real person who we can be sure did for a time occupy in Dickinson's imagination the role of Master (*Letters*, 616). Notice that, as in Hegel's analysis of lordship and bondage, the superior's stature is here conferred by the inferior's consciousness.[17]

Furthermore, underlying or preceding the frequent dyadic hierarchies in Dickinson, we can often discern some struggle between the two parties and even a contest for supremacy. As in Hegel, the relatively stable hierarchy of mastery emerges from a conflict of rival consciousnesses. Mastery's origins in rivalry manifest themselves most clearly in poems in which Dickinson imagines herself as the master. Sometimes this appears as a rather unattrative vindication fantasy.

> No matter—now—Sweet—
> But when I'm Earl
> Wont you wish you'd spoken
> To that dull Girl?
>
> (704)

Elsewhere, rivalry is, from the triumphant master's point of view, simply a necessary part of the hierarchy of rank and dominance.

> Smiling back from Coronation
> May be Luxury—
> On the Heads that started with us—
> Being's peasantry—
>
> Recognizing in Procession
> Ones We former knew—
> When Ourselves were also dusty—
> Centuries ago—
>
> Had the Triumph no Conviction
> Of how many be—
> Stimulated—by the Contrast—
> Unto Misery—
>
> (385)

At least once Dickinson insisted that the relation of idolater to idol was directly reciprocal, one person's gain being the other's loss. "I rose—because He sank— / I thought it would be opposite—" she says when her lover proves to be a "fainting Prince" unworthy of idolization (616).

Even Dickinson's celebrated images of the self as volcano depend for part of their appeal on the lure of vindication and the rivalrous resentment that feeds it. Now I am dormant, peaceful, and unassuming, these poems all say, but once my native forces erupt into view you who have disregarded me will be awed into submission to my true majesty.

> On my volcano grows the Grass
> A meditative spot—
> An acre for a Bird to choose
> Would be the General thought—

How red the Fire rocks below
How insecure the sod
Did I disclose
Would populate with awe my solitude
(1677)

Discriminations can and sometimes must be made among the various situations of mastery. The volcano poems differ from the poems of queenly rank, and both differ from the frequently abject love poems. Likewise, Dickinson's attitudes about mastery and submission are not the same in all poems; sometimes the tone is clearly satirical, sometimes it is celebratory, and most often it is ironic and analytic in a way specific to the poem. However, Dickinson does seem to imagine all the various instances and possibilities as belonging to a single structure. Indeed, many poems go out of their way to conflate logically distinct possibilities. It has long been noticed about Dickinson's poetry that the self's relations to God, father, and lover seem interchangeable with one another, each regularly serving as an analogy for the others and no one especially primary or central. For instance "I'm ceded, I've stopped being theirs" expresses the once humbled self's reassertion against God, father, and also clergy (508). Likewise, the "He" of "He found my being, set it up" is both God and beloved (603).

More suprisingly, the same structure appears vis-à-vis otherwise inanimate phenomena of nature. In contrast to the scene represented in "Four trees," Dickinson usually represents nature as an unremitting quiddity with which the self must battle to avoid a humbling affront.

An ignorance a Sunset
Confer upon the Eye —
Of Territory — Color —
Circumference — Decay —

It's Amber Revelation
Exhilirate — Debase —
Omnipotence' inspection
Of Our inferior face —
(552)

The contest here transforms the epistemological drama of a subject/ object relation into a contest for supremacy between two subjectivities. Elsewhere this contest is played out with quondam friends or peers (as in "No matter now sweet," quoted above, or "A mien to move a queen" [283]). It can also be seen as a contest between parties or faculties within a single self, in such poems as "Like eyes that looked on wastes" (458), "Me from myself to banish" (642), and "Who court obtain within himself" (803).

In its most general form, then, mastery is the structure Dickinson sees as normally obtaining between any two subjects or between any consciousness and some otherness that it imagines as capable of subjectivity. Mastery is also in a more limited sense a principle she sees as underlying conventional forms of authorial control. Her frequent metaphors of order as monarchical are anything but innocent. Dickinson can never either fully reject or fully endorse literary mastery as something she is eager to practice. The challenge for her poetics then is both to imagine some form of power that might transcend the limitations of mastery and to imagine a kind of poetry that might draw upon such power.

2

Style and Sensation

The most striking aspect of Emily Dickinson's poetry is surely the style, however one defines that slippery notion. It is also one that might most seem to align her work with a heroic ideal of authorship. If style is the man himself, then a boldly distinctive manner of writing asserts a man's selfhood boldly. Likewise, telling the truth but telling it conspicuously slant would seem to make a bid for literary glory. Any claim that Dickinson keeps her distance from an ideal of literary mastery must thus consider the aggressive idiosyncrasy of her style.

Even as somewhat tidied up by her earliest editors, the irregularities of syntax and prosody in Dickinson's verse shocked conservative reviewers and virtually disqualified it as poetry in their vew. Although genteel standards of versification have long since lost their sway, the victim of the modernist revolution in taste that ushered in Dickinson's reputation as a major poet, her style has lost little of its singularity. The idiosyncrasies of punctuation and capitalization alone make it impossible to mistake Dickinson's poems for anyone else's, and a number of other stylistic features remain as distinctive as they were in the nineteenth century.

Why did Dickinson invent such an unusual manner of writing? Invention is hardly too strong a word here. Amidst all the uncertainties about how and why Dickinson wrote poetry, the style of her poems stands out as their single most persistent and deliberate aspect. The case can even be made that the achievement of a discernible style is one of Dickinson's chief criteria for what counts as a poem and thus one of the most reliable clues to her otherwise elusive literary goals. Nothing in her work so calls attention to itself as how she selects and combines marks on a page. Indeed, nothing else is so designed to call attention. According to Dickinson's affective understanding of poetry, moreover, the assertiveness of a writer's style plays a crucial role in provoking the reader's response. Beyond any momentary aggrandizement of the authorial self, it contributes centrally to a network of textual relations in which the author's part is never finally that of the master.

Inventing a Style

Dickinson's themes, images opinions, and voices vary considerably from poem to poem, but over the course of her career they do not reveal any notable pattern of uniformity or development. The style, in contrast, is remarkably consistent from beginning to end, and Dickinson's stylistic aims and standards are perhaps even more so. The fully mature poems that she began to preserve around 1860 do not strike off in a new stylistic direction but only intensify, concentrate, and perfect traits already evident in poems of 1858 and 1859.[1] The main developments at this time are an increase in the conciseness she obviously already valued and an increasing boldness in deploying rhetorical disjunctions and syntactic elisions, with which she had already experimented. From about 1858, when she first began making and preserving fair copies, until her death in 1886, the same distinctive features appear over and over again.

The sparse evidence we have of Dickinson's literary apprenticeship strongly implies that her characteristic style did not spring forth spontaneously. She deliberately chose it from among other possibilities, or so it would seem from a pattern that is evident in her letters. More clearly than the poems, which are also more difficult to date, the surviving letters reveal early stylistic experimentation and variation, which then disappears entirely, replaced by a mature, consistent style.

In later years the letters so closely follow the manner of the poems that her editors have convincingly arranged some passages as verse. During the 1850s, however, they show her experimenting with several different sytlistic registers, most of them notably mannered or ostentatiously literary. Several of the letters written to her brother while he was at Harvard adopt a conspicuously Dickensian comic tone, for instance, complete with character sketches and helter-skelter narrative anecdotes. Likewise, a letter of 1858 to her cousin John Graves has been plausibly interpreted as an intentional exercise in the outsetting-bard genre, even Dickinson's counterpart to "Lycidas."[2] That letter is remarkably loquacious, far more so than any letter or poem written afterward. In addition, the letter to Graves begins with a relatively elaborate effort at scene painting, one of the several other features that—along with narrative elaboration and extended characterization of anyone other than the speaker—Dickinson's mature poems and letters flagrantly eschew. Indeed, the letter to Graves stands out even among the other correspondence surviving from that time. By 1858 and 1859, especially in letters to Susan Gilbert Dickinson, to the Hollands, to the Bowleses, to Joseph Sweetser, and to Mrs. Joseph Haven, Dickinson's mature epistolary style has begun to be fully evident: brief aphoristic paragraphs, the omission of explicit signals for a change of topic or tone, and a marked preference for analogy or periphrasis over direct reference.

Because so few letters survive from the years between 1854 and 1858, the break between Dickinson's initial experiments and the emergence of her mature style appears dramatically abrupt in Johnson's edition of the letters. The suddenness is misleading, no doubt, yet the telling thing here is not the exact timing of her development but the almost complete disappearance of alternative literary devices and styles. By the end of the 1850s Dickinson has invented a characteristic style and from then on she uses virtually no other.

At the center of Dickenson's style are a number of highly conspicuous features: the use of dashes in grammatically or rhythmically unorthodox places, the unconventional capitalization of words in the middle of lines and sentences, and the notably short lines, most of which rely on hymn meters and other instances of two-, three-, or at most four-stress lines. These features may seem superficial in comparison with ones that play prominent roles in a poem's meaning: lexical choice, figural language, syntactic patterning, and so on. Yet precisely because they lie on the surface and of all the facets of Dickinson's poetry are literally the most visible, they serve as a stylistic signature, making Dickinson's mature poems instantly recognizable to the reader. There is reason to believe that some or all of these features served Dickinson in the same way, as a badge of literary identity. The features are not evident, for instance, in the few early poems Dickinson herself did not preserve or revise. The absence confirms what the surviving letters suggest: that about the time she began copying poems into fascicles she had established for herself a literary identity primarily characterized by style.

Other features are implicated in Dickinson's early but already mature style, notably including a tendency to elide grammatical and rhetorical connectives. For the moment, however, let us look mainly to the most conspicuous traits—the stylistic signature—as a way of charting the origins of Dickinson's style. The characteristic punctuation, capitalization, and lineation appear in nearly all the poems Dickinson wrote down from 1858 until her death. (The exceptions are poems for which no manuscript exists, notably the texts transcribed by the Norcross cousins.) In this the signature features are unlike other aspects of the style, which belong to a repertoire Dickinson draws upon continually but does not exhaust in every poem.

A number of the poems Dickinson copied and bound into fascicles in 1858 may well have been composed earlier, but only four poems known to have been transcribed before 1858 survive what must have been a larger group of lost, rejected, or abandoned efforts. These four thus provide our only opportunity to compare Dickinson's mature poetic style with what had come before. (Dickinson turned twenty-eight in 1858, and she had apparently deemed herself a poet since 1853, the year of the "Brother Pegasus" letter to Austin.)

Three of these four poems survive only in versions from 1854 or earlier. Dickinson apparently never reworked them after she began saving her poems, and she never transcribed them into the fascicles. The three unclaimed works are numbers 1, 3, and 5 in the Johnson edition: two valentines and a poem sent to Susan Gilbert in 1853. (The one Johnson designates as number 2, which comes from a letter to Austin, was written in prose and rearranged as verse only after Dickinson's death.) All three unclaimed poems are somewhat more conventional in rhyme, meter, and punctuation than the earliest fascicle poems. Number 5 does use the characteristic dashes but restricts them to the ends of lines, where in each case they coincide with a moment of syntactic closure. The three poems thus indirectly corroborate the hypothesis that Dickinson achieved literary maturity with the invention of a characteristic style.

Poem number 4 is unique, the only poem that survives in both a fascicle transcription and a fair copy datable before 1858. The two versions differ only slightly, but the variation is nonetheless the strongest indication we possess of stylistic difference between the poems Dickinson saved and the ones she discarded or neglected. The wording in the two manuscripts is almost identical, but the lineation of the fascicle copy is conspicuously and even arbitrarily less regular. The first version has two six-line stanzas with an *aabccb* rhyme scheme, the trimeter couplets of the *a* and *c* lines varied by dimeter in all but one of the *b* lines. In the fascicle version, however, Dickinson fuses what had been the first two lines, masking the rhyme scheme and creating two unequal, no longer parallel stanzas.

Here is the version Dickinson sent in 1853 to Susan Gilbert:

On this wondrous sea
Sailing silently,
Ho! Pilot! Ho!
Knowest thou the shore
Where no breakers roar—
Where the storm is oer?

In the peaceful west
Many the sails at rest—
The anchors fast—
Thither I pilot *thee*—
Land! Ho! Eternity!
Ashore at last!

And here is the version copied into a fascicle in 1858:

On this wondrous sea—sailing silently—
Ho! Pilot! Ho!
Knowest thou the shore
Where no breakers roar
Where the storm is o'er

In the Silent West[3]
Many—the Sails at rest—
The Anchors fast.
Thither I pilot thee—
Land! Ho! Eternity!
Ashore at last!

The new first line has a dash where an unpunctuated line break had been, and a few other changes in punctuation are also visible. The most striking change, other than lineation, occurs in the first three lines of the second stanza. Along with the single, largely inconsequential change of wording, we get the capitalization of most substantive words and the insertion of Dickinson's most idiosyncratic mark, the intralinear dash that isolates a word from those to which grammar, lineation, and meter would otherwise connect it. Consequently, we get for the first time in Dickinson's poetry a possibility of hesitation and uncertainty about how some words are linked. "Many" no longer quite so automatically modifies "Sails," as it would simply according to the grammar and as it does in the earlier version. Instead, the fascicle version provides the first clear-cut example, albeit a minimal one, of Dickinson's single most important compositional practice. She has arranged the details of the poem in such a way that two or more legitimate but incongruent readings are possible. Is the mark between "Many" and "the Sails" to be construed as a pause, a closer link, an abrupt break, or what? Dickinson's reader is thus for the first time invited to ponder a slantwise text.

This inauguration of a minimal double writing has no major consequences for the reading of the whole poem, at least that I can see, and the presence or absence of a single punctuation mark would seem unlikely to be decisive. On the other hand, we know that comparably minute details could sometimes matter intensely to Dickinson. A brief poem from 1878 portentously declares that "The Treason of an accent / Might Ecstasy transfer" (1358). Less hypothetically, the Springfield *Republican* in 1866 printed the third line of "A narrow fellow in the grass" with a comma at the end. Dickinson complained of this to Higginson on two grounds, first that it had been printed at all (which belied her claim to him that she had no thought of publishing) and second that the newspaper had violated her intention of having no punctuation at the end of the third line: "Lest you meet my Snake and suppose I deceive it was robbed of me—defeated too of the third line by the punctuation. The third and fourth were one—" (*Letters*, 316).

The episode is well known, but its significance remains elusive. Dickinson passes over several other small but potentially consequential differences between the newspaper version and the two manuscripts (one written after the incident) that have survived. The newspaper prints the poem as three eight-line stanzas, for example, as against the five or six shorter stanzas in manuscript. The offensive opening lines appear this way in the newspaper:

> A narrow fellow in the grass
> Occasionally rides—
> You may have met him—did you not,
> His notice instant is.

By contrast, a manuscript dated to 1865 has it this way:

> A narrow Fellow in the Grass
> Occasionally rides—
> You may have met Him—did you not
> His notice sudden is—

And an 1872 copy sent to Susan reads:

> A narrow Fellow in the Grass
> Occasionally rides—
> You may have met him? Did you not
> His notice instant is—
>
> (986)

If the exact punctuation is so important, why does Dickinson add a question mark in the version sent to her sister-in-law? And what difference does the newspaper's comma make, in any case? I suggest we suppose that the 1872 copy partly reflects Dickinson's exasperation with the newspaper version and perhaps also with Susan. (Susan had a role in the newspaper version, it is generally assumed; she is believed to have given Samuel Bowles, the editor of the paper, her copy of the poem.) The 1872 version can then be understood as spelling out or insisting upon a distinction Dickinson had once fabricated more subtly.

By inserting a question mark Dickinson alters the way the line is voiced. A strong caesura appears where a weak one had been, and the obligatory rising inflection of the question form necessitates a stress on "him," which all but destroys the meter. All this is apparently not too high a price to pay for insisting that—contrary to grammar, meter, and normal phrasing—the third line rapidly runs on into the fourth. Without such drastic intervention the enjambment would at best be optional, since the third line otherwise coincides with a phrase boundary. Quickening the pace through enjambment might well have semantic value, for it would anticipate the urgency and fright later secured in the poem by its concluding words, "Zero at the Bone." But the more striking, more Dickinsonian note would be to signal the opportunity for the rapid pacing while at the same time honoring the more conventional possibility. This is what the 1865 version, which has neither question mark nor comma, does best. In allowing two different possibilities (in this case vocally incompatible ones), it accomplishes the usual ends of her slantwise style.

Keep in mind that the reading I have proposed depends on a questionable premise, namely, that the 1872 version makes explicit something Dickinson had always intended but preferred to keep implicit. In addition, it supposes that the 1872 version is as faulty as the newspaper version and for the same reason. Nevertheless, the premise does explain Dickinson's exasperation with the newspaper version. Without the comma, as Dickinson originally wrote the poem, the enjambment of lines three and four is not necessary; indeed, it is only mildly possible. But with the insertion of the comma a deliberate instance of double writing is half erased.

In contrast to Dickinson's occasional fastidiousness about small details, she apparently felt no compunction about violating the integrity of finished poems. She regularly lifted lines and stanzas out of her poems in order to send them to a correspondent, sometimes altering the wording or address in the process and always disregarding any protoformalist thought that poems ought to be seamless, organic wholes. More strikingly, significant differences in meaning sometimes clearly mattered less to her than local stylistic effects. Analyzing the drafts of poem 1386, which was apparently never finished to Dickinson's satisfaction, Porter has pointed out that filling grammatical and metrical slots with a certain kind of diction seems far to outweigh the meaning of the word chosen or its semantic relations with other parts of the poem.[4] As the verb with "Affluence" as its subject or object, for instance, Dickinson variously writes "evolved," "conferred," "bestowed," and "involved." Each choice fits a category defined solely by formal attributes: a one-word verb; a lexical choice that is Latin in origin and hence possesses a certain gravity and abstraction; two syllables with an iambic beat; a preterite tense form marked as such by a *d* that is both stopped and yet does not add a syllable to the root; and a second syllable, beginning also with a fricative. Within the limits of this stylistic type, the words are interchangeable tokens. Yet semantically each denotes rather different activities and sharply different senses of agency; among other differences some are transitive and thus allow a key ambiguity about the grammatical case of "Affluence." Likewise, for an adjective to describe summer's taking or going its way, Dickinson variously and without any apparent criteria other than stylistic proposes "gracious," "spacious," "subtle," "mighty," "gallant," "sylvan," "ample," and "perfect."

An unfinished poem may be a poor example, Dickinson like most poets presumably exploring sound, sense, and style all at once it the process of composing. Yet similarly formal criteria are evident in "The Bible is an antique volume" (1545), which did get finished and sent in fair copy to her nephew. The "warbling" teller that the poem calls for is semantically comparable to the "thrilling" teller of a semifinal draft, but the same cannot be said for all the alternatives she proposes. "Hearty," "bonnie," "warbling," "ardent," "friendly," "magic," "winning," and "mellow" may all spring from one persistent semantic intention, but Dickinson intersperses such divergent possibilities as "typic," "breathless," "spacious," "tropic," and "pungent."

Even more curious an indication of her priorities are the many variants she noted on presumably finished and final copies. Is it that she expected later to make a more authoritative choice? This seems unlikely given the enormous number of fascicle poems for which she noted alternative readings, often several of them. Is it that she expected the unchosen possibilities to remain part of the poem, as if she were constructing her own variorum? Most often the variants are semantically and metrically comparable, but for a number of poems it remains a matter of sporadic debate which choice would be the best. None of these questions can be answered definitively, but one thing seems clear. The effect of the variants is always to multiply possibilities.

The Genealogy of Deviance

Dickinson's style has always attracted considerable attention. Scholars have identified its main features and described them with some care.[5] Generally speaking, this stylistic criticism confirms the grounds on which some early readers and reviewers rejected her work or responded with dismay: the style seems predicated on deviation from available poetic and discursive standards. Not only do such readily visible features as punctuation and capitalization depart from established practices, so also do presumably more important lexical and syntactic choices. As Cristanne Miller has shown, all these features produce a single kind of linguistic effect.[6] In terms of Chomskyan linguistics, all work toward making the deep structure of an utterance unrecoverable, or to be more exact, multiply recoverable. In other words, rather than merely inventive verbal features that with enough time and ingenuity we might confidently renormalize according to the accepted protocols of English usage, these devices are linguistically deviant in a precise and provocative way. They systematically frustrate linguistic competence, which tranformational grammar describes as a capacity to match a surface structure to the deep structure that is its logical origin.

The deviance can be exaggerated, to be sure. Dickinson's meters are almost all based on established hymnology, for instance.[7] Likewise, most of her recurrent images are poetic commonplaces: sun, birds, flowers, bees, butterflies, pearls and other gems, and even lightning and volcanoes. So also are the tropes she uses and indeed her poetry's foregrounding of figurality itself. On the other hand, Dickinson's poems sometimes subvert the established rhetorical postures of hymnology, not to mention its piety. Likewise, although precedents can no doubt be found for each of Dickinson's tropes, the customary abruptness and compression of her figurative language are exceptional.

Other conspicuous features of Dickinson's style more plainly and unmistakably deviate from established practices: the ellipsis of otherwise syntactically or rhetorically obligatory terms, the use of uninflected and hence modally indefinite verbs, and the already mentioned oddities of punctuation and capitalization. Deviance is also evident on a larger scale than details of wording and pointing. Robert

Weisbuch has called attention to the frequent scenelessness of her poems, this being an especially dramatic divergence from nineteenth-century practices.[8] The absence or elusiveness of such representation is a major part of what Jay Leyda has called her poetry of the "omitted center."[9] In poems that by their emotional intensity seem bound to specific, perhaps highly personal experiences or events, Dickinson regularly and conspicuously omits referents, occasions, scenes, narratives, contexts, or anything else that might identify a concrete focus. In brief, Dickinson's style is characterized by the massive violation of lexical, syntactic, rhetorical, and specifically poetic or literary norms.

If we assume as a norm language that calls no attention to its formal properties by deviating from conventions of standard communication (that is, an utterance intended solely to communicate a message), then Dickinson's poetry is richly deviant. That there may in fact be no such norm makes Dickinson's poetry no less rich.[10]

It has sometimes been tempting to explain her verbal eccentricities as the spontaneous expressions of a mind as singular as the language in which it more or less directly manifests itself. An odd style from an odd woman, in other words. Yet Dickinson can hardly be considered a primitive artist, unwittingly fashioning an unprecedented poetic style because of her ignorance of prevailing literary practices and her isolation from established standards and tastes. Quite the opposite, for she clearly recognized and apparently sometimes relished her singularity. That is why she jokingly calls herself "the only Kangaroo among the Beauty" (*Letters*, 412).

Dickinson is not a learned poet, to but sure, but she clearly had a wide acquaintance with the established literary practices of her day. Indeed, she once insisted to Higginson, perhaps out of fear he would think her a plagiarist, that she conscientiously avoided repeating the work of others. "I marked a line in One Verse—because I met it after I made it—and never consciously touch a paint, mixed by another person—I do not let it go, because it is mine" (*Letters*, 271).[11] The image of mixed paint seems to refer specifically to style, an identifiable palette of lexical, grammatical, and rhetorical patterns that is distinct from the finished picture on one hand and its raw materials on the other. As a form of private property, in other words, style is not to be confused with a particular model text or with the general capacities of the English langauge.[12]

In the absence of clear documentary evidence about Dickinson's literary intentions, it has been tempting to see her deviations from established literary practices as a pointed rebellion against them. The temptation has been measurably assisted by the circumstances under which Dickinson was first recognized as a major poet. The recognition began in the 1920s, along with and indeed as part of the modernist rejection of nineteenth-century taste. Because Dickinson's poetry legitimately anticipated several aspects of modernist style, most notably its sparseness and its reliance on discontinuities and disjunctions, Dickinson was largely exempted from the new disdain for things romantic or Victorian She became, in fact, something of a modernist cause, and it was easy to assume that she shared the anti-Victorianism of her champions.

A second, only partly independent circumstance is that the modernist revolution coincided with the emergent institutionalization of American literature as a distinct and worthy object of study. Although necessarily more forgiving of the nineteenth century than their European counterparts, the new Americanists often sought to justify American literature by modernist standards.[13] They accordingly devalued the school of Longfellow and emphasized the protomodernist stature of nineteenth-century writers forgotten or ignored in their own time. It was — and largely remains — a major recommendation for a nineteenth-century American writer to have been spurned by, isolated from, and presumably at war with genteel literary culture. The key figures were Melville and Dickinson, the revaluation of whom assumed legendary proportions. In this context also, then, it has been easy to imagine Dickinson as deliberately rejecting the poetry of Longfellow, Lowell, and Holmes, in spite of the fact that her extant comments on them range from respectful to admiring.

More recently, and also more tentatively, feminist critics have asked if her style might not be understood as pointedly rebelling against a patriarchal literary tradition.[14] Dickinson did take an obvious interest in a number of women writers of her day. Some manner of vocational identification with her sisters is one thing, however, and a stylistic rebellion against her brothers quite another, especially since Dickinson's style has no more in common with that of the women writers she admired than it does with anyone else's. Unlike some nineteenth-century writers, Dickinson did not seem to imagine language or art as to an important degree gendered.[15]

My point is that Dickinson's conspicuously deviant style cannot simply be taken as polemically deviant. All the biographical evidence suggests that, although Dickinson was highly conscious of her style and aware of its obvious distinctiveness, she had no great quarrel with the alternatives favored by her contemporaries and predecessors. Indeed, there is reason to believe that Dickinson sometimes saw herself not as a literary rebel but as heir to a recognizable wing of the nineteenth-century English poetry and that her style was designed to carry out the aims generally ascribed to that wing. As we shall see more fully in a moment, this was the wing sometimes known as the poetry of sensation.

Because Dickinson's work is more commonly seen in the context of American poetry and poetics, especially Emerson's, I should say a word here about literary nationalism. Dickinson seems to have read and absorbed Emerson's work, also Hawthorne's and that of other antebellum New Englanders, and she was clearly familiar with much of the popular American poetry of her day.[16] Yet she appears to have kept her distance from the sense of transcendental unity beckoning Emerson and also from the sentimental assurance of consolation motivating much newspaper verse. Moreover, she was singularly unaffected by the continual campaigns in favor of a distinctively American literature and does not appear otherwise to have distinguished between English and American writings. It may then be that our habit of reading Dickinson almost exclusively in an American context violates both her own more catholic tastes and the actual continuities of American and English writing at the time.[17]

Dickinson refers to admired English writers as often as to Americans in poems and letters, and her only poem even raising the question of national affiliation is "The robin's my criterion for tune," a work that carefully limits the importance of the regional differences on which it dwells. That poem's most memorable phrase is the declaration by the speaker that she sees "New Englandly," which in isolation might be taken as patriotic or sectional affirmation. The words acknowledge her locale, to be sure, but Dickinson calls attention to the origin of the place name by transforming the proper noun into an adverb. This undercuts the usually instantaneously denotative or referential power of the proper name, and it correspondingly amplifies the phrase's textuality, its implication in a network of contexts and associations.

Dickinson's is a new England, that is to say, not a sovereign or autochthonous culture. Regions differ from one another, of course, and so the flora and fauna upon which a New England poet draws will be recognizable. On the other hand, all regions are ultimately interchangeable, for even "The Queen sees like me—Provincially." In other words, even the capital and the provinces do not differ from one another in kind. Moreover, the speaker can easily imagine herself in other, equally provincial locales, writing the poems that would be appropriate to such climes.

> But, were I Cuckoo born—
> I'd swear by him—
> The ode familiar—rules the Noon—
> The Buttercup's, my Whim for Bloom—
> Because, we're Orchard sprung—
> But, were I Britain born,
> I'd Daisies spurn—
>
> (285)

The Influence of Elizabeth Barrett Browning

The main evidence for Dickinson's sense of filiation comes from her response to Elizabeth Barrett Browning's poetry and especially to Browning's death in June 1861. During the crucial and extraordinarily productive year immediately following the Englishwoman's death, Dickinson at times imagined herself as invisibly bidding to fill the place Browning had occupied in English poetry. She seems in part to have seen Browning as the last eminent representative of a particular literary tradition or school, one which Arthur Hallam had baptized the poetry of sensation and which also might be thought of as the romantic faction in English culture after the reign of George III. Hallam had referred to Keats, Byron, Shelley, and the young Tennyson. Other writers who were identified with the romantic wing in early Victorian literary debates, in addition to Browning, included De Quincey, Alexander Smith, and the Brontë sisters, all of whom Dickinson is known to have been familiar with.

Dickinson clearly did not model her verse on Browning's, nor is her style inspired directly by any of the earlier romantic poets whose tradition Browning both championed and continued. The styles of Keats, Shelley, Byron, and Browning differ as much from one another, in fact, as those of any four poets of the times. Dickinson's affinity is rather with the aims, motives, and effects that were ascribed to these poets' work by friend and foe alike and that were understood to bind them together in opposition to the emergent values of Victorian literary culture. These aims appear to have had specific stylistic consequences for Dickinson; in any case, her poetry is by common consent uniquely successful in achieving them. Moreover, the motives generally associated with the romantic wing find expression in a number of Dickinson's remarks about poetry, and tracing this historical context can help us correlate and account for the assumptions underlying such remarks.

Dickinson expressed greater and more persistent admiration for Browning than for any other writer, except possibly Shakespeare. Her enthusiasm is most often explained as one aspect of a recognized interest in the women writers of the era. One of the poems Dickinson wrote about Browning, for instance, pointedly describes her as a nonpareil among woman artists: "Not on Record—bubbled other— / Flute—or Woman— / So divine" (312). On the other hand, assimilating Browning to her female contemporaries does not explain the much greater intensity of response she inspired from Dickinson. Moreover, in the company of George Eliot, George Sand, and Charlotte and Emily Brontë—some of the other women Dickinson admired—Elizabeth Barrett Browning is likely to seem more nearly the least impressive figure than the most.[18] Even the contemporary interest in reclaiming women's literature has not significantly altered the century-old verdict that Browning is a poet of the second or third rank.

In style and theme, moreover, Browning is more nearly Dickinson's opposite than her model. Browning's poems are copious, notably fluent in manner, and sometimes clearly prolix. They directly address the social and political issues of the day, they cultivate a consistent moral earnestness, and they avoid venturing into new or idiosyncratic forms and techniques. In other words, Browning is one of the most unrepentantly Victorian of writers, a fact that may cause some embarrassment to champions of Dickinson as a forerunner of modernism. Browning's poetry also differs from Dickinson's in other respects. The English poet wrote dramatic and narrative verse as well as lyric, most notably in *Aurora Leigh*, the work Dickinson mentions most often. And Browning is also an impressively learned, allusive poet who drew on a wide range of classical and modern European literatures.

How then could Dickinson have admired Browning so fervently? The enthusiasm is more explicable if we recall what Browning's poetry meant to her own times. Although her reputation began to fade soon after her death, during her lifetime she was widely deemed a significant poet. More important, during the 1850s she was perhaps the single most eminent representative of a dwindling band, those who saw Keats, Shelley, Byron, and their followers as the major voices of nineteenth-century English poetry and as praiseworthy inspirations for the literature of the future. In contrast to the numerous and for a long time generally more influential voices deploring the excesses of these poets, Browning remained an outspoken champion of such romanticism. She was, for instance, one of the few established English writers who responded warmly to the Spasmodics.[19] And although her own poetry may now seem unexceptional enough, at the time it was seen as exemplifying the romantic wing's preference for enthusiasm over Apollonian or Polonian sobriety and also its supposed reliance on lush, striking, or even shocking images at the expense of intellectual coherence. *Aurora Leigh*, which is an overtly argumentative poem of considerable intellectual seriousness, was known as much for its metaphoric intensity as for its contribution to public debates or its appropriation of the previously male domain of epic high seriousness.

None of Dickinson's references to Browning unmistakably associate her with the romantic wing or with any other specifically English context; however, in the one Dickinson poem that explicitly refers to Browning, she characterized the Englishwoman as the last representative of a tradition. "Her—'last Poems'— / Poets—ended— / Silver—perished—with her Tongue" (312).[20] The second line cannot be taken literally, but neither is it empty hyperbole. Browning's death means not just the end of her own work but the possibility that what she and Dickinson consider the line of true poets will come to an end. Dickinson's poem was written in 1862, a time when Emerson, Longfellow, and Lowell were the most eminent American poets, when Arnold and Clough were in mid-career in England, and when Tennyson—the most esteemed of them all—had long since discarded the Keatsian mode of his early verse. In other words, the only poets who could possibly have seemed in danger of vanishing with Browning's death were those outside the then ascendant mode we now identify as Victorian.

At the time of Browning's death the split between those who reacted against English romanticism's second generation and those who upheld it had been a matter of public debate for three decades. In 1831, reviewing Tennyson's early poems in the *Englishman's Magazine*, Arthur Hallam contrasted the two wings under the heading of reflection as against sensation. Among the poets of sensation, who stress provocative imagery, intense or exotic mental states, and an immediacy of sensual and emotional impact, Hallam placed Keats, Shelley, and Tennyson. Later contributors to this debate usually added Byron, Leigh Hunt, Thomas Lovell Beddoes, and sometimes Shakespeare (who was also claimed by the other side). Among the poets of reflection, who were said to emphasize contemplative wisdom, rational judgment, and the primacy of moral and philosophical ideas, Hallam singled out Wordsworth.[21] Later critics included the other Lake poets, Goethe, Dante, and often Homer or the Greek tragedians.

Dickinson's sympathies should be clear from the list of poets claimed for each side. Ignoring Carlyle's famous recommendation in *Sartor Resartus*, Dickinson declined to close her Byron and open her Goethe, and indeed she almost never mentions any of the poets whom the Victorian wing championed. On the other hand, she refers often to writers from the romantic wing, usually with considerable enthusiasm. In other words, the various references in Dickinson's letters to admired English poets amount to an emphatic declaration of allegiance, as much by the names omitted as by those included. Within the context of Victorian debates over the proper course for English poetry, Dickinson opts firmly for the romantic wing.

There is even some reason to believe that she stretched the truth in order to make her allegiance clear. To Higginson in 1862 she wrote: "You inquire my books—For Poets—I have Keats—and Mr and Mrs Browning. For Prose—Mr Ruskin—Sir Thomas Browne—and the Revelations" (*Letters*, 404). This answer can certainly not be taken as unvarnished truth; Dickinson's interest in Keats is difficult to confirm but it is obviously less intense than her immersion in Shakespeare. Moreover, Higginson had mentioned both Browne and Ruskin in his "Letter to a Young Contributor," a fact that raises the suspicion of Dickinson's seeking, at this very early stage in their acquaintance, to ingratiate herself with him. On the other hand, Dickinson's list makes considerable sense in the context of contemporary literary debates. Browne's prose and the Book of Revelation are both metaphorically extravagant, for instance. Likewise, Ruskin, although otherwise an advocate of mid-Victorian earnestness, insisted in his criticism on the affective power of poetry, and he had called *Aurora Leigh* "the first perfect poetical expression of the age."[22]

Dickinson is unlikely to have read Hallam's 1831 essay, but she may well have encountered similar distinctions and arguments for one or the other side in the writings of Clough, Kingsley, Keble, Dobell, Arnold, and a host of anonymous or forgotten reviewers. One contribution to the debate that we know she read is Sir Henry Taylor's preface to *Philip van Artevelde*. Austin Dickinson owned an 1835 edition of this verse drama, and Dickinson alludes directly to the play in "If those I loved were lost" (29).[23] Taylor objects to the "sensibility," "fervor," and "profusion of images" in the "highly-coloured poetry" he sees as dominant in his day, singling out Shelley and Byron for extended censure.

[They] wanted, in the first place, subject matter. A feeling came more easily to them than a reflection, and an image was always at hand when a thought was not forth-coming. . . . It did not belong to poetry in their apprehension

. . . to infer and instruct. On the contrary, it was to stand aloof from everything that is plain and true; to have little concern with what is rational or wise; it was to be, like music, a moving and enchanting art, acting upon the fancy, the affections, the passions, but scarcely connected with the exercise of intellectual faculties.[24]

The crucial contrast, in other words, is between a poetry appealing to reason or moral wisdom and one appealing mainly to affective, emotive intensity. For Dickinson the chief attraction of the poetry of sensation would be that it provoked or stimulated the reader through the "Press / of Imagery," as against instructing the reader through the grace and profundity of its ideas (582). Dickinson makes virtually no distinction in her work between sensations and ideas and certainly indicates no preference for one over the other. But she is uneasy about assuming the moral authority a didactic poetry would entail, and the idea of poetry as reliable, positive instruction is flatly incompatible with the epistemological and eschatological uncertainty pervading her work.

Taylor calls for an author of the sort later to be known as the Victorian sage, a figure of calm wisdom and masterly advice to the reader about how life should be lived. Dickinson, however, turns again and again to precisely those topics on which no such wisdom or advice is possible. As she says in several ways and on several occasions, "the unknown is the largest need of the intellect" (*Letters*, 559). To prefer the unknown or unknowable precisely because it is beyond reach was by Dickinson's time a romantic commonplace, and in one early poem she echoes the equally commonplace notion that knowledge threatens enchantment and romance. "It's finer not to know / If Summer were *an Axiom*— / What sorcery had Snow?" (191). In her version of this theme the unknown is a general need rather than one distinctive to the noble soul, and it forms a necessary part of the life of meaning.

> How human Nature dotes
> On what it cant detect
> The moment that a Plot is plumbed
> It's meaning is extinct—
>
> (1417)

Meaning lives, in other words, only until it is securely or confidently grasped. The same poem goes on to defend Dickinson's lifelong concern with the theme of immortality.

Of subjects that resist
Redoubtablest is this
Where go we —
Go we anywhere
Creation after this?

(1417)

Or, to make the pun more explicit, the most greatly redoubtable arises from the most and greatest doubt. Immortality is on this account her "Flood subject" not simply because, like the biblical flood, it is an inherently great theme but because it floods the mind with possibilities, none of which can be definitively ascertained (*Letters*, 454).

Doubt and uncertainty usually lead to anguish, in Dickinson's speakers and presumably her readers also. Eschewing the consoling or ennobling wisdom generally favored in the critical opinion of her time, Dickinson clearly cultivates anguish, partly because she views it as authentic. "I like a look of Agony / Because I know it's true —" (241). More important, like such apparent opposites as bliss or joy, anguish is a particularly intense emotion, and Dickinson consistently values intensity above all else. In this she remains true to the values of the romantic wing as against its Victorian critics, who generally shunned intense but possibly idiosyncratic moments in favor of a broader, more balanced and comprehensive view. Matthew Arnold's 1853 repudiation of *Empedocles on Etna* exemplifies this shift in values. Arnold refused to reprint the poem because its portrait of supposedly unrelieved human suffering lacked the balance and wholeness he was coming to prize over more idiosyncratic situations.

Arnold's position deserves some attention, not only because Dickinson may have read him but because he represents a nineteenth-century version of the standards sometimes wrongly applied to Dickinson by twentieth-century critics. Arnold faults modern poetry in general and Keats's *Isabella* in particular for the same reasons Porter and Blackmur fault Dickinson's poetry. *Isabella* lacks "Architectonice." Although a "treasure-house" of "vivid and picturesque turns of expression," Keats's poem is "utterly incoherent," like the all too frequent poems of the day that "seem to exist merely for the sake of single lines and passages; not for the sake of producing any total impression."[25] Now Arnold's standards are hardly despicable or indefensible, but the point is that they mark a clearly defined position in the history of literary controversy, not a set of self-evident values.

Browning's appeal for Dickinson has one other important facet. In addition to serving as a model of a successful woman poet and representing a literary faction Dickinson favored, Browning conveniently died just at the time when Dickinson's poetry was beginning to flourish. Until Browning's death Dickinson never once refers to her in any of the surviving poems, letters, or rumors and reports of conversation. In the year to year and a half afterward, however, Dickinson mentions her in five letters (out of the thirty-eight extant from the period) and writes at least three memorial poems: "Her 'last poems'" (312), "I went to thank her" (363), and "I think I was enchanted" (593). (Browning's husband, Robert, likewise receives no mention before Elizabeth's death but gets referred to frequently afterward.) One other poem, "Ourselves were wed one summer—dear" (631), likewise reads on the basis of internal evidence as an elegy for Barrett Browning. As a context against which to set all these memorials, recall that Dickinson is known to have written only one other poem to or about a person with whom she was not directly acquainted: the elegy for Charlotte Brontë beginning "All overgrown by unmoving moss" (148). The surviving references to Browning probably represent only a fraction of the interest Dickinson expressed at the time, for her fascination was widely known to her friends and acquaintances. By the summer of 1862 three persons had sent her pictures of the deceased poet, or so she said in offering a spare to Higginson (*Letters*, 415).

It seems likely, in other words, that Browning's death precipitated a change, or at least a marked increase, in the appeal she held for Dickinson. The American poet had no doubt been reading Browning's poetry over a period of years, but only in death did the English poet assume a central place in her imagination. Moreover, survivorship is a crucial theme in each of the poems Dickinson wrote about Browning. Her relation to the other poet is defined as much by the fact of Browning's death as by the virtues of her poetry, her person, or her place in English literary history.

Poem 363, apparently the last written of the three, is an unremarkable account of a graveside visit, and indeed nothing in the poem identifies the subject as Browning or even as a writer.[26] Poem 312, however, concludes with an extraordinary fantasy of becoming the dead poet's bereaved bridegroom.

> Nought—that We—No Poet's Kinsman
> Suffocate—with easy wo
> What, and if, Ourself a Bridegroom—
> Put her down—in Italy?

The difficult first two lines of this stanza are clear about one thing. A contrast exists between the speaker's response and the easy woe one would expect from a mourner who is unrelated to the dead poet. More curiously, the lines identify the otherwise easier and more conventional response with suffocating, as if letting go of Browning too lightly would threaten the life of the poet writing the text we are reading. The actual bridegroom is Robert Browning, of course, also a poet, as Dickinson would have known, and in most of the verse he had published by that time an ardent disciple of Shelley. In alluding to the already famous story of the Brownings' elopement and comparing Robert's grief to her own, Dickinson effectively places herself alongside him as Elizabeth Browning's literary heir. Dickinson's pronoun is "Ourself," the conspicuously royal plural including herself, the actual widower, and perhaps any other as yet uncelebrated poetic survivors who are not content to suffocate or merely to lament that "Silver—perished—with her Tongue."

A partial confirmation of this reading comes from a letter she wrote to Samuel Bowles, while he was touring Europe in 1862. "Should anybody where you go, talk of Mrs. Browning, you must hear for us — and if you touch her Grave, put one hand on the Head for me — her unmentioned Mourner" (*Letters*, 410). What is striking here, as Ellen Moers notes, is not the avidity of Dickinson's interest but the reference to herself as an *unmentioned* mourner.[27] Dickinson certainly made no secret of her vicarious grief, so to specify herself as an unmentioned mourner makes sense only in contrast to mourners who are mentioned, i.e., more visible to the public. Those would certainly include Robert Browning and perhaps others who by this time had memorialized Browning in print. In other words, Dickinson's phrase suggests an edgy awareness of those who might more visibly or legitimately claim to be Browning's heirs. Whether or not she envies their mention, she at least wants to stake a claim of her own.

Whether "Ourselves were wed one summer" refers directly to Browning or only draws in part upon Dickinson's reaction to her death, it is the edgiest of the four memorial poems. It is also the only one of the four which is addressed to the deceased and which thus in some regard seeks her approval of the speaker's claims. The poem includes several biographically suggestive details. One is to the June in which the addressee's vision, wedding, coronation, and perhaps also death — these may be four metaphors for the same moment of exaltation — have occurred. Another is to the addressee's sunny, blooming, transoceanic, and hence possibly Italian home, which is contrasted to the speaker's frosty northern climate. The poem also echoes several images and situations from the three memorial poems identified by Johnson, notably in characterizing Browning's effect on Dickinson as darkness and in associating the facts of Browning's death and Dickinson's continued life with a vision of marrying and widowing. As in "Her 'last poems,'" the vision clearly works to bind the women more closely and thus give Dickinson a share in the dead woman's glory.

> Ourselves were wed one summer—dear—
> Your Vision—was in June—
> And when Your little Lifetime failed,
> I wearied—too—of mine—
>
> And overtaken in the Dark—
> Where You had put me down—
> By Some one carrying a Light—
> I—too—received the Sign.
>
> 'Tis true—our Futures different lay—
> Your Cottage—faced the sun—
> While Oceans—and the North must be—
> On every side of mine
>
> 'Tis true, Your Garden led the Bloom,
> For mine—in Frosts—was sown—
> And yet, one Summer, we were Queens—
> But You—were crowned in June—
>
> (631)

The key claim in the first line, which links the speaker's eminence to the addressee's, is significantly ambiguous. If speaker and addressee are wed to one another (like Robert and Elizabeth, whose marriage actually took place in September), then the former shares grievingly but assuredly in the latter's glory. If two independent but parallel weddings have taken place, then the speaker's derivative stature is more suspect, but she is also freer to make her own way. To put the same point in a different perspective, the speaker appears undecided whether she wants to be as much like the addressee as possible. As a result the somewhat elaborae rhetoric of comparison she has initiated falters at the end, undercutting the expectation of a bold claim of identity.

That the addressee's vision/wedding/coronation has priority, the speaker clearly acknowledges. (The variant last line is even more emphatic: "but Your's was first—in June—.") Initially then the speaker insists upon similarities which would confirm her likeness to the dead queen: the summertime wedding, the failing lifetime and growing darkness, and the reception of some mysteriously salvational sign. Both the last two stanzas begin with a marker of concession ("'Tis true"), which we normally expect will be used to set up a stronger reiteration of the positive claim. In other words, we expect a "'tis true" to legitimize and strengthen a "nonetheless," whether the latter is uttered or only implicit. However, rather than strongly reasserting her claim, Dickinson only begins the reversal characteristic of this rhetorical pattern, giving it but one line as against the six lines of concession before reversing again to a final line that once more concedes difference: "But You—were crowned in June." Where the structure leads us to expect a resounding claim about the speaker's and addressee's closeness, we get only a nervous or abrupt recognition of distance. Where we are prepared to accept similarity, even equality, the speaker confesses secondariness.

Some nervousness about survivorship and belatedness can also be faintly heard in "I think I was enchanted," the most important of the memorial poems and arguably the one in which Dickinson fully comes to terms with Browning. The poem differs from the other three in emphasizing Browning's formative influence as much as Dickinson's survivorship. Yet like most elegies by one poet for another, it stresses the survivor's imaginative responsive as much as the dead poet's majesty.

> I think I was enchanted
> When first a sombre Girl—
> I read that Foreign Lady—
> The Dark—felt beautiful—
>
> And whether it was noon at night—
> Or only Heaven—at Noon—
> For very Lunacy of Light
> I had not power to tell—
>
> The Bees—became as Butterflies—
> The Butterflies—as Swans—
> Approached—and spurned the narrow Grass—
> And just the meanest Tunes
>
> That Nature murmured to herself
> To keep herself in Cheer—
> I took for Giants—practicing
> Titanic Opera—
>
> The Days—to Mighty Metres stept—
> The Homeliest—adorned
> As if unto a Jubilee
> 'Twere suddenly confirmed—
>
> I could not have defined the change—
> Conversion of the Mind

Like Sanctifying in the Soul—
Is witnessed—not explained—

'Twas a Divine Insanity—
The Danger to be Sane
Should I again experience—
'Tis Antidote to turn—

To Tomes of solid Witchcraft—
Magicians be asleep—
But Magic—hath an Element
Like Deity—to keep—

(593)

The enchantment is at first so powerful that it overwhelms Dickinson's powers of expression, although her power to tell has ipso facto returned by the time she writes this poem. The time scheme is important here. Dickinson's frequently retrospective poems often strongly distinguish the moment of telling from the moment told about. The normal narrative tense in English is the past, to be sure, but Dickinson regularly exploits the grammatical norm as an ontological symbol. Her several past-tense accounts of dying are the most famous examples, for they fantastically project the moment of telling into some afterlife. Furthermore, she proclaims in one poem that intense experience is incompatible with articulateness. "If I could tell how glad I was / I should not be so glad—," the poem begins (1668). The same poem goes on to characterize the moment of intensity as a time "When I cannot make the Force / Nor mould it into Word." Whereas one might expect a two-part distinction, between the force of gladness and the eventual wording of it, Dickinson distinguishes three phases. Rather than an immediate consequence or constituent of experience, the force later to be worded is Dickinson's creation, something she has made in response to the experience but only after the intensity of the experience has waned.

All this bears on the praise for Browning in "I think I was enchanted" because that poem provides something of a model for the ideal relation between the experience of reading and the act of writing, in this case Dickinson's youthful reading of Browning and her writing of the retrospective poem. Dickinson writes from a time well past the initial enchantment, indeed from a time when the enchanter is dead, so the apparently lasting "Conversion of the Mind" that Browning's poetry has occasioned cannot quite be the same as the "Divine Insanity" of the initial enchantment. If nothing else, the power to tell has revived, although without necessarily bringing with it the

"Danger to be Sane." Dickinson speaks from a middle state that is neither the mundane sanity of her life as a "sombre Girl" nor the mute, giddy "Lunacy of Light" she had experienced on first reading Browning. Thus immediately after insisting that "I could not have defined the change—" (note the verb tense), she rather effectively defines it as a "Conversion of the Mind." ("Change" can also refer to the change in nature's appearance, however, and the poem does acknowledge that defining the change as a conversion is not the same as explaining it.)

The middle stanzas of this poem consist of fairly extravagant images for the speaker's condition after she has read the foreign lady. More specifically, the images depict how the world appears to her in this new middle state of consciousness. The images are without exception Dickinson's own. In other words, she passes over the opportunity to make complimentary allusions to Browning's verse or to borrow any of Browning's own abundant metaphors for the value and effect of poetry. As in "If I could tell how glad I was," the force of the enchantment is something Dickinson prefers to make herself, rather than to take it over from the texts initially causing the enchantment.

One can infer only so much from the dog that did not bark, but it is curious that here and elsewhere Browning's avowed influence leaves so few marks on Dickinson's poetry. Were it not for the testimony of the letters and the one uncontestable reference in "Her 'last poems,'" I doubt the influence would ever have been suspected. To be sure, several critics have claimed to find sources in Browning, especially *Aurora Leigh*, for a number of Dickinson's poems. Source-hunting is a notoriously subjective sport, however, and I find most of the claimed borrowings to be doubtful. Either the similarity between the supposedly related passages is slight or both passages can as easily be ascribed to poetic commonplaces. Even one of the single most convincing instances is not quite a direct borrowing. Dickinson's "I died for beauty" (449) almost certainly draws on Browning's "A Vision of Poets" but both poems owe as much to their common source in Keats.

"I think I was enchanted" emphasizes the speaker's state of mind rather than the enchanter who has caused it. This culminates in an assurance that the enchanter's death poses no threat. The poems can always be reread. That the "Tomes of solid Witchcraft" should outlast their author may seem unremarkable. Yet Dickinson's noting this fact softens the stress that her imagery of magic and enchantment might otherwise put on the exotic, unique, or distinctively personal power of the magician. In other words, it is not the magician's irreplaceable presence that effects the magic. Moreover, by the end of the poem, when the present tense makes its only appearances, "Magicians" is conspicuously plural. A poem beginning with the singular event of reading the equally singular "Foreign Lady" ends by quietly assimilating her to an anonymous company of bygone literary magicians. The company presumably consists of the same poets whom Browning's *Last Poems* ended. Here, however, the devastation recorded in poem 312 is absent. Not only is magic like diety because it lasts, the speaker is in possession of the magicians' lore, the tomes of solid witchcraft.

Browning's death may have increased the power her poems had upon Dickinson or even helped focus Dickinson's ambitions, but there is no reason to doubt Dickinson's testimony that the poems strongly affected her long before she began to compose the testimony. In fact, the relation Dickinson articulates between herself and Browning represents an ideal transaction between author and audience, one that shapes Dickinson's anticipations about how she herself wants to be read. Dickinson values Browning's poems first and foremost for the intensity of their affective power, that is, for their ability to produce the enchantment. This power is distinctive enough to Browning and her poems to justify singling her out for what never quite amounts to idolatry. Because Browning shares the power with earlier poets of sensation, she can be understood more to hold it in trust than to wield it in the exclusive or privative way a Carlylean poet would.

Although they elicit enchantment, Browning's poems do not much shape the actual content of Dickinson's experience. Dickinson responds to Browning's power by representing not the world Browning's poems have revealed but the world Dickinson herself makes and molds into word in the wake of her mental transformation. In other words, Browning's poems stimulate Dickinson to go and do otherwise, seeking perhaps the same intensity of response in her own readers but seeking it through a poetry that in style and theme bears little relation to Browning's. The difference between Browning and Dickinson does not dishonor the older poet or her poems; rather it honors them precisely for stimulating the conversion that allows Dickinson to invent her own witchcraft.

Dissemination

Browning's influence inspires or legitimizes what I have called an ethic of productivity. Dickinson's invention of a conspicuously idiosyncratic, deviant style, her affective view of poetry, and her allegiance to Browning and the romantic wing are all linked by a literary enterprise designed to enchant and to astonish without also impoverishing the reader. Like most writers, Dickinson modeled her own writing on her experiences as a reader. However, unlike an Augustan poet respectfully imitating a classical predecessor or a post-Miltonic ephebe battling the anxiety of influence against a titanic precursor, Dickinson imagined that the reader should play as prominent a part as the author. What an author has created thus initiates at best a richly productive process of response. This necessarily makes the author's role somewhat less gloriously imposing than in "This was a poet." Rather than an idolized immortal who is "Exterior—to Time" and rather also than the autonomous creator and owner of his own riches, "Himself—to Him—a Fortune," the poet becomes the more modestly honored initiator of a process that continues long afterward.

The ethic of productivity is proclaimed most explicitly in "The poets light but lamps," where authors are praised as agents of circumference. Circumference here requires for its dissemination the refracting and hence coproductive response of subsequent ages. It is still the poet's product but it also now continues to exist only through its furtherance by future generations.

> The Poets light but Lamps—
> Themselves—go out—
> The Wicks they stimulate—
> If vital light
>
> Inhere as do the Suns—
> Each Age a Lens
> Disseminating their
> Circumference—
>
> (883)

The lamps here may in part be taken as poems, in which case the text proposes only a truism: poems containing a genuinely vital light continue to spread their influence well after the author has died. Yet Dickinson refers to the poets as stimulating the wicks of these lamps, an odd way of describing the composing of a text. The verb suggests that the things primarily lit and stimulated by poets are their readers, an interpretation which would both fit with the image of poets going out as lamps do and also allow us to fill in the poem's characteristically elliptic syntax. If the wicks or readers stimulated by the poem shine with a vital light, then those readers will last or inhere just as suns (and poets) do, for they will become by their refracting and magnifying responsiveness agents of light in their own turn. The circumference thus disseminated belongs in part to the original poets ("their" referring by way of "they" to "Poets"), and it also belongs grammatically and actually to the lamps and wicks as well, for the responsive readers are poets themselves, either in the literal sense of composing poems inspired by the earlier generations or in the figurative sense of responding in some other, equally co-productive way.

Each age repeats the process of dissemination. This means that it would be difficult, maybe impossible, to locate whatever original center there may have been for the unending process or to identify the first source from which the light began to radiate in stepwise phases. Consequently the poets named in the first line may as well be found in the middle of the chain as at its beginning. That is why every noun until the final, iterative phrase is plural. Poets, lamps, wicks, and suns represent the roles played out successively by each person and each age. Circumference is singular, to be sure, and with its plural possessive pronoun the word asserts that there is some single phenomenon or effect jointly produced, transmitted, and received by all the agents who fill these roles. But circumference in this sense can have no single author and cannot be coextensive with some meaning that a magisterial poet has disclosed once and for all.

The poets of dissemination are in large part the poets of sensation as Dickinson understood and admired them. According to the prevailing mid-Victorian view that she shared, the romantic wing of nineteenth-century English poetry emphasized intensely rendered scenes and images, especially exotic ones. It is easy to see that such poetry might be understood as stimulating responses without dictating them. Indeed, the debate over the poetry of sensation mainly concerned its moral consequences, not its objective properties or the kind of imagination capable of engendering it.

The difference corresponds to the differing lines of descent that can be traced to the romantic wing by Dickinson on one side and modernist poetry on the other. Yeats, for instance, cites Hallam's review of Tennyson as a chief source for the principles of his poetry, but he understands the review as buttressing a poetics centered almost exclusively on the nature of artistic imagination.[28] At mid-century on the other hand, the controversy over the romantic wing largely concerned such poetry's power to arouse dangerous sensations and feelings in the reader. The other side prized objectivity, balance, and wholeness because it sought to harness the admittedly evocative powers of poetry to ennobling and morally responsible ends. Dickinson accepted the Victorians' stress on the effects of poetry, and indeed she essentially defined poetry in terms of what it does. Yet she also opted for the romantic wing's intensity and force as against the Victorians' edification and ennoblement.

Browning herself is a formidable moralist, and her poetry sounds to modern ears the edifying note stereotypically associated with Victorian moralism. Dickinson read Browning's poetry for its power to enchant, however, not its didactic wisdom, and through Browning she seems to have seen the romantic wing as legitimizing a poetry designed to stimulate rather than to instruct. In her famous remark to Higginson about how she recognizes poetry (quoted in the previous chapter), Dickinson even makes the kind and intensity of the response curiously independent of the poem's contents or its author's intentions. This too is characteristic. Separating the reader's experience from the author's intentions and authority—the author's presence, ultimately—is crucial to Dickinson's poetics, so much so that Dickinson will sometimes exaggerate the distance. She even suggests that poetry can dispense with representation or communication, thus radically divorcing the reader's response from anything the poet might have designed.

> "Lethe" in my flower,
> Of which they who drink[,][29]
> In the fadeless orchard
> Hear the bobolink
>
> Merely flake or petal
> As the Eye beholds
> Jupiter! my father!
> I perceive the rose!
>
> (1730)

The images of flower, drink, bird, and orchard join rather clumsily in this very early poem, but the effect partly reinforces the emphasis on the audience's role. If poetry is variously an intoxicating drug and a flower of rhetoric, what the audience perceives in the fadeless orchard of its responsive revery is not necessarily an image conveyed by the poem and certainly not one they receive passively. Even the identity and value of the flower/poem are perceived as the eye beholds them, rather than as nature determines them or the poet speaks them. The final lines, which may refer to what the speaker sees while she writes, then assert only the poet's identification of the flower as against other, presumably also legitimate identifications. I behold the rose; you behold the sunflower; he, she, and it behold snowflakes or hyacinths. The lines also place the speaker/poet in a

49

reader's position in relation to the divine author of nature. In responding to Jupiter's creations she insists that what she perceives competes in validity with whatever he may have set before her.

Dickinson's understanding of poetry has been compared to Poe's, for the obvious reason that he is the only other significant American writer of the day to articulate an affective theory of literature.[30] Moreover, Poe's affective theories are militantly antididactic, a cardinal principle being the gulf separating truth and beauty. There is an instructive and equally obvious difference, however. Poe insists upon the writer's calculation of the effects he elicits and his careful manipulation of the reader's response. In other words, Poe writes from an author's perspective, often taking the knowing and superior tone of a master craftsman sharing trade secrets with the public. Dickinson, however, usually writes from the perspective of the responding reader. In letters and poems she continually depicts herself remembering, experiencing, or anticipating the affective forces she clearly values in art. "The love a life can show below," for instance, provides a dizzying and virtuoso list of responses to the "diviner thing" that "In Music— hints and sways."

> 'Tis this—invites—appalls—endows—
> Flits—glimmers—proves—dissolves—
> Returns—suggests—convicts—enchants—
> Then—flings in Paradise—
>
> (673)

Style is not the only literary resource capable of eliciting such effects, but a style conscientiously predicated on deviance is especially well designed to disseminate circumference. Indeed, deviance per se is provocative, the eccentricity of Dickinson's style importantly contributing to a widely recognized intensity and to an enigmatic quality at least as widely recognized. Dickinson's poetry offers the evocative, intensified language characteristic in one way or another of most poetry. By means of its exceptional strangeness, furthermore, her poetry forestalls the cultural and linguistic codes that might otherwise allow us to extract an authoritative message.

Even the features of Dickinson's stylistic signature further dissemination. For example, isolating words or phrases with dashes and capital letters (and also, in the earliest poetry, with frequent quotation marks and underlinings) partly decontextualizes their semantic resources, slowing or interrupting the cumulative effect of the poem so as to invite the reader to linger more attentively over their full potential as single words. This foregrounding of linguistic potentials is also a kind of deviance, in that it interrupts the automatism of some forms of communication. Furthermore, Dickinson's dashes as much join as they separate words, providing thereby a positive power of combination in addition to the usual ones found in grammar, meter, and rhyme. The distinctive effects occur when, rather than reinforcing one another, the links scatter in different directions.

In addition to syntactic and lexical deviance of a sort that lends itself to linguistic analysis, the most richly provocative aspect of Dickinson's poetry may be its figurative intensity. It is a common claim in contemporary criticism that figurality is crucial to literary language and that it is also the feature which most fully resists codification and certainty.[31] The claim was not unheard in Dickinson's time, and she would certainly have agreed with Emerson that "an imaginative book renders us more service at first by stimulating us through its tropes than afterward when we arrive at the precise sense of the author," demurring only at his assumption that we always ought so to arrive.[32]

One response to this sort of style is suggested by poem 711. "Strong Draughts of Their Refreshing Minds" are what "enables Mine," that poem insists, concluding by exclaiming "How powerful the Stimulus / Of an Hermetic Mind." The poem offers another instance of reading as empowerment, which here is imagined as enabling the speaker to endure a desert as though she carried her own resources. "Through Desert or the Wilderness / As bore it Sealed Wine." "Hermetic" also derives from the image of a sealed jar, thus identifying "Their" minds with the speaker's predicament, and the word carries as well the usual extended sense of the esoteric or enigmatic. The stimulus is conveyed, in other words, not only by the intoxicating contents of the jars but by their provocative mystery. The claim extends an already noted motif, the intellect's need for the unknown as a spur to its own determination of meaning. A text whose contents are tantalizingly elusive stimulates the reader more effectively than one bearing a readily accessible message. "The Riddle we can guess / We speedily despise" (1222). Here, moreover, the hermetic stimulus of their minds enables mine to become as theirs are, a conveyer of sealed wine.

Judging from the recorded responses, however, the effect of Dickinson's sometimes hermetic stimulus has as often been intimidation as liberation. A deviant style risks being taken as an esoteric one and hence as the deliberately veiled but doubly authoritative speech of a remote master. I am almost exaggerating, but Susan Howe recently has had the honesty or the bad judgment to confess just such a response in print.[33] And more generally, so accustomed are we all to decoding texts, receiving authorial meaning, and referring the effect of an artwork to the artist's intentions that Dickinson's provocative indeterminacy can be genuinely unsettling. The temptation always is to silence or explain away the insistent equivocality of the poems. Yet when the singular surface features of Dickinson poems regularly yield up multiple deep structures, leaving us no linguistic rationale for selecting one over another, it should be clear that the disclosure of meaning is not Dickinson's primary enterprise.

3

Cherishing Power

It would be hard to overestimate the presence of the Romantic sublime in the nineteenth century.

Thomas Weiskel

Beyond the mastery of a Carlylean poet's disclosure of meaning lies a different configuration of poetry and power, Dickinson believes. Indeed, if any single motto could characterize her entire poetic enterprise, it would be the following recommendation addressed to her sister-in-law. "Cherish Power—dear," the poet advised Susan Gilbert Dickinson in an undated note written about 1878. "Remember that stands in the Bible between the Kingdom and the Glory, because it is wilder than either of them" (*Letters*, 631). This note enjoys no special status in Dickinson's correspondence and has heretofore received little attention, yet it manages to epitomize the commitments shaping Dickinson's entire body of work. The literary and spiritual ambitions endorsed by the letter to Susan both acknowledge the prominence of mastery and outline a means of working around its otherwise extensive reach.

In the doxological conclusion to the Lord's Prayer as it appears in Matthew 6 (the King James translation only), three divine prerogatives are linked: the kingdom, the power, and the glory. Dickinson's advice sharply distinguishes power from the other two, a pair which revealingly includes monarchical sovereignty and hence the idea of control as mastery that we have already noticed. Dickinson recommends cherishing power rather than seeking it, wielding it, or submitting oneself to it. These other ways of appropriating power would all be forms of mastery; each either presupposes a dyad of dominant and submissive parties or can be fully accounted for by the logic of such dyads.

Cherishing power may differ. It certainly leaves room for the personal will to power at the heart of mastery, and it can include as well the dyadic opposite of such will, a desire to submit oneself entirely to the other's majesty. But it also intimates an oddly impersonal intention to foster power, to keep it going or to magnify its scope while remaining at a distance from it. This intention goes beyond the closed circuits of mastery or at least seeks to. Dickinson's advice thus may not succumb so easily to the literary power relations manifested in "This was a poet." To the extent that it succeeds, a poetics based on cherishing power opens Dickinson's otherwise characteristically romantic enterprise to a different sort of project. The resulting poetry regularly mobilizes the themes and stances of heroic mastery but also refuses to be limited by them. In other words, Dickinson's work performs a sort of jiujitsu on the poetics of mastery, drawing much of its strength from the resources of domination, submission, and the intersubjective rivalry underlying them while at the same time seeking to turn those resources toward different ends.

As well as proper techniques or a sound method, jiujitsu requires deftness, a quality that cannot be guaranteed in advance. In other words, the poetic implications of cherishing power do not by themselves constitute a way around mastery, and indeed the two main implications are not only vulnerable to such a structure but put themselves rather directly in its way. Before turning to these two, then, the one leading us to the rhetorical commitments underlying Dickinson's style and the other to her engagement with the sublime, let us first examine some simpler instances of how Dickinson imagines power. Like time to Saint Augustine, power is one of those notions which if no one asks me to explain, I know, but which if I wish to explain to someone who asks, I know not. Some clarification at least may forestall confusing Dickinson's sense of power with the currently influential notions deriving from Foucault. Dickinson's frequently metaphysical or specifically theological understanding of power overlaps with Foucault's, but Dickinson almost entirely lacks Foucault's institutional imagination and she often sees knowledge as power's opposite, not its accomplice.[1]

Two of Dickinson's cognates for power are dominion and discipline, each an aspect of mastery. More specifically, dominion is Dickinson's main term for the kind of power wielded by a master, and discipline is a key honorific for the willing minion's regimen. Both terms also apply readily to a politics of authorship, dominion signifying the Carlylean poet's hegemony over the reader and discipline the usually eager acceptance of instruction from some external or internalized monarch.

On the other hand, both cognates sometimes front upon wilder, less restrained notions of power, the one distinctively represented for Dickinson by the doxology concluding the paternoster. Consider "Dominion lasts until obtained," which empties out the idea of dominion and also by means of an allusion to Keats implicitly correlates artistic communication with relations of power.

> Dominion lasts until obtained —
> Possession just as long —
> But these — endowing as they flit
> Eternally belong.
>
> How everlasting are the Lips
> Known only to the Dew —
> These are the Brides of Permanence
> Supplanting me and you
>
> (1257)

The first lines assimilate dominion to one of Dickinson's few unequivocal themes, the superiority of seeking to attaining. Other versions of this persistent theme more explicitly echo a romantic commonplace which Dickinson clearly endorsed, namely that the boundless intensity of longing dwarfs the finitude of any actual satisfaction of the desire.

This poem differs from its cousins, however, because it contrasts the obtained dominion or possession not to the uncompleted quest for them but to a quite different activity, the one which endows as it flits. One riddle in the poem then is who or what the first stanza's "these" might be, these beings that endow and flit. The answer would seem clearly to be butterflies, or possibly bees. By pollinating the flowers they flit among, butterflies endow those flowers, enabling their continuing generation. "Lips / Known only to the Dew" would then be leaves or petals, in which case the second stanza's "These," namely the "Brides of Permanence," could refer to either party in the botanical marriage, the endowing insects or the endowed plants.

Butterflies are proverbially ephemeral, but here the physical transitoriness of any one butterfly recedes before the permanent role that the species plays in maintaining natural fecundity. Dominion lasts only as long as it is longed for, which Dickinson usually thinks will be forever, but even such a prolonged desire might be less eternal than the endless cycle of generativity celebrated here. Pollination would accordingly become an organic counterpart to the ethic of productivity discussed briefly in the first chapter. Butterflies eternally belong because they help generate plant life for new generations of butterflies to kiss. Moreover, they do this by endowing their brides rather than possessing or taking dominion over them. The alternative, up to and apparently including rape, is a regular feature in Dickinson's other poems about flowers and bees; examples include "Did the harebell loose her girdle" (213), "Like trains of cars on tracks of plush" (1224), and "A bee his burnished carriage" (1339).

If the word "endowment" generally designates a kindly and beneficent bestowal, one that establishes the recipient in, on, and as its own, pollination is even less domineering than endowment in general. It merely transfers from one plant to another (or one part of a plant to another part) a substance that at no point actually or properly belongs to the transferring, catalyzing agent. Were it otherwise, were the butterflies and bees giving something of their own to the flowers, then presumably the entire transaction could succumb to a dialectic of dominion and possession, that is to say, of mastery. The gift of what truly belonged to the butterfly would then confirm his superiority and priority.

The link between pollination and esthetic production is strengthened by the allusion to Keats, whose most famous ode can be construed as presenting much the same point. The Grecian urn preserves the depicted lovers' never quite consummated kiss, thus eternalizing carnal desire by sublimating it to an esthetic stasis. Keats may or may not share Dickinson's usual reservations about such stasis, but in this case silence and slow time are productive means rather than ends in themselves. The still unravished bride of quietness on the urn endows the one in the poem. Reading the urn generates the poem, and that in turn helps give rise to Dickinson's responsive lyric. Such generativity is a power Dickinson deeply cherishes. It is also one she usually sees as distinct from or even threatened by dominion, which is defined by an authority established in the past rather than some capacity still open to the future.

Discipline may seem a more attractive literary possibility than dominion, particularly if one sympathizes with Blackmur's belief that it is the virtue Dickinson most lacks. Like Blackmur, Dickinson understands discipline as internalized mastery, a regimen for curtailing and redirecting the self's natural, perhaps wayward, indulgent, or capricious practices. More specifically, she links the attainment of self-mastery to the braving of adversity. "Power is only Pain— / Stranded, thro' Discipline," as she most memorably and—it would seem—approvingly put it. Yet the whole of the poem in which these lines appear sets disciplined power against an image of intoxication that the poem unambiguously rates as a mightier power.

> I can wade Grief—
> Whole Pools of it—
> I'm used to that—
> But the least push of Joy
> Breaks up my feet—
> And I tip—drunken—
> Let no Pebble—smile—
> 'Twas the New Liquor—
> That was all!
>
> Power is only Pain—
> Stranded, thro' Discipline,
> Till Weights—will hang—
> Give Balm—to Giants—
> And they'll wilt, like Men—
> Give Himmaleh—
> They'll Carry—Him!
>
> (252)

The poem has plausibly been read as celebrating discipline, sobriety, and hence the sort of firm self-control Dickinson is sometimes thought to lack. "Control [of pain] is the key. Control is power. And in this poem, at any rate, delight cannot be controlled."[2] The reading certainly identifies much of the contrast between joy and pain, a contrast that in other poems ("I like a look of agony" [241], for instance) results in prizing the latter for its greater authenticity. On the other hand, delight is not on that account condemned or ignored, for the poem maintains a humorous, even giddy tone that sets it apart from Dickinson's normally grim, clinical investigations of psychic states. The comically wilting giants, the tipsy admonition to the pebble, and the bathetic, nearly nicknaming reference to Himmaleh as "Him" conspire against soberly binding oneself to a discipline of pain endured and hence controlled.

A key image appears in the word "stranded," which the following line encourages us to gloss as woven or braided. Pain would then be transformed into power by braiding it into the usable strength of a rope or whip (one of the arcane meanings of "discipline" being a whip or scourge). "Stranded" can also mean abandoned, of course, left high and dry as by shipwreck or betrayal. To control pain by braiding it into a useful power entails keeping it close at hand and thus continuing to bear it, as the giants bear the mountain on their backs. Understood as abandonment, however, stranding locates pain and also the kind of power it fosters at a distance from the self. Similarly, in the first stanza the speaker wades a grief that is clearly separate from her, specifically from her body, whereas the intially separate joy gets incorporated as intoxicating drink. So also does balm. The image uniting the two otherwise divergent stanzas is thus a contrast appearing in each. On one side is an upstanding self who metaphorically shoulders or strides across painful experiences and on the other a staggering, wilted figure who imbibes or absorbs joyful, soothing ones, the experiences in both cases being represented as liquids.

Whereas "Dominion lasts until obtained" argues for the inferiority of dominion to endowment, "I can wade grief" is less polemical in its comparison of two kinds of power. Intoxication by joy is clearly mightier than disciplined sobriety, but sobriety may have the advantage in being a power wielded by rather than against the self. In other words, if one is concerned to use rather than to cherish power, drunkenness is the loser. Elsewhere, of course, Dickinson more unstintingly celebrates drunkenness. The difference is that Dickinson's more sentimental poems about intoxication emphasize the drinker's responsiveness rather than the liquor's power. To be a "Debauchee of Dew," as in "I taste a liquor never brewed," is to claim a power variously and generously bestowed by air, dew, summer days, and other unmastering and unmasterable sources of delight (214).

To be a debauchee of dew is not necessarily to oppose discipline or to combat it. A more succinct and profoundly nonoppositional contrast is inscribed in the advice to Susan about cherishing power, for cherishing power is likewise not a strategy for overthrowing the kingdom or snatching the glory. Either such version of fighting fire with fire would directly oppose the oppositional structure of mastery and thus itself succumb to the structure.

The typically half-jocular, half-oracular letter of 1878 to Susan is not directly about poetry, but it aptly summarizes the literary credo which Dickinson had by then practiced for twenty years. Like many of Dickinson's poems and a number of her letters to frequent correspondents, this one omits any reference to topic, context, or occasion. Unlike poems, on the other hand, letters are finitely addressed speech acts as well as texts, and they accordingly presuppose a shared context and contact that can sometimes be reconstructed. The allusion to the Lord's Prayer, for instance, echoes a similar remark in a letter dated 1864, also to Susan Dickinson, that more clearly associates the scriptural passage with imagination and will. "I knew it was 'November' but there is a June when Corn is cut whose option is within. That is why I prefer the Power—for Power is Glory, when it likes, and Dominion, too—" (*Letters*, 432).

Susan Dickinson is an especially appropriate recipient for momentous but veiled pronouncements on art. She had once been a literary confidant of the poet and continued in the 1870s to be the recipient of more poems than anyone else. The pious Susan would also have been a fitting addressee of the poet's theological wit, which here and elsewhere plays heretically less with the truth of Christianity than with the justice of its political economy. Most of all, throughout the long and often tumultuous relation between the two women, Emily Dickinson often showed an intense mixture of affection and rivalry that led her to justify herself more aggressively, regularly, and seriously with Susan than with any other correspondent.

In the 1878 letter the poet advises choosing among the divine attributes listed together in the doxology. This act of choice seems to have no theological or homiletic precedent, for the three attributes represent a single liturgical formula that, as a matter of fact, has only doubtful authority as scripture.[3] Dickinson's understanding of "Kingdom" is clear enough from the term she substitutes in the 1864 letter, "Dominion," and from her other uses of monarchical imagery. A Kingdom, regal dominion over properties earthly and supernal, represents the cardinal form of rule as mastery.

"Glory" is slightly more difficult to explicate, because there are at least three distinguishable contexts that contribute to the term. Glory may be imaged by voice, a centripetal chorus of praised directed to God or, by extension, to some earthly hero. Or it may be imaged by light, the axially illuminating nimbus adorning holy personages in much Christian art. In most of Dickinson's uses of the word, "glory" seems synonymous with fame and thus perhaps implies praise by voice, but one poem transcribed by Susan centrally and explicitly associates such glory with brightness. The opening lines are: "Glory is that bright tragic thing / That for an instant / Means Dominion" (1660). The third context, which intersects the other two, is military fame, particularly and originally the honor paid to some chieftain at a triumphal procession. In the Old Testament sources for the doxological phrase, God's glory is the honor due the Lord of Hosts for defeating Israel's enemies.

Linking the different senses of glory and uniting them with the idea of the kingdom is that all four stipulate some singular, commanding center; glory organizes and hierarchically dominates the space around it. As voice, for example, glory is directed inward toward its object, whereas as a nimbus it radiates outward, yet in each case it establishes a single focusing object which portions all that surrounds it. Both the Kingdom and the Glory exemplify the structure of mastery, in other words, for they construct a definitive hierarchy of command. Both also reinforce the association Dickinson makes between mastery and design, because both serve as well to organize the subordinated and peripheral region that lies about them. It is not only that they are elevated and thus distinct but also that their minions look to them and heed their authority.

According to most understandings of the term, Power also ought to belong on the side of mastery, particularly if one discounts Dickinson's claim about its wildness. In the 1864 letter, for instance, Power clearly dominates the other two in the sense of being mightier, more inclusive, and more comprehensive. It thus arguably plays the monarch to the kingdom's more restricted sovereignty. Power's superior scope is reiterated in an 1868 letter to Higginson. "When a little girl I remember hearing that remarkable passage and preferring the 'Power,' not knowing at the time that 'Kingdom' and 'Glory' were included" (*Letters*, 460). On the other hand, inclusion is not precisely domination. Moreover, Dickinson does insist on power's wildness. This wildness is pointedly given as the cause of Power's standing between the Kingdom and the Glory, a claim which is both puzzling and intriguing. Is it that by virtue of its wildness Power, in conformity with the 1864 text, exemplifies a primus inter pares, supporting and sustaining the other two? Or does the scripturally and liturgically authorized sequence show us a wild Power being custodially restrained by sober, orthodox attendants? In either case the wildness contrasts sharply to the order and stability of the centered and centering agents.

Both explanations of the scriptural sequence and perhaps the very act of reading allegorically this extract from the 1878 letter are vulnerable to a charge of overinterpretation. I have cited what corroborating evidence I can find, including some of Dickinson's several other references to the triplet in Matthew 6, but surely it is not enough to establish a persuasively authoritative reading. Dickinson may or may not have intended such fanciful extravagance in the letter, yet such extravagance is the kind of reading Dickinson's poems regularly solicit and just as regularly receive. Interpreted as I have suggested, the letter insists that power stands in the center, in the middle of the doxological triptych and as the recommended object of our cherishing, and yet in its wildness power seems inevitably an agent of disorder. If the interpretation seems too contrived, however, then we are left with an epistolary counterpart to Dickinson's most gnomic poems, a text which sparkles with wit and the promise of wisdom but which, as far as I can discern, makes little recoverable sense. In other words, should one doubt the allegory, one gets in its place a text that enacts what the allegory advises: honors a power that both centers and destabilizes, both commands attention and disperses coherent understanding. Furthermore, although this coinciding of the text's constative and performative effects may inspire some confidence, the brevity and obliqueness of its language still makes the passage more a stimulus to the reader's powers of response than a decisive communication of authorial meaning.

Power and Style

This motif of a central wildness, specifically of a textual agency that both focuses and scatters meaning, is one of the two chief consequences that can be drawn from Dickinson's advice to cherish power. I take the motif to designate the explosive, slantwise force that by 1862 she understood to be at her disposal in poetry. If cherishing power is construed as honoring a central wildness in language, then it prizes both the positing of some meaning, focus, or center and at the same time, and by means of a wildness inherent in that posited center, the dispersing, undoing, or disrupting of it. This is more familiar than it may sound. We have already glanced at the notion of double writing while investigating the origins of Dickinson's style. In addition, several well-known critical concepts similarly account for textual functioning in terms of simultaneous but opposed operations.

Among the established accounts of double writing are deconstruction, New Critical notions of irony or tension, and the Formalist concept of defamiliarization. Each theory tends to emphasize a negative or antithetical moment, corresponding to the dispersal or undermining of positive signification. However, each notion also necessarily presupposes a positive, thetical operation as well, one which produces the object of dispersal in the first place. In other words, each contains an affirming, positing, or organizing moment as well as a negating or disaffirming one. The two moments rarely if ever simply cancel one another out but instead coexist uneasily or indeterminately.[4]

Regardless of how one accounts for it theoretically, the motif of a central wildness describes effects familiar to most readers of Dickinson's poetry. Riddling, provocative, and idiosyncratic intensities of language are found in varying degrees in almost every poem she wrote.

As an example of Dickinson's double writing that also discloses the broader implications of the practice, let us examine "Tell all the truth but tell it slant." Not only does it exemplify Dickinson's characteristically slant verbal strategies, the poem explicitly argues in their favor. Yet its effects belie the confident tone with which the argument is conducted. Here is the poem:

> Tell all the Truth but tell it slant—
> Success in Circuit lies
> Too bright for our infirm Delight
> The Truth's superb surprise
> As Lightning to the Children eased
> With explanation kind
> The Truth must dazzle gradually
> Or every man be blind—
>
> (1129)

As directly as any poem Dickinson ever wrote, this one posits a message. The gist of the poem is clearly a recommendation that truth be stated obliquely, lest sudden or direct exposure to it damage us. Furthermore, the poem is organized as a serial repetition and amplification of the single central theme. Dickinson less develops her theme than rewords it. Each of the poem's four complete but unpunctuated sentences (line 1, line 2, lines 3–4, and lines 5–8,) advances a self-contained variation of what the first already states with reasonable fullness. The second line, for instance, parallels and reiterates the first mainly by altering the linear "slant" to a curvilinear "Circuit," thereby advantageously suggesting circuitousness as well.

Repeating a single theme in several vivid and rather direct versions makes the poem itself strikingly uncircuitous, it would seem, particularly in comparison to the elliptical, periphrastic, and catachretic extravagances of many Dickinson poems. The repetitions work to limit what more extravagant poems license, attention to any waywardness, equivocality, or recalcitrance in a poem's details. In details, however, is where Dickinson usually finds the cherished wildness of language. "Superb," for instance, must primarily be taken as a word of praise, representing the worthiness of truth and the desirability of our being dazzled by it, though the word can have more negative connotations: pride, haughtiness, even cruelty. Similarly, "infirm" mainly signifies a regrettable but forgivable weakness we are all said to have, our irresolution about bearing truth. However, the term can also suggest a more thoroughgoing incompatibility between truth's brightness and our delight. The legal meaning of the world is "invalid," as of an infirm title to a piece of property; that meaning would ascribe the incompatibility more to the essence of truth and delight than to a curable weakness in delight. Finally, "surprise" chiefly denotes the suddenness of our being delighted by truth, a slantwise telling accordingly being recommended so that the brightness is not too astonishing. On the other hand, "surprise" belongs grammatically to the truth, not the telling or our response. The grammar may make a difference, for when surprise is ascribed to an active agent rather than to a recipient, it commonly implies aggression. Macbeth's surprise of Duncan would thus be his unexpected attack upon him. (A manuscript variant for "bright" is "bold," which likewise makes truth the agent that intends its own shocking advent.)

I do not call attention to these generally more sinister possibilities in the first four lines in order to propose that they make up the poem's true but covert theme. About a work that less insistently repeated a single, central exhortation (and perhaps had a looser structure than this one), one might plausibly claim just that. In considering "Renunciation is a piercing virtue" (745), for instance, no respectable interpretation could fail to notice the image of laceration which is inherent in "piercing" and which ironizes the commendatory sense of "valuably keen or emphatic." Here, however, the repetition of the central theme discourages such regard for semantic deflections, which otherwise can often be crucial in reading Dickinson. The question then is what effect or function to ascribe to the combination of reiteration and potential waywardness.

In fact, without ceasing to reaffirm the central theme, the poem's repetitions gradually pull free of it. The more the poem insists, the more it raises up divergent possibilities. The epic simile that begins the second half of the poem, for instance, seems designed to reinforce once again the need for slantwise telling, but the analogy it proposes breaks down on close inspection. Lightning is surely an image of truth, for instance, and children of ourselves, truth's beholders. But how exactly does an "explanation kind" ward off the dangers of direct exposure to truth? A child, frightened by a storm, may be reassured by its parents, but the child's vulnerability is not thereby lessened. If we assume an elided auxiliary in line 5, understanding it to say that the lightning is or must be eased by an unnamed adult's explanation, we are offered a highly unlikely claim. Explanations do not ease the force of a storm. Imaginary dangers may be dispelled, but the real ones are quite enough; and this poem offers no support for the possibility that truth only seems dangerous to the childishly ignorant or superstitious. Alternatively, if we construe "eased" as a verb in the active voice, the poem claims that lightning itself eases up by means of some kind explanation, muffling its force on our behalf. This is meteorologically unlikely, to say the least. Either way we construe the syntax, lightning remains the same potentially deadly bolt of electricity.

This fact might encourage us to glance back to the second line and wonder if we have not overlooked a ghastly, proleptic pun in "Circuit." Closing such a circuit would then be the lightning's success, anyway its natural destiny, but read in that way the rhythmically and rhetorically evident parallelism of lines 1 and 2 would be sharply disrupted. We would now be advised to tell it slant to avoid a murderously successful circuit. The second line then offers itself up to two contradictory and incompatible readings, an obviously dominant one cued by the repetitions in the poem as a whole and by the links to the first line and also a subordinate one cued retroactively as it were by the imagery in lines 5–8.

The phrase "dazzle gradually" contains the same problem in miniature, though here it is not the sense of the phrase that is in question but its felicity. The words make an oxymoron that in most respects seems admirably constructed. Such figures are usually striking, and here the effectiveness is reinforced by vowel assonance. But dazzling gradually is the act to which the simile in lines 5 and 6 is being compared. And one function of the comparison is to put asunder what the oxymoron hath writ. It insinuates that no phonetic or rhetorical trick ought to convince us, like some grownup's hasty story to frightened children, that dazzling gradually is anything more than a comforting but preposterous fiction.

According to the insinuations of the lightning image, then, we can never see or grasp the truth's illumination. Unless the truth dazzle gradually, at best a miraculous event, we are all blind. We *are* blind, that is to say. If we play Ben Franklin, seeking truth in a thunderstorm, we blind ourselves at the moment of success. If we sensibly eschew such folly, then we are blind in another, more traditional sense. Not having seen the light, we wander in error and falsehood, perhaps comforting ourselves with kind but false explanations on the order of Santa Claus, the tooth fairy, and a prescientific mythology of thunderbolts. Moreover, the "we" apparently includes the poet, who claims no exemption from infirmity. This further destabilizes the poem's nonetheless emphatic truth claims. Supposedly truthful and unmistakably confident statements emerge from a place of blindness, the situation perhaps thereby disaffirming the negative insinuations and the cheery exhortations as well.

The hermeneutic zigzag of truth and error, blindness and enlightenment, or affirmation and insinuation may itself be a little dazzling. Indeed, the razzle-dazzle may be the point, and the zigzag is certainly the method. Dickinson's double writing *differs itself*, always actively and often flagrantly, from any singularity it has itself signified. This poem accordingly works by both repeating and displacing the exhortation made in the first line, without ever arriving at a point where the divergent possibilities are gathered up into some more comprehensive or coherent view. Moreover, the divergences from whatever we take as the first or primary reading do not collect into some single, rival counterargument, as with a text that says one thing on the surface and another covertly or esoterically. Consistently antithetical propositions about whether the light of truth delights can be read out of the poem, but the other displacements and deflections from the central exhortation are more fragmentary and uncertain. The first part of the poem insinuates, for instance, that truth may be a malevolent aggressor giving the lie to our fatuous expectations of delight. The second half, however, makes the danger more impersonal or even, if one takes seriously the possibility of the lightning kindly explaining itself, an unfortunate and unintended consequence of an otherwise considerate natural force. Likewise, the sinister possibilities offer neither a contrary justification for the value of slantness nor a covert recommendation that truth be told some other way or avoided in silence.

The self-differing significations of "Tell all the truth" can be separated and diagramed more easily than their counterparts in other poems, but a comparably central verbal wildness is at work throughout Dickinson's poetry. This wildness is, indeed, a chief effect of her literary style, and under other names and descriptions ("riddle," for instance) may be the best-known aspect of her poetry. However, we know more about the repertoire of techniques contributing to wildness than about Dickinson's reasons for fostering it so conspicuously. The more challenging question then is why Dickinson wrote this way. And part of the answer can be seen in the fact that, typically, "Tell all the truth" focuses mainly upon the effect that some expression will have on an audience.

In other words, like "This was a poet," "I reckon when I count at all," and numerous other poems or remarks on poetry from Dickinson's letters, "Tell all the truth" imagines literature from the point of view of the reader. Although cast as advice to an author, it defines truth telling in terms of the effect on an audience, not of the author's powers and predicaments nor of the textual properties of the utterance.

As we have seen earlier, the effect Dickinson most prizes from her own reading is affective intensity, especially if—as in the poetry of sensation—such intensity does not coercively disclose meaning. Dazzling can accordingly be something of an end in itself, whether or not it happens gradually and whether or not it conveys truth. And Dickinson's form of double writing thus differs somewhat from each of the theories it otherwise resembles. For example, a slantwise style differs from deconstructive effects in being intentional and voluntary.[5] By contrast the rigorous undecidability explored by Derrida or de Man and formalized earlier by Gödel (at least for syntax) surpasses any unitary subject's intention or will; indeed, it bespeaks a propositional machinery autonomically generating meanings it cannot master.

More than the majority of Dickinson's poems, "Tell all the truth" meets New Critical standards of formal integrity. The poem's wildness thus could be considered to exemplify irony, tension, or paradox, these three being roughly interchangeable terms for the ideal state of formal equilibrium achieved when divergent possibilities are suspended in a single artistic monad. Unlike most of the New Critics, however, Dickinson shows very little concern with form as such, and she manifests a positive dislike for achieved stability. Indeed, her willingness to disrupt formal integrity in order to achieve some specific, local effect is the despair of critics such as Blackmur. More generally, poems for Dickinson are not ends in themselves, which exist in an esthetic space ideally transcending other aspects of life, but rhetorical stimuli, which exist in an equally ideal space of elite readers and writers.

Finally, Dickinson's rhetorical and stylistic wildness differs also from defamiliarization, although both share a concern with producing effects and responses in the audience and both are deliberate, voluntary phenomena. A Formalist account of "Tell all the truth" might say that is defamiliarizes stale, habitual notions of truth, freshening the reader's understanding by showing us the object—here, truth—as we had not previously seen it, that is, as a powerful and dangerous thing. On the other hand, the idea of truth as dangerous, even deadly, is as conventional as the rosier view and if anything has the older pedigree. More important, the poet has not masterfully and authoritatively exposed our inadequate understanding in favor of a better one or even for the austere joy of a purely negative cognition. She cannot be credited with bestowing wisdom where foolishness prevailed before, because her own wisdom is highly doubtful. Like New Criticism, Russian Formalism generally imagines the poet as a genius, a master, someone who can imagine or envision or fabricate what lesser mortals cannot and who can convey the products of the imagination to us mortals. Dickinson, however, eschews such imaginative authority. Indeed, quite as much as the many poems explicitly dramatizing the speaker's quest for certainty, understanding, or knowledge, "Tell all the truth" may be said to end in authorial bewilderment. It differs itself not only from univocal meaning but from its own authority to determine meaning.

The point of these comparisons can perhaps be put more succinctly by saying that for Dickinson poetics is always at the service of rhetoric rather than the other way round. Her style may loudly call attention to itself, but it does not usually do so as a construction to be admired in its own right or as evidence of authorial genius. Like all the other isolable devices contributing to the double writing of "Tell all the truth," Dickinson's conspicuously deviant style is part of a larger rhetoric of stimulus. It is meant to cherish a power that extends considerably beyond the author's direct control.

The Sublime as Design

Dickinson's slantwise or double writing may differ itself from any magisterial pose of authority, thereby skirting Carlylean mastery, but such a technique certainly also risks avoiding coherence. Were cherishing power only a program for fostering the mercurial capacities of language, it would simply reinforce the split between force and design. Not so the other chief implication of cherishing power, although at first glance this might appear to be the case.

In taking power as the object of cherishing (rather than, say, beauty, truth, love, or whatever), Dickinson opts for an esthetics of the sublime. The difference between the kingdom and the glory on one side and power on the other exactly parallels the commonplace distinction in eighteenth-century esthetics between the beautiful and the sublime. On one side are order, balance, and the inherently pleasurable link between the mind's conceptions and nature's forms. On the other are energy, might, and magnitude, all envisioned as inherently volatile and exciting. In Dickinson's imagination the categories translate as the orderly and the wild.

The two categories neither divide all possibilities between them nor form a neatly binary opposition. As we have already seen from Dickinson's letters, power includes the other two prerogatives. The same is true of Dickinson's other common names for sublimity, "awe," "tremendousness," "transport," and so on, none of which precludes what she normally calls "beauty." Moreover, in the books and magazines available to Dickinson the picturesque was nearly as prominent an esthetic category as the sublime or the beautiful.[6] Nevertheless, Dickinson clearly imagines the esthetic—that is to say, the appreciation of natural or artistic phenomena—as dividing between what she sometimes calls prose and poetry, the former given over to order and the latter to force. And in virtually every instance in which she is obliged to choose between them, Dickinson unmistakably prefers the sublime; she invariably values force and intensity over harmony, stability, and order.

The preference for the sublime may at bottom be a matter of temperament rather than deliberate belief, and it sometimes may reflect or contribute to Dickinson's willingness to sacrifice design to force. On the other hand, the sublime is also a powerful structuring principle, one capable of giving shape to numerous aspects of an artist's enterprise. As Thomas Weiskel and other modern critics of romanticism have shown, from the middle of the eighteenth century onward, the sublime became an increasingly important and prevalent poetic structure.[7] Dickinson's poetry takes the established patterns of the romantic sublime and gives them an additional twist, one which works to circumvent the otherwise deep complicity between sublimity and mastery.

The specifically structural consequences of a commitment to the sublime can appear at three levels. In the first place, because the sublime is a phenomenal category, it links and thus gives shape to a variety of otherwise discrete kinds of experience, and it also specifies their value. More specifically, in Dickinson's poetry it identifies for us the conceptual bridge between idolatrously beloved Masters, internal psychic turmoils, and objective natural phenomena as various as sunsets and snakes. All are apprehended according to the magnitude of their affective intensity, and all are valued for precisely that. Indeed, there would seem to be a perspective in Dickinson's imagination from which all such experiences are interchangeable; each kind certainly can be a metaphor for any other.

The sublime also shapes artistic representations of such experience, providing a vocabulary of forms and more specifically a repertoire of narrative or quasi-narrative phases. Third, it can give shape to the wider artistic projects designed to foster sublimity, selecting certain kinds of content and expression as worthy and also establishing a distinct hierarchy of overall goals and designs. A corollary of this third stuctural consequence extends beyond poetics to rhetoric. The same design linking her poems to one another and to a common enterprise helps organize her understanding of the transactions among the poet, the poem, and a reader.

As Weiskel has brilliantly demonstrated, a single pattern can be seen to underlie all the differently accented representations of the sublime in literary practice and in critical or philosophical theory. Weiskel's synoptic model derives most directly from Kant's accounts of the dynamic and mathematical sublime, but it draws also upon Longinus' primarily rhetorical sublime, the natural sublime as represented by Burke and earlier eighteenth-century critics and poets, Hegel's negative and dialectical sublime, the Wordsworthian egotistical or positive sublime, and Freud's account of sublimation and related defenses. According to Weiskel, the sublime is always organized as some form of sudden encounter with otherness, usually as incarnated in some specifically sublime object which the subject apprehends as grand, dreadful, majestic, authoritative, enticing, and so on, depending upon the specifics of the situation. The encounter always proceeds according to a three-phase sequence that in one form or another and with one rationale or another can thus be regarded as the invariant structure of the romantic sublime.

In the first or *normative* phase, before the alterity has been apprehended, the subject relies upon what will later be seen as habitual modes of thought and feeling. He or she may not be content with such conventional modes, but no other possibility presents itself, except perhaps a utopian dreaming that lacks any more tangible experiential validity. The *traumatic* phase commences with the apprehension of an object, which variously and often simultaneously entices the subject, disrupts his or her habitual modes of consciousness, and challenges the subject's dignity by means of the drastic contrast opened up between its powers and his or her own. So intense is the experience the object has precipitated that the world usually contracts to a dyadic relation of subject and alterity. Finally, in the *reactive* phase or the moment of what is sometimes called *sublimation*, the subject experiences elevation, empowerment, and a release from traumatic assault. The new state of consciousness may be regarded as the restoration of blocked or occluded power, and it may be regarded also as an influx of fresh resources that the subject can now make or claim as his or her own. In either case, it is an exhilaration so powerful and vivid as to be self-evidently valid.

As an introduction to the structure of the sublime and a springboard toward examining Dickinson's unorthodox handling of it, consider the following well-known poem.

> A little Madness in the Spring
> Is wholesome even for the King,

> But God be with the Clown—
> Who ponders this tremendous scene—
> This whole Experiment of Green—
> As if it were his own!

(1333)

The clown's response to spring exactly corresponds to the empowering elation first identified by Longinus as the quintessential moment of the sublime.

Our soul is uplifted by the true sublime; it takes a proud flight and is filled with joy and vaunting, as though it has itself produced what it has heard.[8]

More specifically, the clown interprets the moment as his appropriation of what would otherwise be an alien power, the tremendous force of spring.

The poem focuses mainly upon this moment of appropriation, which is the third phase in Weiskel's model, but we can nonetheless easily enough reconstruct the others from the imagery. The first or normative stage precedes any apprehension of springtime's force. King and clown have gone about their customary duties, perhaps in winter or under the influence of any weather that fails to inspire spring's madness. The two personages are conventionally contrasted ones, and their respective duties of ruling the kingdom and providing it amusement represent the salient range of habitual, uneventful behavior in the poem. To the king primarily belongs power and proud dominion; to the clown belongs a joy perhaps tempered by the exigencies of his subordinate state.

The second or traumatic phase arises in Weiskel's schema from encountering some phenomenon that abruptly challenges normal habits, beliefs, and perceptions. Spring is not universally understood in our culture as a disruptive force, much less an abrupt one, but Dickinson here stresses the unexpected majesty of the seasonal change more than is usual even for her. An earlier draft referred to the "sudden legacy" of new greenery, and both the earlier and the final versions characterize the scene as "tremendous." The primary sense of the word here is awe-inspiring, literally causing one to tremble, as before the might of what Kant calls the dynamical sublime. As it happens, the more colloquial sense of tremendous, some vast magnitude that is difficult for one to take in as a whole, is also relevant. (According to the *OED*, this more hyperbolic sense was in use by the early 1800s.) Again, vastness is not a conventional attribute of spring, but it is fitting to the immensities of Kant's mathematical sublime, which is set off by large, uncountable quantities of sensory data.

Whether occasioned by an apprehension of power, of vastness, or (as here) of both inextricably, such a break in the normal continuum of experience precipitates confusion. More specifically, the disorientation suffered is one that usually measures the majesty of the object against the subject's own now humbled or threatened powers. At the same time, the subject may feel solicited, even inspired, by the other's superiority; the characteristic awe induced by the traumatic phase combines both admiration and fear. In other words, at this point the object at once "dowers" and "deprives" (1675). Dickinson underplays any threatening aspect in "A little madness," but it exists in the direr possibilities of "Madness" and in the quaking response tremendousness ought etymologically to trigger.

The traumatic stage may be initiated by the object, which can thrust itself into consciousness with the unexpected majesty of spring's first advent; however, the stage is then experienced as a moment of blockage, one that affects the subject's movements and powers. Or, to describe the same thing from a different perspective, during the second phase the emphasis shifts from the properties of the external phenomenon to the subject's relation to the object.[9] The mind is unable to comprehend the object, unable to take it in perceptually and conceptually as it was able to do with previously encountered phenomena. It accordingly feels a new and belittling sense of its own inadequacies, upon which it may begin to dwell, even to the point of forgetting about the object that instigated the humbling. Here the concern with the self's native or legitimate powers comes through in the contrasting reponses of king and clown. The king, exemplar of duly established authority, discovers his relative impotence. Unlike nature he cannot command trees to bear leaves. His ensuing "little Madness" is said to be "wholesome," that is, primarily salutary in the sense of a healthily chastening reminder of his limits. The word also punningly conjoins a "whole" that is discontinuous with and beyond his power by comparison to the "some" he legitimately commands. Similarly, the clown, a stock figure of both powerlessness and foolishness, is provoked to the uncharacteristic act of pondering. The usual antics no longer suffice.

The third or reactive stage is the center of the poem. In this phase the object and sometimes even one's relation to it as a wholly external thing fade before the advent or the recovery of the self's loftiest powers. What had previously threatened one's dignity or rebuked one's

capacities is replaced by a feeling of elation, liberation, and empowerment. No longer the manifestation of otherness, the object is now seen
as an aspect or an extension of one's internal powers. As Longinus
suggests, the turn comes partly because one now identifies with and
hence mentally subsumes the otherness.

Theories of the sublime differ from one another mainly in their
understanding of the mechanisms of reactivity, but all agree in endorsing its actuality. The prestige of the sublime depends not upon pene-
trating reflections about why it works but upon the self-legitimizing
and self-authenticating fact that it does work.

There is a depth in those brief moments which constrains us to ascribe
more reality to them than to all other experiences. For this reason the argument which is always forthcoming to silence those who conceive extraordinary hopes for man, namely the appeal to experience, is forever invalid and
vain.[10]

In "The Over-Soul" the alternative to sublimity for Emerson would
be the mundane contingencies of ordinary experience. More commonly, as at the beginning of *Nature* or throughout "Self-Reliance,"
the alternative is an acceptance of previously established authority.
The latter context is what Dickinson most strongly suggests in "A
little madness."

For the king, apparently secure enough in his royal authority, the
reactive phase appears only as a mild case of spring fever, an inocu-
latory mania upon which he will not presumably think to act in times
to come. The tonic effect of spring will then have largely served only
to reconfirm his socially established elevation. By contrast and with
the poem's at least partial approval, the clown reactively sees spring
as "this whole Experiment" and "as if it were his own." The first phrase
Dickinson settled upon only after trying more than a dozen others,
ranging from the original "sudden legacy" to "gay Apocalypse," "whole
experience," "whole Astonishment," and "whole Periphery." The advantage that "Experiment" has over alternative head nouns is that
the poem then depicts spring's otherness both as an object and as the
creation of some transcendent subjectivity. So indeed do sublime objects regularly imply transcendent powers or daemonic and divine
agencies. Indeed, the sublime frequently advertises itself as the primary means of human access to such powers.

Dickinson's choice has more specific thematic consequences also.
Behind any experiment must be an experimenter, it would seem, but
that is an ideologically neutral role that can shift easily among the

various candidates: God, nature, and the clown. "Apocalypse," in contrast, would be a gift of (hence initially the legitmate property of) God and nature; similarly, "astonishment" would mainly be limited to the clown. The final choice thus deftly negotiates the transition or tranformation from spring's tremendous force to powers the clown can imagine as his own. Experiments can belong to anyone; anyone can imaginably instigate them. Self-initiating growth, abundant vitality, unconstrained joy, and a more than royal dominion can thus plausibly become the clown's to try out.

We are not yet done with this poem, which also contains elements that importantly diverge from the romantic sublime, but its general adherence to the three-phase structure should by now be apparent. "A little madness" is actually less an example of the sublime than a second-order representation of it, a poem that depicts the experience retrospectively and externally rather than from the inside. Dickinson's more typical poems represent one or another phase of the sublime at its most immediate and forceful, but they only sometimes display or directly imply the entire narrative sequence. Almost all the many poems dealing with an experience of crisis, ecstasy, or struggle thus fullow some part of the pattern, but the intensity of focus on a single phase can mask the larger context.

Consider "It was not death," a reasonably typical and highly regarded representation of the kind of psychic crisis so frequent in Dickinson's poems, here one that specifically threatens her perceptual, epistemological, and verbal powers. The poem exemplifies as well what has perceptively been singled out as Dickinson's propensity for writing in the aftermath of some overwhelming experience.[11] The poem is further typical in not identifying the empirical situation that might have precipitated the crisis. These three characteristically Dickinsonian features are in most respects independent of one another. To understand the poem in the context of the romantic sublime, however, is to see that all three are consequences or manifestations of a single structure.

> It was not Death, for I stood up,
> And all the Dead, lie down —
> It was not Night, for all the Bells
> Put out their Tongues, for Noon.
>
> It was not Frost, for on my Flesh
> I felt Siroccos — crawl —
> Nor Fire — for just my Marble feet
> Could keep a Chancel, cool —

And yet, it tasted, like them all,
The Figures I have seen
Set orderly, for Burial,
Reminded me, of mine—

(510)

The poem continues for another three stanzas, lingering all the while in retrospective bafflement at the moment when some catastrophic force has disrupted all normal modes of understanding. In other words, the poem speaks from the traumatic phase, at a moment when the object has already been occluded and the speaker is beginning to reflect on her newly dwarfed powers. The sublimity of this blockage is most evident in its magnitude, which Dickinson insists is absolute and hence insurmountable.

The challenge is both to the identity of the threatened speaker, who nonetheless apparently speaks from a moment when the threat has subsided or been overcome, and to "the Figures I have seen," that is, to previous experiences, nameable phenomena, and known categories that might accordingly serve to define "it" and thus defend her against its disruptiveness. The experience is "most, like Chaos— Stopless," but even such names as those for absolute disorder will not quite do. Defining the phenomenon as chaos would be oddly comforting, for by its very linguistic intelligiblity the term would supply a cognitive hold on the experience, defining as absence what the speaker could then know she has lost. In other words, "Chaos" would itself indirectly constitute the "Report of Land" that could "justify—Despair."

This is as bleak a poem as any Dickinson wrote, so one is tempted to consider it a cri de coeur, an artful depiction of authentic helplessness. And since there are many such poems, one is equally tempted to suppose that she must have suffered greatly. Be that as it may, the appeal of such bleak experiences as this poem depicts goes beyond their factuality, their intensity, and whatever gain may be involved in wording an otherwise wordless experience. Such experiences promise the unique exaltation of the sublime. Rather than looking only backward and then perversely mystifying or making invisible the very thing one looks back at, the experience of sublime trauma stands pointedly between the initial shock of the sublime and the promised transcendence. "The tint I cannot take is best" precisely because it most sharply challenges the speaker's powers, promising triumphant "Moments of Dominion" if one can only gain access to the next phase (627).

For Dickinson, however, an abject "Discontent / Too exquisite—to tell" is as likely an outcome as elevation. Triumphant sublimation is by no means guaranteed, especially from within the traumatic phase, Dickinson's most common standpoint and indeed the most common in romanticism generally.[12] Moreover, Dickinson regards even positive sublimation with considerable suspicion; the dominion foreshadowed in "The tint I cannot take" is clearly a form of mastery.

In this regard look once more at "An ignorance a sunset," which represents the natural sublime as a struggle for mastery between perceiver and object.

> An ignorance a Sunset
> Confer upon the Eye —
> Of Territory — Color —
> Circumference — Decay —
>
> It's Amber Revelation
> Exhilirate — Debase —
> Omnipotence' inspection
> Of Our inferior face —
>
> And when the solemn features
> Confirm — in Victory —
> We start — as if detected
> In Immortality —
>
> (552)

Overcoming the ignorance in which the sunset's sublime omnipotence leaves us appears here as a combat between the subject and the sentient, willful, or even aggressive alterity incarnated in the natural phenomenon. In a fashion that we will eventually see as characteristic of the Dickinson sublime, the poem stops short of saying that the victory belongs to the speaker or the object, but it also makes clear that a victory for one of the parties in the dyad can be the only resolution of such encounters. The stakes of this contest are likewise clear from the speaker's suspicion that she has been detected in immortality. Within or beyond the empirical phenomenality of the sunset is the supersensible, which Dickinson almost always describes in theological terms.

Until the final stanza, where the "solemn features" cannot definitely be attributed either to "Omnipotence" or to "Our [heretofore] inferior face," the poem represents the apprehension of the sunset according to the usual three-phase pattern of the sublime encounter. The initial consequence of encountering the sublime object is "ignorance." More specifically, as in "It was not death," previously reliable categories of knowledge such as color and circumference are helpless to deal with the object. The experience is predictably humbling, but here it is also enticing. The revelation at once debases and exhilarates, as the speaker comes to understand the sunset as a figure for omnipotence and to take the entire episode as a thrilling challenge.

Rather than simply the inanimate occasion of a startling experience, however, the omnipotent other she faces in the sunset is an agency that has designs upon her. It deliberately inspects her, measuring her powers against her own, or so it seems to the speaker as the moment is undergone and as she is held spellbound by the object. Because both parties are understood as struggling with the other, the outcome must be victory for one or the other. Although the polarity can and does reverse during an adventure of the sublime, the relation between self and other necessarily remains a hierarchy of domination and submission.

If the romantic sublime thus centrally involves a poetics of mastery, out of the writings of Dickinson's own time the paradigmatic figure of the one seeking such mastery would be Robert Browning's Childe Roland, as Harold Bloom has frequently argued. The romantic sublime specifically lends itself to heroic questing, in other words, of a sort Dickinson most vivdly represents in her poems of apocalyptic journey: "I saw no way, the heavens were stitched" (378), "Our journey had advanced" (615), and a number of others. Or from the writings to which Dickinson more frequently adverted, the figure would be Jacob wrestling with the angel in Genesis. "Pugilist and Poet," Dickinson called Jacob in a late letter, one in which she also astonishingly rewrote scripture. Her Jacob says to the angel "I will not let thee go except *I* bless *thee*" (*Letters*, 1042, my italics).[13] As aggressive, heroic poet of the sublime, in other words, the victorious Jacob proudly reserves even the power of blessing to himself.

As poet, on the other hand, a victorious Jacob would become the Carlylean master, dominating readers because incarnating for them the angelic tremendousness he had overcome. For a poet to achieve the romantic sublime is for that poet or his works to become sublime, thereby precipitating in responsive readers the same kind of struggle for mastery Dickinson undergoes in "An ignorance a sunset." This means that, at least from Dickinson's perspective, the sublime is never only a formal category, one pertaining simply to the contents and expressive devices in her poems; it is also a rhetorical category, one that directly implicates the worldly fate of her poems and the roles that she and her readers are able to play in relation to them.

Lest it seem fanciful that the otherwise reasonably self-contained, formal sequentiality of the sublime might open directly onto such questions, we should note that in assimilating sublime textual encounters to the forms of sublime adventure represented in texts Dickinson is by no means eccentric. A link between rhetorical and experiential patterns has been present in the notion of the sublime throughout its history. Ever since Longinus' *Peri hypsos* first isolated and identified the notion of sublimity, a privileged or paradigmatic occasion for it has been the situation of reading. Mary Arensberg conveniently summarizes more recent notions of the link, quoting parenthetically from the key passages in Longinus.

1. The experience of the sublime is an affective or emotional response (joy and ecstasy) to *power, authenticity,* or *authority.*
2. This *power* is perceived in a moment (like a "lightning flash") through the effects of speech and language.
3. The sublime moment is preceded by a disruption in normal consciousness ("parts all matter this way and that") whose equilibrium must be restored.
4. Equilibrium is seemingly restored through an identification with that *power* or *authority* ("exalts our soul as though we had created what we merely heard") and a *repression* of that power.
5. The repression takes the form of a *defense* (in this case [in Longinus, that is] *mimesis*) in which the reader makes the sublime her own.[14]

Like Dickinson, Arensberg emphasized the agonistic basis of the sublime, characterizing the reading of a powerful text here as the reader's partly unconscious struggle to maintain or restore balance and a sense of his or her own powers. At least loosely this is the conflict played out in "This was a poet," and as we shall see in subsequent chapters the ethical charms of the sublime are precisely those of mastery as it is envisioned in that poem. One challenge for Dickinson then is to find some way of circumventing mastery without giving up the experiential intensity she values or the promise of transcendence that the sublime always holds out. More generally, as this challenge may suggest, the romantic sublime is less an answer to Dickinson's problems than the matrix in which they appear. Her own unorthodox version of the romantic sublime then specifically responds to such problems.

A second look at "A little madness" will give us a preview of Dickinson's strategy. Kings normally lose out in literary comparisons with clowns, especially in the Shakespearean plays likely to have been Dickinson's main inspiration for using the pair of figures. This poem is no exception. The king's little madness is notably inferior to the clown's greater one; the king's response certainly does not measure up to the criteria of the true sublime. Yet Dickinson does not simply endorse the more extravagant responsiveness of the clown. She also hesitates about the vaunting and usually self-aggrandizing idealism implicit in the clown's elevation and normally an integral part of the romantic sublime. The equivocation appears here in a simple but striking double meaning. "God be with the Clown" may be read as a blessing, one that expresses delighted approval of the clown's imaginative possession of the springtime. The concluding exclamation point, an especially rare punctuation mark for Dickinson in the 1870s, corroborates that approving sense. God is with such wonderful clowns, she says, even if by stuffier standards the clown's state of mind is a fantastic madness. Such derangement would only confirm the holiness of the delusion. On the other hand, the phrase is grammatically a subjunctive petition or prayer, formulaically appropriate to expressions of good will but nonetheless requiring some need of what is wished for. God help such poor deluded clowns, the poem would then say, for no one else can.

In either reading the poem recognizes the subjective actuality of the sublime experience—the clown is not pretending or merely hoping—and it recognizes as well the superiority of the clown's elevation to the king's paltrier reaction. Whereas the first reading endorses the sublime wholeheartedly, however, the second regrets it or at least reserves approval.

The divergence between these two possibilities for reading Dickinson's attitude to the clown is not in itself remarkable. We may, for instance, take it as another example of Dickinson's double writing. Emblematically, however, much depends on how Dickinson judges the clown's reaction. On one side, an excellent case can be made for the romantic sublime as a comprehensive structuring principle for her work. According to such a view, the clown's admirable elation would represent one instance of a state regularly solicited, valued, or encouraged by Dickinson's poems. Consider, for instance, some of the most obviously valorized terms in Dickinson's psychic and metaphysical idiolect. "Tremendousness," "transport," and a number of others directly translate into admiring images the characteristic features of the sublime. Likewise, "degree" regularly measures vaunting elevation, and "circumference" in large part can be understood to designate ownness, that which before or after the sublime encounter belongs properly to the self rather than to the other. In addition to these more private terms, a number of Dickinson's other key words borrow directly from the traditional lexicon of sublimity. "Dread," "awe," "abyss," "infinity," and "exhilaration" were all clichés of sublime diction before Emily Dickinson was born. Other borrowings from the established discourse of the sublime include a metaphorics of height and depth and a poetic landscape amply supplied with mountains, volcanoes, whirlpools, oceans, chasms, and horizons.

The case for the sublime is a version of one that is in fact commonly assumed by Dickinson's commentators: that her poems are to be understood as episodes in a continuous spiritual venture and thus, however that venture is specified, that the poems belong to the genre of the romantic quest. For Dickinson to deem the clown's final estate the highest and worthiest of accomplishments would confirm the case. Weiskel's model would then provide a skeletal but complete plot for a grand narrative structure in which a great many of Dickinson's poems could find their place. And the essential project of her work would be the quest for a more than human wholeness of being, the state she most frequently terms "immortality."

The case is incomplete, however. Dickinson cannot quite bring herself to endorse the clown's state unreservedly. Indeed to do so, by the fatally centripetal logic that sublimity and mastery share, would make the speaker of the poem the clown's inferior, defensively imitating in words what she cannot or at least has not accomplished in direct experience. In other poems as well, Dickinson always keeps some distance from the heroic ideality of achieved sublimity. Here she offers her own reader the two sharply bifurcated possibilities for construing "God be with the Clown." This is, amidst considerable variation and diversity, the quintessential maneuver of the Dickinson sublime. Articulating experience according to the three-phase structure of the romantic sublime and thus at least partly affirming its general validity, Dickinson nonetheless lingers on the threshold of a full commitment to the reactive phase. Her hesitation defers to the reader a choice that if made by the poet would constitute her claim to the Carlylean role.

Notice, incidentally, that the clown in "A little madness" only happens on the sublime rather than deliberately seeking it out, yet the poverty of his stature in comparison to the king's apparently provides sufficient motivation for seeking sublimity. The normative phase of the sublime, which is characterized by established habits and conventions, has as its affective correlative in Dickinson and in most poets a sense of dissatisfaction, blankness, or even outright despair. An aptitude for the sublime requires need, or at the very least a readiness to acknowledge the limitations revealed by the traumatic phase. As Weiskel remarks of Blake's Urizen, a mind convinced of its own sublimity cannot in fact experience the awful or sublime moment.[15] Unlike the clown, the happily established king may simply not need fresh exaltation badly enough.

4

The Rhetoric of Stimulus

I have argued that Dickinson held an affective theory of poetry primarily modeled on her own experiences as a reader, that she carefully and conscientiously invented a deviant style, and that such style is particularly well suited to eliciting the effects she most valued in her own reading. These arguments fall just short of a claim that Dickinson specifically designed her style to achieve those ends. We simply cannot be sure how deliberate her strategy may have been. If the affirmations of "Tell all the truth" can be trusted, Dickinson did specifically intend her style to be provocatively deviant. Elsewhere, however, there is little indication that Dickinson imagined style to have especially close or important links with literary affect. Moreover, if style might once have been an explicit or troublesome issue for her, the rapidity with which she developed a mature style and the consistency with which she then maintained it argue that for most of her career the matter of style had been long and satisfactorily settled.

Not so the other features of Dickinson's rhetoric of stimulus. Unlike style, they regularly get thematized in the poems, sometimes as issues Dickinson explicitly worries and sometimes as principles she expressly argues or avows. From among Dickinson's views about poetry, language, and the circuits of communication and dissemination, three categories are important here: her beliefs about the relation of cause to effect, intention to consequence, and stimulus to response; her meditations on the legitimacy of apparently natural forms of symbolism; and her notable preference for modeling literary textuality on letters sent to some correspondent, that is, on epistolary scenes that dissipate or dissimulate the otherwise singular presence of a speaking voice.

Like any rhetoric, Dickinson's is constitutively social. On the other hand, the tenets of Dickinson's rhetoric also work to accentuate her reclusiveness. It has often been remarked, for instance, how mutedly Dickinson registers the major event taking place while she wrote most of her poems, namely the Civil War. Yet as this next poem implies, rather than being imaginatively negligible, such public and historically significant affairs are so potent that they must be carefully kept at a distance.[1]

> The gleam of an heroic Act
> Such strange illumination
> The Possible's slow fuse is lit
> By the Imagination.
>
> (1687)

Like the glory of a Carlylean poet, that of a valiant soldier apparently threatens to overwhelm Dickinson. Between the gleam and its possible outcome Dickinson thus inserts a specifically imaginative stage, carefully attributing the consequences of the heroic act to the creatively responding imagination rather than to the hero. In other words, she construes the act as if it were a heroic poem, giving to the elaboration of a response the same three-part process we noticed in "If I could tell how glad I was." Likewise, she assimilates this process to the otherwise narrowly literary ethic of dissemination and productivity. The heroic act is valued primarily in terms of what it may eventually stimulate from "the Possible." Just as reading a text has historically been the paradigm for all encounters with the sublime, including seemingly more worldly ones, so in the Dickinson sublime the primarily literary ethic of productivity can be a model for ethos in general.

"The gleam of an heroic act" employs an imagery of fire, light, and explosion, Dickinson's usual metaphoric resource in poems about response and stimulus. All of these images connote a sudden outburst, which is belied by the process Dickinson actually describes. "Slow fuse" serves the function of "dazzle gradually" in "Tell all the truth," in other words, that of putting an instantaneous force at the service of leisurely regard. This is the common theme of all the aspects of Dickinson's rhetoric: between a stimulus and the ideally productive response some form of delay or distance must be provided. Here it is the slowness of the fuse; in "The poets light but lamps" it is the interval between one age's lens and the next one's; and in the Browning poems it is the gap opened by Browning's death.

On the other hand, such delay obviously compromises the affective intensity Dickinson prizes and also the immediacy, even shock and surprise, that usually characterizes the advent of the sublime. Presumably it is not a day or a week after reading a book that Dickinson first feels as if the top of her head were taken off and thus knows the book is poetry. Her best-known poem on the subject likewise depicts painting, music, and poetry as arts to which one responds without delay.

> I would not paint—a picture—
> I'd rather be the One
> It's bright impossibility
> To dwell—delicious—on—
> And wonder how the fingers feel
> Whose rare—celestial—stir—
> Evokes so sweet a Torment—
> Such sumptuous—Despair—
>
> I would not talk, like Cornets—
> I'd rather be the One
> Raised softly to the Ceilings—
> And out, and easy on—
> Through Villages of Ether
> Myself endued Balloon
> By but a lip of Metal
> The pier to my Pontoon—
>
> Nor would I be a Poet
> It's finer—own the Ear—
> Enamored—impotent—content—
> The License to revere,
> A privilege so awful
> What would the Dower be,
> Had I the Art to stun myself
> With Bolts of Melody!
>
> (505)

This may be Dickinson's single most exuberant celebration of affect, particularly to the extent that the three stanzas are strictly parallel and the three arts thus exactly comparable in their effects. Poetry does seem to differ from painting and music, however. The first two stanzas are similar in structure and meaning, each articulating in the second line the preference for a role over a particular act. In other words, each contrasts being the person who responds— "I'd rather be the One"—to performing the act which provokes the response. Neither the painter nor the musician appears, only their arts, whereas the third stanza brings in the person of the poet for comparison to the person of the audience. More exactly, it compares being the poet with being a person who has been synecdochally reduced to acknowledging a passive, readerly role. The "I" who in earlier stanzas chose being "the One" elevated by painting and music can now only "own the Ear." Similarly, whereas the first two stanzas give us wondrous, extravagant accounts of responding, the last stanza passes over such details to dwell on a more contemplative reaction. And this reaction is not to the poem but to the poet imagined as the authority behind the work of art.

In other words, what starts out by celebrating the affective intensity of art ends by verging on the situation depicted in "This was a poet," helpless fascination with the power, license, and privilege of the magisterial poet and a correspondingly humbling recognition of one's own impotence. Even the "sumptuous—Despair" evoked by painting does not oblige the audience to be content with revering the artist. Dickinson accordingly concludes by fantasizing a superlatively autoaffective art of which she could be the potent author without giving up the role of astonished reader.

Painting, music, and poetry are all equally capable of astonishing, but only poetry also threatens to dominate. No reason is given in "I would not paint a picture," but from what we have observed elsewhere we can surmise that mastery is closely associated with disclosing meaning. And more than nonverbal arts, at least as they were beginning to be understood in Dickinson's times, poetry traffics directly in the stipulation and conveyance of meaning.

Whatever the reason for poetry's distinctive status in "I would not paint a picture," there and elsewhere poetry is represented as giving rise to three distinctive, sometimes inseparable effects: an astonishment or amazed sense of elevation that for Dickinson defines all powerful arts, a pronounced awareness of the artist who has created the work, and a sense of helplessness and inferiority at the contrast between his powers and our own. The first of these is inherently desirable. Indeed, it belongs to the general promise of the sublime, as the metaphors of elevation and uplift in this poem suggest. Even the second effect, the personalizing which distinguishes poetry from music and painting, does not necessarily disempower the reader, as the example of Browning shows. Dickinson's rhetorical aim is thus to deter the third effect without compromising force and intensity. In general Dickinson seeks to accomplish this by introducing or emphasizing various forms of delay in the chain of conveyance between author and reader.

Intention and Effect

Even a Carlylean author does not necessarily set out to beggar the reader, and Dickinson usually makes it clear that his magisterial stature is primarily a creature of the reader's idolatry. In other words, the chief consequence of his poetry is largely independent of his intentions. With remarkable persistence Dickinson claims that this is true of all utterances and indeed that the intentions behind any stimulus do not determine its effects. An example is the three-stage process by which one utterance eventually responds to another or to some different kind of instigation. The hero's deeds may set off an elaborate chain of events, culminating in the possible's explosion, but they do not decide the shape of that explosion. Contrary to use of "stimulus" in behaviorism, Dickinson's use of the term and the idea always belies determinism and it regularly also denies milder forms of causality.

Most of Dickinson's statements about stimulus and response have to do with language. For example, the consequences of a remark need have nothing to do with the intentions of the author, who may have assisted in provoking them only inadvertently.

> A Man may make a Remark—
> In itself—a quiet thing
> That may furnish the Fuse unto a Spark
> In dormant nature—lain—
>
> (952)

As in "The gleam of an heroic act," Dickinson uses an imagery of explosion that departs from the usual expectations about causality. The spark, notice, is in the recipient and the fuse in the words spoken, contrary to the more conventional image of an author's words setting a reader's imagination on fire. Indeed, although the poem's second stanza cautions us to discourse with care, the explosive power of our words seems to come entirely from their unbidden stimulus of the reader's dormant and unpredictable nature.

The same motif of unintended but devastating effects also appears in a more explicitly literary context.

> A Word dropped careless on a Page
> May stimulate an eye
> When folded in perpetual seam
> The Wrinkled Maker lie
>
> (1261)

This apparently is why Dickinson writes:

> A word is dead
> When it is said,
> Some say.
> I say it just
> Begins to live
> That day
>
> (1212)

This is one of the more banal of Dickinson's poems, but its sentimental bravado depends upon a sentiment deserving some notice. The life of language is found in the effect it has on an audience, not in the inherent vitality of the utterance and certainly not in the preverbal genius of the author. As we have seen, Dickinson concurs in the frequent Victorian emphasis on literary effect, but she goes against the grain in detaching effect from authorial intention. She sometimes goes astonishingly against the grain in absolving authors of reponsibility for the effects their words elicit.

> She dealt her pretty words like Blades —
> How glittering they shone —
> And every One unbared a Nerve
> Or wantoned with a Bone —
>
> She never deemed — she hurt —
> That — is not a Steel's Affair —
> A vulgar grimace in the Flesh —
> How ill the Creatures bear —
>
> (479)

The diction of this poem suggests a drawing room context, not a literary one, and the speaker carefully refrains from approving of the woman's actions. Nevertheless, the poem imagines an extraordinary dislocation of effect from agency, intention, source, or cause.

A distancing of effect from intention obviously furthers Dickinson's affective aims, because it grants power to the reader. The stimulus a poem provides can always exceed the conveying of some meaning or effect controlled by the poet.

> Could mortal lip divine
> The undeveloped Freight
> Of a delivered syllable
> 'Twould crumble with the weight.
>
> (1409)

The discarded second stanza of this late poem indicates that Dickinson refers here to "the Minds / That told the Truth to me." The phrase makes it clear that Dickinson grants a certain authority to those minds. But the truth they tell seems mainly a sort of raw material for the reader. The fuller truth whose weight Dickinson remarks is not the possession of those who create and deliver the syllables. The freight of their messages awaits development, which apparently only daring readers can supply. Furthermore, they supply it by divining with their lips, that is, by a responsive utterance of their own rather than some merely passive or receptive understanding.

The detachment of seminal acts from disseminated and disseminating consequences pervades Dickinson's writings more fully than can be demonstrated by means of poems that explicitly describe the process. So also does the distancing of causes from effects, stimuli from responses, and intentions from results. With some exceptions the poems I have been citing are not among Dickinson's most interesting or accomplished. Rather than exemplifying or enacting a rhetoric of stimulus, they talk about it or even argue explicitly for it. On the other hand, if this explicitness somewhat belies the effect argued for, it clearly testifies to the deliberateness of Dickinson's affective poetics and perhaps even to its willed or strategic character.

Dickinson's explicit claims for the priority of effects over origins culminate in two poems that draw directly upon traditional philosophical debates. "To hear an oriole sing" argues unequivocally that the tune is "of within" rather than "of the Bird":

> To hear an Oriole sing
> May be a common thing—
> Or only a divine.
>
> It is not of the Bird
> Who sings the same, unheard,
> As unto Crowd—
>
> The Fashion of the Ear
> Attireth that it hear
> In Dun, or fair—
>
> So whether it be Rune,
> Or whether it be none
> Is of within.
>
> The "Tune is in the Tree—"
> The Skeptic—showeth me—
> "No Sir! In Thee!"
>
> (526)

87

The oriole disappears from the poem after the second triplet, and as author of a song the oriole is only minimally relevant to any meaning the song conveys. The bird "Sings the same, unheard, / As unto Crowd." In other words, although Dickinson grants the actuality of the bird's act regardless of whether anyone perceives it, she attributes to the perceiving ear all powers of construing the act. The dispute is not over epistemological or ontological skepticism. Rather it concerns the power of deciding whether the song is "Rune" or "none," and Dickinson unequivocally asserts that the listener determines this, not the bird. Indeed, not only does the difference between hearing the tune as common or divine depend upon the listener, so does the difference between hearing the tune and not hearing anything. Dickinson specifically writes that the fashion of the ear attireth (in order) *that* it hear, rather than attireth what it hears. All hearing is hearing-as.

Whereas "To hear an oriole sing" diminishes the equivalent of the author in favor of the creativity of the ear, "Perception of an object costs" goes further in all but banishing the authority we might expect the stimulus itself to possess.

> Perception of an object costs
> Precise the Object's loss—
> Perception in itself a Gain
> Replying to it's Price—
> The Object Absolute—is nought—
> Perception sets it fair
> And then upbraids a Perfectness
> That situates so far—
>
> (1071)

Rather than objects as external stimuli we have only the mind's perception of the object and the equally mental idea of a Platonic "Object Absolute." (The last four lines may perhaps be construed as indirect discourse, the reply of the mind to the question of price, in which case the object absolute would be the original object rather than its perfected, Platonic form.) The "Object Absolute—is nought," an assertion that joins three separable claims. First, the object absolute is nothing in comparison to perception; it has no value, presumably because it is unattainable. Second, the object absolute does not exist; it is a fictitious ideal or a fantasm and moreover one constructed by perception itself rather through some power of the object to represent an ideal. Finally, the object absolute exists but only as a nothing, a no thing, a mental construct to which no material phenomenon corresponds. Thus, to say that perception sets it fair means not only that the object absolute is unblemished and pleasing but that such "Perfectness" is set or posited by the apparatus of perception, not by some inherent quality of the object.

The claims here nicely buttress Dickinson's case for the responder or perceiver, but it should be noted that the poem allows for more misgivings than "To hear an oriole sing." Whether the gain of perception is fair recompense for the loss of the object remains an open question. Moreover, the acknowledgment that the object has been lost belies the poem's seemingly Kantian equanimity. The object itself never appears as such, and while its stimulating a perception may count as appearing, this does not quite establish a distinction between noumena and phenomena, things as they unapproachably are in themselves and things as they appear. To have lost the object presumes that one has initially experienced it through some other means. In Dickinson's world this other means would presumably be the overwhelming, often paralyzing, and usually unspeakable power of an object's presence. Contrary to the Husserlian outlook she has been said to anticipate, Dickinson experiences presence in a more visceral way than by perception.[2]

"Perception of an object" for the most part supports Dickinson's usual emphasis on effect over stimulus, and like the other poems examined in this section it does so by explicitly arguing for the priority of effects. This priority also gets manifested in a quite different and often poetically more interesting fashion. On different grounds and mainly with reference to different poems, Roland Hagenbuchle has also pointed out that Dickinson characteristically effaces origins or causes in favor of consequences and delayed responses. He makes the case through an analysis of Dickinson's tropes, particularly in poems that do not overtly reflect on the form of consciousness they exhibit. Dickinson's imagery is unusually dominated by the metonymic substitution of mental effects for objective causes and of subjective responses for external stimuli, Hagenbuchle argues, both in poems identifying the objects and scenes they describe and in the famously periphrastic texts that conspicuously avoid naming the object.

Again and again in her poems Dickinson represents the effects on a speaker's mind of objects, events, and persons whose identity the reader can often only guess at. The strategy wholly dominates the most perphrastic poems, such as "A route of evanescence" (1463) or "It sifts from leaden sieves" (311), where the teasing exuberance and unpredictability of the responses make it clear that Dickinson's figures are more counterterms of her own devising than anything determined by the object itself.[3] Indeed, the energy and copiousness of the style in "A route of evanescence" are often read as deliberately challenging the power of the never-named locomotive.

In other words, Dickinson's metonymic descriptions exemplify an extravagantly free responsiveness, here to extraverbal stimuli rather than to texts or messages. Likewise, consequences again take priority over origins. These poems also perhaps manifest with special clarity Dickinson's rhetorical solicitation of her own readers. According to Hagenbuchle, "Metonymic tactics tend to impose especially great and occasionally excessive demands on the reader, even though it must be admitted that he finally comes into his own. At the same time, it becomes increasingly difficult to verify one's findings by reference to the text."[4] It is not clear to me what Hagenbuchle means by saying that the reader finally comes into his own, but the phrase is an apt one for the aims of Dickinson's affective poetics. A poetry designed more to stimulate responses in the reader than to control them or instruct the reader's imagination is indeed an art that encourages a reader's coming into his own.

Like a number of critics before and since, Hagenbuchle emphasizes the tantalizing obscurity of Dickinson's imagery and the frequent difficulty a reader would have in verifying understanding against the authority of the text. Her eclipsing of intelligible design by figural force helps prevent the poems from successfully practicing their designs upon us. In other words, affective metonymy is one instance of the split between force and design, here seen not as a problem to be overcome but as a particularly effective example of Dickinson's rhetoric of stimulus. Similarly, Dickinson's famously striking first lines, which so often allude to an experience or context that remains veiled throughout the poem, typically arouse fascination by their verbal ingenuity or their emotional and conceptual force. They also remain at least for a while, enigmatic and thus help to delay the reader's production of a satisfactorily concluded response. More generally, Dickinson's poetics of the absent center regularly teases us into supplying what seems to be missing. In this sense, even the most flagrantly inventive readings of Dickinson's verse—biographical fantasies, for example—have a certain validity, one measured not by fidelity to truth or sense but by an ethic of imaginative productivity.

Natural Symbolism

Diminishing the authority of intentionality helps ward off the author's dominion, but to the extent that conveyed meaning is itself a threat the author is not the only enemy of responsiveness. No authorial master appears in "There's a certain slant of light," for instance, but the scene certainly imposes "Heavenly Hurt" as it inscribes upon the soul "internal difference, / Where the Meanings, are" (258). Typically such moments are spurned as painful, perhaps overwhelming, and also craved as an intensity beyond the quotidian. In other words, they belong to an esthetics of the sublime. And a chief issue, particularly in the wonderfully multivalent line "None may teach it—Any," is the authority or legitimacy of the meanings written within. If, as the tone of the poem suggests, the meanings manifest some natural or supernatural order, then the self can only accede to them. If, however, as in other instances where response is prolonged, the slant of light only marks or rearranges the internal differences, which the self then as a separate act gives meaning to, a crucial freedom to determine meaning is maintained. Indeed, we once again have a three-part process: the stimulus of the light, the inscription of the internal differences, and the interpretation of these signifiers by the no longer helpless soul.

The poetic and rhetorical issue broached by "There's a certain slant of light" is the possibility of natural symbolism. As a rule, romantic writers have searched eagerly for some form of symbolism that might claim natural or supernatural sanction, thereby transcending mere custom. Dickinson is more wary than most, however, and her practices differ revealingly from her two most important American predecessors, Poe and Emerson. Both otherwise mutually hostile poets endorse some form of natural symbolism as a guarantee of poetry's validity and hence of the authority of the genuine poet. The main difference between Emerson and Poe on this is that Emerson's natural symbolism promises to deliver spiritual truth, whereas Poe is less interested in truth than in beauty, that is, esthetic and affective intensity.

Poe's affective theory depends prominently on the belief that certain images have a natural or inevitable effect on us. We cannot help but be moved by the image of a dead woman, Poe tells us in "The Philosophy of Composition," and true to his word Poe makes use of that image time and again in his stories and poems. Similarly, although Emerson's ideas otherwise differ as much from Poe's as Poe could demand, Emerson articulates an explicit doctrine of natural symbolism in *Nature*.

1. Words are signs of natural facts.
2. Particular natural facts are symbols of particular spiritual facts.
3. Nature is the symbol of spirit.[5]

Elsewhere in *Nature* and more broadly in the writings of both Emerson and Thoreau this theory authorizes a general project of combating the corruption of modern langauge. Both Concord writers thus seek an etymological renaturalization of the original symbolic power of words.

By contrast Dickinson's poetry regularly works to denaturalize the available symbolic resources of our condition and culture.[6] Etymology, for instance, less often confirms or reforms a current usage than gives it a comeuppance, as we have already seen in reading the zigzags of "Tell all the truth." More generally, the scattering and focusing forces of Dickinson's style necessarily make use of variously sanctioned linguistic resources but also invariably put such resources in question.

Sometimes the questioning extends to the codes or sanctions themselves. Consider "Essential oils are wrung," one of Dickinson's few poems that pay more attention to authoring than reading.

> Essential Oils — are wrung —
> The Attar from the Rose
> Be not expressed by Suns — alone —
> It is the gift of Screws —
>
> The General Rose — decay —
> But this — in Lady's Drawer
> Make Summer — When the Lady lie
> In Ceaseless Rosemary —
>
> (675)

Like perfume, poetry requires the manufacturer to do violence to the naturally given source. The latter is treated as raw material that must be all but destroyed in order to get at the concentrated essence. The artificially derived essence is markedly superior to the natural resource, however. It outlasts the natural source and also the lady, who seems here mainly to be the recipient of the perfumes and poems but could well also be their maker.

The analogy of perfume to poetry is only implicit, of course, for the poem employs an extended metaphor without ever quite identifying the tenor. Nevertheless, every reading of this poem I have found makes that identification, and indeed the image of the flower, raw material of the perfume, is a conventional figure for poetry and/or poetic language. We have seen Dickinson use such imagery elsewhere. The apparently elementary issue of identifying the tenor in fact epitomizes the poem's scrutiny of symbolic resources. On the one hand, the poem argues for denaturalizing the given, but on the other it depends for intelligibility on the culturally given and thus naturally authoritative association of flowers and poems. (Wittily extending the commonplace from flower to attar does not, I take it, constitute an instance of putting the screws to the language's given resources.)

Attacking a symbol while depending upon it exemplifies the usual slantwise practices of Dickinson's style, which are also evident elsewhere in the poem. The capitalization of most nouns and adjectives lends a personificatory drama to the statements, encouraging our taking attar, rose, screws, and the others as metaphors. In addition, several verbs exhibit a characteristic absence of inflection, enhancing the poem's linguistic strangeness and perhaps lending sententious power to the clause in the second and third lines as well as giving "make Summer" a portentous force. More interestingly, Dickinson pointedly juxtaposes high and low registers of diction, "Essential Oils" with "wrung" and "Attar" with "Screws." Finally, the punctuation adds to the strangeness and also contributes to more specific effects, such as the clash of registers in the first line and the seeming reluctance in the third of conceding any expressive power at all to suns.

As these instances testify, Dickinson's deviant style most often exerts pressure only on particular acts or moments of signification. In this poem, however, the pressure increases to the point of challenging the codes, protocols, and sanctions which make any particular moment possible. We are encouraged to look for further gifts of screws, both by the poem's explicit argument and by the uncertainties that the more obvious instances of deviance raise. For example, several words in the poem appear to be additionally motivated by their potential as anagrammatic puns. "Expressed" is the most obvious candidate, since it is an otherwise odd selection for the way sunlight nurtures roses. It contains "pressed," however, which is what the screws of an attar-extracting machine do, and its punning attribution of expressive intentions to the sun licenses our seeing the perfume-making as a metaphor for poetic expression. To express is to utter or move to the outside what is contained within, and here expression requires destroying the original container. Likewise, "essential" contains within it the phonemes for "scent," redundantly corroborating oil and attar, and "essence," another synonym for perfume, is both the root of the word and a phonic component of it. The sounds and the letters of the text can thus be taken apart and meaningfully recombined, indeed recombined in a way that strikingly enhances the poem's surface meanings. The process of decomposing and resynthesizing words is a linguistic counterpart to crushing roses to release their scent.

Excavating morphemes in this way requires us to take the words of the poem as momentary combinations of letters and phonemes rather than as elemental signs. Moreover, once started there may be no stopping the excavation, for the "ooze" of oil can be found in "screws." I see no gain from noting this quite possibly coincidental sound effect, but that is my point. At least two things happen when one begins to split apart words. First, normal lexical and syntactical protocols lose some of their authority, for the text gives up "secret" morphemes that are not necessarily bound by the linguistic codes governing words in the surface text. Second, the sheer randomness of language's power to evoke meaning makes an appearance as a source for the poem's effects, alongside more familiar sources such as determinate linguistic and cultural codes or a particular author's powers of selecting and combining words toward some determinable purpose.[7]

These two effects open a certain distance between the signifiers of the text and the usually inseparable signifieds. The poem's foregrounding of the codes and protocols at work in signification culminates in the last word of the text. Several things combine to call attention to "Rosemary." First, it may be the single most metrically dissonant word Dickinson ever placed in a poem. For seven and a half lines the poem has galloped along to an iambic beat varied only by the possibility of extra syllables in line 5 (where "General" can easily be elided to two syllables rather than three) and in line 6 (where some effort may be required to pronounce "Drawer" in two syllables rather than one). Fitting "Rosemary" into that pattern is possible only by doing violence to the usual pronunciation of the word. Moreover, the word does some violence to the poem's rhyme scheme, which is otherwise a strict *abab* pattern, at least if one can attribute strictness to the partial rhyming of the last phoneme in each line rather than the exact rhyming of the full syllable. "Rosemary" does partly echo the [ôr] of "Drawer" but in its penultimate syllable, the last syllable more nearly rhyming with the long *a* of decay and the long *i* of "lie." Second, the word contains within it "rose," the only word or morpheme used more than once in the poem's previous thirty-eight words. Anagrammatism can run amok here, too, for "Rose," "Mary," and "Rosemary" are all candidates for the otherwise anonymous lady's name.

In the language of flowers, rosemary signifies remembrance (and constancy), a fact that Shakespeare's Ophelia would have taught Dickinson had she not known it from the popular courtship rituals of her day.[8] This meaning is certainly appropriate to the genteel context of the lady with perfumes, sachets, or poems in her drawer and also to the argument, which concerns making or representing the bygone summer when the rose bloomed and the lady lived. On the other hand, introducing at the last moment a conspicuously artificial, non-linguistic code calls attention to the more naturalized linguistic codes at work up to that point. For instance, the multiply and ambiguously deictic "this," to which the poem attributes so much, may seem less like a riddle whose meaning we ought to determine than an instance of language's power to posit in the absence of any determinable referent. The pronoun can refer to the attar of rose, it can reflexively refer to the text of the poem at hand (a possibility made less resistible by the fact that Dickinson kept her own poems in a drawer), and it could even refer to a pressed flower or an aromatic sachet of the sort one might expect to find in such places. All of these can be mementos of summer's rose.

Introducing flower symbolism does not deny the efficacy of these decodings of the pronoun; if anything, it might impress us with the author's resourcefulness. But the conspicuously artificial flower code does make it considerably more difficult to take any single code as natural or authoritative, for the mechanisms of signification are inevitably hindered by self-consciousness about semiotic processes. Moreover, the metrical and phonic clumsiness of "Rosemary" makes it the poem's prime example of a gift that only machinery can produce.

I shall not insist upon it, but all this strikes me as furthering the identification of "this" with the poem at hand, a possibility that itself would add to the text's foregrounding of semiotic mechanisms. Attars, sachets, pressed flowers, and any other conceivable derivative of an actual rose are at least in part expressed by suns. The derivative's visual or aromatic reference to the natural rose of summer remains an iconic or a material link, however much violence the manufacturing process may require. On the other hand, not only is the poem a linguistic object without any such link, this poem does not even attempt to depict summer by means of vivid language. No single resource, natural or cultural, stands as this poem's necessary origin or its raw material. In claiming that "this" will make summer, although the general rose decay, the poem insists that its efficacy will continue after the roses of summer have decayed, after roses in general or as a species have vanished, and apparently even after the idea of roses has disappeared.

We cannot even quite attribute all the poem's effects to the author, although she is certainly the main operator of the machinery. By foregrounding and denaturalizing other ways of perpetuating an absent summer and more generally by enacting language's power to signify both through and beyond the usual conventions of poetic dis-

course, the poem may curiously make good on the claim that this—
this poem, this kind of poetry, and the autonomous signifying power
of the word "this"—can make summer when everything else has decayed. Yet it does so not by means of any natural symbolism or even
a legitimized cultural code but through the local, patently artificial,
and even contrived machinations of the "this," in other words, of this
particular poem.

"Essential oils are wrung" pays as little notice to the reader or
to reading as any poem Dickinson ever wrote, yet the aggrandizement
of "this" works in favor of the reader's capacity to disclose the meaning of the deictic. It does so primarily by working against any more
general philological authority, whether such a thing be grounded in
nature, culture, or divinity. In place of such an authority, the poem
effectively exercises and thus honors the "consent of Language / This
loved Philology" named in "A word made flesh," a poem that does explicitly correlate language's powers and the reader's. Although this
latter poem is widely read as celebrating the qualities inherent in the
ideal poem and describing the miracle of ideally inspired composition, the first of the two stanzas contemplates the Logos from the recipient's point of view.[9]

> A Word made Flesh is seldom
> And tremblingly partook
> Nor then perhaps reported
> But have I not mistook
> Each one of us has tasted
> With ectasies of stealth
> The very food debated
> To our specific strength—
>
> (1651)

The central metaphor is food, clearly enough, and more specifically
the Eucharist as a literal scene of ingestion. The odd, perhaps colloquial
forms of the participles "partook" and "mistook" call attention to their
common root in acts of taking. Initially, as would be appropriate for
a communion rite, our taking is a rare and fearful taking part, in which
we may easily be imagined as accepting God's word/flesh from solemn and suitably ordained ministers. The speaker then reconsiders,
wondering not only if she has been mistaken in her first thought but
in effect if it is at all possible to mis-take such food as a word made
flesh. Here in "ectasies of stealth" we each partake on our own. The
initial trembling makes a furtive reappearance in "debated," a word
derived from "bate," which means to flutter one's wings violently in

anger or fear, especially as a hawk does. On the one hand, food debated to our strength has been decided upon in open, public discussion. On the other, we hawks have ourselves agitatedly fluttered about it.

The speaker's doubt that one can mis-take a Word accords well with an affective theory of poetry. One could really be mistaken only if the word's power of signifying meanings and directing intensities were alien to the recipient and thus capable of legitimately thwarting his or her needs. This might prove to be the case if such power were natural, divinely sanctioned, authorially decided, or wholly a creature of publicly debatable standards of discourse. Here, however, in a rare and wondrous vision of mutuality, one of the few genuinely utopian moments in Dickinson, the word naturally fits our specific strength. The uncanny match perhaps suggests that the word's power depends upon how strongly we can respond to it, a possibility that other Dickinson poems would corroborate. This poem does not otherwise imply that we have a share in the process of consumption, but it does joyously affirm the "consent of Language," its capacity and even eagerness to be taken by us.

Letters

In the poems examined so far in this chapter acts of reading, listening to music or bird song, looking at painting, and hearing someone speak have all been treated as interchangeable instances of an audience's situation. At times, however, Dickinson is more insistent that poems are written texts. She then most often imagines them as like letters and the speech-act situation of poetry as like the sending and receiving of letters. "This is my letter to the World," one of her best-known poems announces itself. The cloying pathos of that poem should not distract us from an important reminder that it offers. Like a letter's, a poem's message is normally "committed / To Hands I cannot see" (441), which puts the power of judging the message and also the author in the hands of the reader. That reader, moreover, may always leisurely "con the faded syllables" (169), lingering over the text long after the occasion of its utterance and even—as in the poem just quoted—after the author has died.

Reading letters has other advantages as a model for reading in general.

> The Way I read a Letter's—this—
> 'Tis first—I lock the Door—
> And push it with my fingers—next—
> For transport it be sure—

And then I go the furthest off
To counteract a knock—
Then draw my little Letter forth
And slowly pick the lock—

Then—glancing narrow, at the Wall—
And narrow at the floor
For firm Conviction of a Mouse
Not exorcised before—

Peruse how infinite I am
To no one that You—know—
And sigh for lack of Heaven—but not
The Heaven God bestow—

(636)

The insistence on the privacy of letter reading is obvious, even ob-
sessive, apparently because of the specific and understandably intimate situation of receiving a letter from a lover. On the other hand,
the lover is designated as "no one that You—know." Directly invoking
a third-party addressee, presumably the reader of the poem, rather
shockingly violates the privacy of the lovers and thus may forcefully
remind us that letters can be read by persons other than those to whom
they are addressed. Moreover, contrary to the poem's subsequent par-
ticularity, the speaker refers initially to "a" letter, that is, any letter
and not just this one and not only the ones from her lover. The result
is to generalize the effect of a love letter to all letters. All may allow
one to "Peruse how infinite I am" and "sigh for lack of heaven—but
not / The Heaven God bestow." Any letter can stimulate the exhila-
rating responsiveness Dickinson prizes.

In agreement with what we have seen earlier, this responsiveness is at least partly independent of the contents of the text or the
intentions of its author.

Going to Him! Happy Letter!
Tell Him—
Tell Him the page I did'nt write—
Tell Him—I only said the Syntax—
And left the Verb and the pronoun out—
Tell Him just how the fingers hurried—
Then—how they waded—slow—slow—
And then you wished you had eyes in your pages—
So you could see what moved them so—

(494)[10]

The author addressing her text here certainly has urgent intentions about what she wants it to communicate. Though denying she is a "Practised Writer," she has nonetheless "worked" the letter so hard that she "almost pitied it." Yet she recognizes that even such intensely labored effort will not control her reader's response, and so she hopes the letter might convey the page she did not write. Similarly, the wish that the pages had eyes applies at either end of the chain of communication. Just as the recipient cannot see what moved the author's pen-holding fingers so, the author likewise cannot see what in her text will move the recipient's letter-holding fingers — or his heart — as he peruses the letter.

For both the author and the reader written letters contrast most sharply with words spoken in face-to-face exchange. "A Pen has so many inflections, and a Voice but one," Dickinson notes in apologizing for misunderstanding a correspondent's intentions and at the same time backhandedly taking note of the scriptive powers she so obviously cherishes in her own writings (*Letters*, 470). Written words have the disseminating potential she elsewhere values highly, in other words, whereas spoken ones are more singularly determined by the speaker. "We bruise each other less in talking than writing, for then a quiet accent helps words themselves too hard" (*Letters*, 463). Dickinson is preemptively apologizing here for any offense her letter might give, and again the apology contrasts the speaker's power to control effects with the writer's inability even reliably to deter unwanted ones.

The absence of authorial control over epistolary messages and their consequent disseminative power may be why, when this power does not need to be forestalled, "A Letter is a joy of Earth / It is denied the Gods" (1639).

A Letter always feels to me like immortality because it is the mind alone without corporeal friend. Indebted in our talk to attitude and accent, there seems a spectral power in thought that walks alone— (*Letters*, 460)

The justly famous remark may owe something to a commonplace distinction between the ideality of language and the material finitude of human life, but Dickinson's primary distinction is between written and spoken words. It is less human corporeality's finitude than its presence that inhibits thought's spectral power. By being bodily present to one's words, a speaker controls them more effectively and directs the reader's response more fully than a letter's author ever can. This is an idea Dickinson seems genuinely to have lived by. Beginning in the 1860s she increasingly and notoriously shunned the bodily presence of other persons, while at the same time continuing or perhaps even increasing the voluminous correspondence indicated by her surviving letters. Dickinson's reclusiveness has complex motives, no doubt, yet given her obviously acute sensitivity to all manner of external stimuli we can reasonably suppose that she found it difficult or threatening to manage the bodily presence of other persons. Moreover, reclusiveness is not quite the right word, for she maintained a lively interest in the doings of her many correspondents. The guarded privacy of epistolary communication thus had the advantage of releasing the spectral power of thought (both the author's and the reader's) while deferring the overwhelming intensity and authority of presence.[11]

According to Sharon Cameron, presence is the unrepresented, probably unrepresentable center from which many of Dickinson's poems then depart into language.[12] It would then also be, as I suggested earlier, the grasp that objects have on her and she on them before perception can begin its costly work. Presence in Dickinson's writing can be defined according to fairly simple, prereflective notions, and it usually does not move far from them. Presence first and foremost emerges from spatial nearness, the simple and empirical circumstance of propinquity. The appearance of presence out of nearness is most clearly depicted in "Four trees," which we have already scrutinized. That poem also hints at the potency such common, barely mediated experiences can have. In addition, presence is also the temporal immediacy Dickinson usually indicates by the simple present tense, the temporal coexistence of a subject and some object that has not yet been lost to perception.

Letters are good, I have been saying, because they defer presence. On the other hand, the ordinariness of presence regularly occasions the extraordinariness of the sublime, an experience to be cherished in part precisely because of its intense presence. Just as I have for some time been tendentiously reading "This was a poet" as an allegory of all that Dickinson shuns or rejects in authorship, ignoring the appeal that mastery has to her, so my comments on presence so far have one-sidedly emphasized its threat. In fact, Dickinson usually expresses at least some ambivalence about the power of presence. The issue is always the self's freedom and pride as against the conceivably greater gain that might come from submitting to the authority or majesty of presence. Consider, for instance, "The brain is wider than the sky," an examination of mental powers which concludes in the following stanza with a contrast between writing and voice.

> The Brain is just the weight of God—
> For—Heft them—Pound for Pound—
> And they will differ—if they do—
> As Syllable from Sound—
>
> (632)

(More specifically, the contrast is between the mediations of a language system and the immediacy of sound, but Dickinson elsewhere seems to associate syllables primarily with writing. And indeed syllabification is, according to more recent views, one of the instances of spacing that make all verbal institutions a kind of writing.)[13]

In the poem's first two stanzas the brain easily masters natural phenomena: "The one the other will absorb— / As Sponges—Buckets —do." In each case the mastery proceeds by a process of containment which demonstrates that the mind, the comprehending agent, is larger than the comprehended object. God, however, cannot be grasped so blithely. If the brain differs from God, it is as syllable from sound, a relation categorically unlike that of a container and its contents. How does a syllable differ from a sound? Perhaps it does not differ at all or not by much, the human mind thus slyly being equated with God. However, a syllable does partition the continuum of sound, transforming the aural presence into a cognitive form and thus distancing it in the way any mediation does. On the one hand, then, the analogy credits the brain with transforming, taming, or humanizing the awful presence of God. On the other hand, sound and hence presence is the source and the energy that drives language, perhaps even drives us to language, just as God is the creator of the human mind, and so the transformation into syllable is an example of human weakness.

The same distinction and a similar ambivalence appear in the following poem, which more directly concerns heroic authorship and Dickinson's response to it.

> Just as He spoke it from his Hands
> This Edifice remain—
> A Turret more, a Turret less
> Dishonor his Design—
>
> According as his skill prefer
> It perish, or endure—
> Content, soe'er it ornament
> His absent character.
>
> (848)

The builder of the castle, who rather resembles God the Creator as Dickinson both cherished and scorned him, takes a justifiable pride in his creation. It stands as a monument to the builder both because his skill of execution has accorded precisely with his design and because the building has lasted. Any change would dishonor the design; it would tamper with his originating intention and thus violate the continuing control over the edifice established by that inaugural intention. As is, however, the building delivers an unmistakable message: This was a Builder.

On the other hand, the last line slyly notes that it is only his absent character the building how ornaments. (By contrast, the Carlylean poet's continuing presence, agency, and control are all pointedly obscured in poem 448 by the monumental but also unrecoverably elliptic grammar: "This *was* a Poet—It *is* That" [my emphasis].) To the glorious, possibly vainglorious builder the creation is a kind of speech. The odd phrase "spoke it from his Hands" clearly establishes the building as a kind of utterance or expression, and by way of "bespoke" it may also suggest a successfully executed contract between design and skill, intention and achievement. Yet contrary to the presence a speaker manifests to his speech, the builder is irrevocably absent from the edifice and his building hence a kind of text. Once the castle has been spoken from his hands and he has absented himself from it, it becomes another letter to the world that can take it as it will.

Privacy and Fame

Is there not something perverse in characterizing Dickinson—of all the poets in the English language perhaps the single most notoriously private—as primarily and distinctively orienting her poetry toward stimulating the reader? Certainly Dickinson did not go out of the way to ensure that her poems had readers, and we have heretofore found it easy to suppose that she gave little thought to the audience for her poetry. Indeed, she is known to have resisted entreaties that her poems be published. If Dickinson is indeed the private poet she has so often been described as being, does that not preclude any claim that her poetics is deliberately affective?

Some aspects of her privacy actually work the other way. The obscurities of Emily Dickinson's verse and the many conspicuous difficulties she placed in the way of ascertaining some authorially intended and sanctioned meaning work to enhance the reader's freedom of response. Moreover, the aura of mystery that she obviously prized invites an increased fascination with unraveling the author's secrets. (This is an invitation many readers have clearly accepted.) Her refusal to solve or minimize the mysteries or otherwise to direct her reader more forcefully preserves speculative possibilities even as it tantalizes our desire to speculate. To Higginson, Samuel Bowles, Susan Dickinson, the Hollands, and the Norcross cousins—her closest correspondents and the ones among whom she most often circulated her poems—she never once suggests how a poem of hers ought to be understood. Similarly, when she insists to Higginson, perhaps with some disingenuousness, that it is not she but a "supposed person" and a "Representative of the Verse" who speaks in the poems, she minimizes personal authority at the same time that she guards her privacy (*Letters*, 412).

Nevertheless, one cannot affect readers without somehow reaching them, and the circulation of poems to one's correspondents seems a poor substitute for publication. Dickinson's reluctance to publish seems variously and complexly motivated, but nothing indicates that she feared being read by strangers or that she wished to keep control over who would see her poetry. Of the forty-two persons to whom she is known to have sent poems, at least one (Higginson) was at the time a complete stranger, and six of the others (Daniel French, Thomas Gilbert, Benjamin Kimball, Eben Loomis, Thomas Niles, and Gertrude Vanderbilt) were at best distant acquaintances or persons she never met face to face.[14] Furthermore, in at least one poem she flatly declared that without someone to respond to it an object of beauty would lose its reason for being.

> The Rose content may bloom
> To gain renown of Lady's Drawer
> But if the Lady come
> But once a century, the Rose
> Superfluous become—
> (880)

Her declaration to Higginson that she had no thought of publishing seems to have been at least partly a face-saving response to his criticism. A more serious objection to publication appears in the following well-known poem.

> Publication—is the Auction
> Of the Mind of Man—
> Poverty—be justifying
> For so foul a thing

Possibly—but We—would rather
From Our Garret go
White—Unto the White Creator—
Than invest—Our Snow—

Thought belong to Him who gave it—
Then—to Him Who bear
It's Corporeal illustration—Sell
The Royal Air—

In the Parcel—Be the Merchant
Of the Heavenly Grace—
But reduce no Human Spirit
To Disgrace of Price—

(709)

The objection here is not to reading or being read but to the contamination of art by commerce.[15] Happily without the need to earn her living by the pen, Dickinson rejects entirely the notion of selling the work of her mind to editors and publishers. The poem may thus well originate from the events she described to Higginson in 1862.

Two Editors of Journals came to my Father's House, this winter—and asked me for my mind—and when I asked them "Why," they said I was penurious—and they would use it for the World—(*Letters*, 404–5)

As well as stingy, penurious means indigent, and we may recall that the auction she refers to in the poem would at the time have primarily meant a distress sale or indeed one caused by the seller's bankruptcy. It would thus have been an occasion of public shame.

About "Publication is the auction" the more interesting question is, if thought and poetry are not commodities one can purchase, to whom do they belong and how? The sarcastic references to selling "Royal Air" and merchandising "Heavenly Grace" suppose that they actually cannot or should not be privately owned, but this is not necessarily to say that they cannot be owned at all. In the third stanza Dickinson does specifically identify two figures in a chain of conveyance to whom thought properly belongs. If "Him who gave it" is the "White Creator" and that being is understood as God, then "Him Who bear / It's Corporeal illustration" may include us all. Having been created in God's image, our bodies are literally corporeal illustrations of his thought. However, if the giver is a secular poet, starving perhaps in the Johnsonian garret Dickinson alludes to, then the other figure is the productively responsive reader we have seen elsewhere.

Such a person bears the corporeal illustration of the thought in several senses, from carrying about a physical text to two less mundane meanings. He or she may bear in the sense of enduring the astonishment of reading the text, and he or she may bear in the sense of responsively giving birth to an act or another text that also corporeally illustrates the thought. The latter possibility would link the reader more closely to "Him who gave it," even make the reader another giver of thought in his turn.

Bearing a corporeal illustration can then require a double strength, of reading as well as of something like writing. Although some of the poems I have discussed may imply that the reading stimulated by Dickinson's poems is open to all, this does not quite appear to be the case. The free and active reading Dickinson imagines demands a great deal of the reader, perhaps just as much in theory as her poems do in practice. Moreover, several of her poems clearly presuppose or flatly state that her poetry is meant for an elite. A biographical reminder may perhaps amplify this. As Charles Anderson and other have noted, when she was young Emily Dickinson at several times indicated that she felt herself set apart from others by her belonging to a select group of like-minded fellows.[16] One instance is the Five, the group of girlhood friends whom she continued to seek out well after the others had begun to drift apart. Another is the Dickinson family itself, which she and indeed all the other members felt was set apart from the normal run of Amherst citizens. Related both to the Five and to the sense of the Dickinson family as special was the social group centered upon Austin, herself, and Lavinia in the late 1840s. This one seems to have defined itself in contrast both to the parental generation and to other groups of young people. The common denominator of these three groups, which distinguishes them somewhat from otherwise comparable sets of like-minded persons enjoying the fruits of belonging, seems to have been the emphasis on conversation and especially on verbal skill.

The evidence here is sparse and anything but conclusive, but the letters and recollections from this time suggest that Emily Dickinson and her peers defined themselves as being specially possessed of verbal quickness and cleverness. Joseph Lyman, for instance, emphasizes Emily Dickinson's verbal inventiveness in his own self-consciously literary word portrait of her: "[a] mouth made for nothing and used for nothing but uttering choice speech, rare thoughts, glittering, starry misted figures, winged words."[17] His letters at the time he belonged to the Dickinson circle likewise stress the talking that went on. Verbal playfulness is what Emily's youthful letters also emphasize and what she prized in Austin's when he writes to her from Boston.

> Your letters are richest treats, . . . the only "diffikilty" they are so very *queer*, and *laughing* such hot weather is *anything* but *amusing*. A little more of earnest, and a little less of jest until we are out of August, and then you may joke as freely as the Father of Rogues himself, and we will banish care, and daily die a laughing! (*Letters*, 117)

Moreover, Dickinson clearly trusts Austin and others to appreciate the play of her own language. The trust may be most evident in her bantering rebuke of Austin's request—was it tongue in cheek?—that she write more plainly.

> You say you dont comprehend me, you want a simpler style. *Gratitude* indeed for all my fine philosophy! I strove to be exalted thinking I might reach *you* and while I pant and struggle and climb the nearest cloud, you walk out very leisurely in your slippers from Empyrean, and without the *slightest* notice request me to get down! (*Letters*, 117)

If all this is so, the sense of belonging to and addressing a verbally gifted elite both changed and deepened as she grew older. As I have already mentioned, at about the time that she first invented her distinctive poetic style, the style of her letters changed also, becoming even less forthcoming to a recipient not already in tune with her. Dickinson clearly recognized and perhaps rather enjoyed the fact that others found her baffling. "All men say 'What' to me, but I thought it a fashion" (*Letters*, 415). Even in letters to those who were not her intimates, however, she rarely compromised verbal agility for the sake of wider intelligibility. Of the poems this is even more true. Apparently she was willing to throw pearls before those she suspected of being swine (Higginson is the most notable victim), trusting that others before had appreciated her powers and either that new candidates for this elite might appear or that her more poorly endowed acquaintances might grow into the role. Programmatically unwilling to dictate how her work was to be taken, she was thus content to create the poetic stimuli in the hopes that appropriate respondents might appear.

I offer this biographical interpretation without great assurance, because we simply do not know much about how Dickinson's most intimate acquaintances reacted to her poems or her conversation. The belief in a literary elite is unmistakable in some of the poems, however.

If the foolish, call them *"flowers"*—
Need the wiser, *tell?*
If the Savans "Classify" them
It is just as well!

Those who read the "Revelations"
Must not criticize
Those who read the same Edition—
With beclouded Eyes!

(168)

As the concluding stanza makes clear, the apparently misnamed or unappreciated flowers in the scare quotes are the flowers of rhetoric found in literary texts:

Low amid that glad Belles lettres
Grant that we may stand
Stars, amid profound *Galaxies*—
At that grand "Right Hand"!

This early poem is uncharacteristically modest in petitioning for a humble place in the cultural pantheon, but it does make a clear distinction between the elite who stand among belles lettres and the foolish or pedantic who do not.

Other poems on the same subject make a similar distinction and more directly characterize the elite in terms of their powers of response.

Reportless Subjects, to the Quick
Continual addressed—
But foreign as the Dialect
Of Danes, unto the Rest.

Reportless Measures, to the Ear
Susceptive—stimulus—
But like an Oriental Tale
To others, fabulous—

(1048)

The syntax at the beginning of the second stanza can be normalized as "reportless measures are a stimulus to the susceptive ear." However, Dickinson's arrangement more clearly juxtaposes the ear's capacity and the measures' stimulus, further emphasizing susceptibility's role in constituting the measures as a stimulus. Only the quick even recognize the measures as a stimulus, in other words. Similarly the poem beginning "His Mind like Fabrics of the East" compares the elite respondent to a "humble Purchaser" of the goods no one else can buy: "That one should comprehend the worth / Was all the price there was" (1446). The poem makes clear that such purchases are rare, for only a mind as capably furnished as the one named in the first line can respond with such comprehension.

For a writer who so avoided putting herself forward, Dickinson ponders the nature and possibility of fame with striking frequency in her poems. Fame is a central theme in nearly a dozen poems written after the middle 1860s, by which time she seems to have firmly set herself against a public literary career. Indeed, some of these poems seem to rationalize the mismatch between her public invisibility and a desire for recognition. In "Fame of myself to justify" (713), for instance, the speaker insists that her own opinion of herself is far more important than a "Name" and a reputation that is "Supreme." Similarly, in poem 1427 she says that "Fame's consummate Fee" is that one has "To earn it by disdaining it."

The richest of her meditations on fame likewise denigrates mere notability and concludes that those who concern themselves about fame thereby profane the quality for which fame might be deserved.

> The Clover's simple Fame
> Remembered of the Cow—
> Is better than enameled Realms
> Of notability.
>
> Renown perceives itself
> And that degrades the Flower—
> The Daisy that has looked behind
> Has compromised it's power—
>
> (1232)

The contrast here is between self-regarding celebrity and true recognition of value, each of which is associated with a different sense and a different kind of reception. Renown's vision is the inferior kind, understandably enough given the common association of empty vanity with gazing at oneself. What may be less obvious is why such vanity should compromise power and what the power might be. The superior sense is taste, in the pointedly banal image of a cow eating clover. Dickinson uses eating or digestion as a metaphor for reading and other sorts of mental consumption in a number of poems, but it may have a distinctive function here. Ingesting food provides strength to the eater, of course, and as ruminative animals with an especially complex digestive system cows receive their food and gain nourishment from such "responding" in conspicuously active ways. The analogy between food and digestion on the one hand and a vigorous response to them on the other is thus more than usually apt. Furthermore, the power compromised when the flower looks behind at its accomplishments is apparently its power to stimulate a vigorous, nourishing response. Indeed, the uneaten plant in this poem has no accomplishments. Literary achievement requires the reader to consume the text, simple fame then following to the extent that the reader remembers and admires the stimulus to this action.

In another version of poem 1232 the last four lines read:

> Renown perceives itself
> And that profanes the power
> The Daisy that has looked behind
> Has forfeited the Dower

The power is thus a dower, a gift received from someone else rather than a native property of the flower. (The legal term "dower," as a distinct from "dowry," is the portion of a deceased husband's estate allotted to the wife during her lifetime. The portion can be forfeited by failure to honor the conditions established by the husband's will.) This suggests that looking behind, as distinct from but also like perceiving oneself, refers to comparing one's renown with that of those from the realms of notability, the writers from whom one has by reading them received the dower. Yet this power, like one's own, exists not in the authoring but in the being consumed.

5

The Dickinson Sublime

Numerous peculiarities in Dickinson's style can be accounted for by her affective understanding of poetry and her correspondingly disseminative aims and practices. So also can much of the unusual combination of intensity and enigma her poetry regularly achieves. Allegiance to a rhetoric of stimulus describes only one part of Dickinson's literary program, however; the other part derives from Dickinson's commitment to the esthetics of the sublime, the second corollary of cherishing power. Like the romantic sublime of which it is a distinctive, heterodox version, the Dickinson sublime is a kind of discipline, an array of motives, values, and practices which gives rise to specific poetic structures and structural categories. Whereas the rhetoric of stimulus thus presides over a micropoetics of diction, syntax, and other local effects, the Dickinson sublime governs the larger designs in and among the poems.

We have already examined the general structure of the sublime as it appears in a few Dickinson poems and introduced the question of that structure's complicity with a poetics of mastery. In this chapter we will consider some additional ways in which the sublime shapes Dickinson's work and some other kinds of poems in which its influence is visible. Then, after having thus seen some of the variety in Dickinson's engagement with the sublime, we will look more closely at the problem of mastery. First, however, let us see just how the sublime can work to organize a specific poem, in this case an apparently maladroit or irresponsible one.

There is no real doubt about Dickinson's affinity for sublime intensities or her talent for calling up such intensities in her poems. Even Dickinson's severest critics have generally conceded that her style is provocative and energetic; the doubts have come in asking if she harnesses the rhetorical energy to a distinct or coherent purpose. Might not such criticism blame Dickinson's poetry for effects she actually cherishes? In isolation a commitment to the rhetoric of stimulus could excuse or indeed legitimize such effects. Dickinson's rhetorical allegiance could thus well be taken as requiring the absence of broader patterns and purposes, since it entails displacing from author to reader much of the usual burden of closure and of the determination of meaning. Such a rhetoric would bid fair to rationalize what by other standards would seem the author's abdication of responsibility.

The possibility is not entirely hypothetical, for the unfettered exercise of one's native powers often seems in Dickinson's work to be its own justification. A number of her poems expressly celebrate various kinds of heedless and self-delighting energy, and several others identify restrictions on such power with drabness, tyranny, and repression. Some go further. "The duties of the wind" not only praises the blithely unregulated, capricious power exemplified by the wind, it then flaunts the same kind of power in its own structure. In the last stanza, at a seemingly climactic moment in the otherwise orderly development of her topic, Dickinson suddenly, startlingly, and perhaps indefensibly abandons the poem.

> The duties of the Wind are few,
> To cast the ships, at Sea,
> Establish March, the floods Escort,
> And usher Liberty.
>
> The pleasures of the Wind are broad,
> To dwell Extent among,
> Remain, or wander,
> Speculate, or Forests entertain.
>
> The kinsmen of the Wind are Peaks
> Azof—the Equinox,
> Also with Bird and Asteroid
> A bowing intercourse.
>
> The limitations of the Wind
> Do he exist, or die,
> Too wise he seems for Wakelessness,
> However, know not I.
>
> (1137)

No power in all of Dickinson's poetry, with the possible but by no means certain exception of God, is as unconstrained as the wind is here. The poem celebrates the wind as a force that answers to no one. It does not even answer to itself, at least if it is understood to be endowed with wakelessness. Possessing such a negative trait would mean that it could not waken to a level of consciousness or intentionality separable from the actions it performs. A wakeless wind exists wholly and exclusively in its acts and powers, in other words.

Even what are called the wind's duties consist only of being itself, without regard for purpose, consequence, or consistency. With respect to consequence, for example, it is all the same to the wind whether the exercise of its powers threateningly escorts floods or nobly ushers liberty. The poem conspicuously avoids distinguishing dire from happy consequences, obliterating in the second line any difference between launching or propelling ships—one sense of casting them—and casting the same ships about or adrift. Furthermore, the wind's duties are indistinguishable from its pleasures. Both amount to dwelling Extent among, a particularly marvelous phrase for untroubled autonomy. As the object of "among," the noun "Extent" signifies environment, the wind's surroundings and its field of play: the wind wanders freely within the whole of a presumably vast extent. In addition, because Dickinson reverses the normal word order of the preposition and its object, "Extent" also takes on an adverbial force. As an adverb or verbal particle it designates *how* the wind exists within that extent. It does so by dwelling among, that is to say, by being at ease with, at home amidst, and unestranged from that which, so the rest of the poem says, the wind utterly dominates. The result is to make the wind an integral part of its world but at the same time also able to act upon that world without constraint or hindrance. This is utmost freedom, one which pays no price in homelessness or detachment and which has no needs or desires not immediately answered to.

That the speaker admires the wind's freedom seems evident throughout the poem, and in the last line she abruptly and astonishingly emulates it. Seemingly on the verge of discerning limits to the wind's powers, Dickinson suddenly breaks off both the inquiry and the poem. The act might well anger a reader who has obligingly been following the poem and taking its concerns seriously. Dickinson's confession of ignorance in the last line certifies that she could now care less about what she has for more than a dozen lines asked her reader to attend to carefully. In breaking off the poem Dickinson acts with exactly the blithe caprice previously attributed to the wind, taking no more responsibility for the themes her poems has raised than the wind does for whether it speeds our ships or sinks them. The poem can accordingly be read as a hymn to independent, unregulated force, one that then blatantly and rather maladroitly becomes an example of such power. Like "To be alive is power," "Mine by the right of the white election," and certain other exuberant poems, this one both endorses and exercises a power unconditioned by regard for discipline, coherence, consistency, or consequence.

Yet the exercise of power in this and similar poems is not entirely unregulated, after all. For one thing, the poem itself adheres at least until the last line to a carefully ordered stanzaic and rhetorical parallelism. Like many of her poems, furthermore, this one is most appropriately grasped as an act of mind, a text whose topic is as much the speaker's attempt to come to terms with the wind as the wind itself. I have called the poem celebratory and hymnlike, but this is at best a half-truth. Although Dickinson overtly characterizes the wind as lawless and unconditioned, she also organizes the poem according to a series of terms designed to circumscribe its capacities: duties, pleasures, kinsmen, and then—explicitly—limitations. If one considers pleasures to be more insidious restraints on freedom than duties, because they are internal to the subject and thus more difficult to oppose, then the series escalates from stanza to stanza, as if probing for one that would be sufficiently telling. The power of Dickinson's language to define the wind thus works against the wind's freedom, not necessarily as its opposite or its open enemy but certainly as a burden upon it. The concluding line is consequently less arbitrary, though no less drastic, than it may first appear. The "I" surfaces in that line explicitly, but it has been implicit throughout as the agent directing the poem and the consciousness engaging the wind's sublimity. Dickinson, in emulating and thus joining with the wind's capriciousness, the aspect that has most resisted her definitions, abandons the neutrally descriptive stance of the opening stanzas, but she emphatically keeps faith with the theme of the speaker's relation to the wind, which has been the underlying topic throughout.

She also thus keeps faith with the sublime, which in retrospect we can see all along to have been the governing mode of the poem. As an act of mind, "The duties of the wind" manifests the three-phase structure of the dyadic contest with a sublime object: a normalcy before the advent of the other, a traumatic disruption visited here both on the world and on poetic subjectivity, and a reactive or sublimating assertion of power. The quintessential third moment of the sublime appears in the suddenly altered or reversed relation to the wind, the abrupt change from the poet's representing the wind as an alien force to her manifesting in her own speech the very force previously represented as the wind's alone. To recall Longinus' words once more, the true sublime is experienced as a moment of elevation and empowerment, when the soul takes a proud flight and is filled with joy and vaunting, as though it had itself produced what it has only heard. In this case, and not untypically, the moment is also a quiet triumph over the wind. The limitations Dickinson invokes in the last stanza are obscure, tentative, and halting, but they have one thing in common. Each asks if characteristically human attributes apply to the wind, specifically finitude and consciousness. In calling the wind "too wise" for wakelessness, Dickinson emphatically endows it with a mental capacity (as she had already done with "speculate"), but the phrase is hardly complimentary. Her next line effectively devalues wisdom or knowledge in comparison to doing as one pleases; to "know not" is thus to establish one's superiority to one who is "wise." At the end then Dickinson essentially trades places with the wind, bestowing upon it the feebler cognitive powers she has been exercising heretofore and adopting for herself the power of blithely dwelling extent among.

Sublime Quality

Two distinguishable senses of sublimity can be observed in "The duties of the wind," each with a somewhat different kind of appeal in Dickinson's poetry. The relations between the speaker and wind that I have just been describing exemplify the orthodox romantic sublime, which is above all a structure of events as apprehended by and involving some subject. Historically, the sublime became an important source of poetic structure only with the advent of romantic subjectivity as a major literary topic. The greatness once imagined as belonging to particular, extraordinary objects of representation came regularly to be sought or claimed by the poetic self or by such surrogates for the questing authorial consciousness as Hyperion and Childe Roland.

As well as a noun requiring the definite article and designating a structure of events, "sublime" can also be an adjective. Logically, empirically, and for the most part historically prior to the structural sublime is the qualitative sublime, the extraordinary attributes or properties of the sublime object. Dickinson herself uses "sublime" adjectivally. The word is not especially prominent in her lexicon, particularly by comparison to terms describing some phase of the romantic sublime: "awe," "astonishment," "transport," and the like. When it does appear, however, it is always used in the qualitative sense, as an honorific designation of the mighty, the dread, and the challenging. In a comic valentine of 1852, for instance, *"sublime"* is the italicized climax of a series ascending from "fatal," "fine," and "heroic" (3). Twenty years later she calls conjecturing about the afterlife a "Theme [as] stubborn as Sublime" (1221).

In "The duties of the wind," the qualitative sublime is obviously represented by the wind's insouciant power. In and of itself, however, power need not be sublime, only when it manifests the appropriate wildness. Power becomes sublime, that is, when it is capable of opening or revealing some disruption in the ordinary fabric of life. Although the wind itself is heedless of consequences, what the poem calls its duties all amount to upsetting stability. Ships get cast about, winter ends, floods arise, and liberty gets ushered in. In a small way, echoed more largely elsewhere, each of these duties thus marks a break in some previous order.

The appeal of such regularly dangerous, even disastrous ruptures should be clearer in the following poem, which may be Dickinson's most succinct account of the qualitative sublime.

> A nearness to Tremendousness—
> An Agony procures—
> Affliction ranges boundlessness—
> Vicinity to Laws
>
> Contentment's quiet Suburb
> Affliction cannot stay
> In Acres—It's Location
> Is Illocality—
>
> (963)

As in "A little madness," sublimity is tremendousness, a superlatively affective intensity. What tremendousness does is make available the experience of a realm that is otherwise hidden, remote, and discontinuous with normalcy. Here it allows us first to apprehend or conceptualize the boundedness of whatever law or locality normally defines our quiet suburban life. It then shows that what lies beyond the boundary is not some other location but the boundlessness of illocality, that is to say, a transcendent or supersensible zone that is in all ways incommensurate with location. The appeal of the qualitative sublime is thus access to this transcendent realm, which Dickinson often represents in Christian terms. The contrast between locality and illocality is accordingly one version of the prevailing ontological discontinuity in Dickinson's work. Variously expressed as the gap between this world and the next, life and afterlife, earth and heaven, or time and eternity, the rupture is widely recognized as pervading Dickinson's work.

One difference between the qualitative and the structural sublime is that the discontinuity revealed in the former need not be personal. In spite of the speaker's agony and affliction, the gap between locality and illocality is an objective or conceptual one. By contrast, the essential discontinuity in "The duties of the wind" is not the physical disruption caused by the wind but the metaphysical contrast between the wind's powers and the poet's. What the wind's actions primarily reveal to the poet, surely albeit silently, is the inability of her words and her wisdom to limit or define the wind's power. This is a gap that cannot be closed, only crossed, and so Dickinson does just that in the last line.

Elsewhere, as one moves toward the structural aspect, the affect itself is discontinuous. Indeed, this is one test of genuine sublimity, that it affects the self so powerfully that the response cannot be singly categorized. The difference appears in the following poem as the differing effects morning and noon produce.

> Of this is Day composed
> A morning and a noon
> A revelry unspeakable
> And then a gay unknown
> Whose Pomps allure and spurn
> And dower and deprive
> And penury for Glory
> Remedilessly leave
>
> (1675)

If "Whose" in line 5 refers solely to noon's "gay unknown" rather than to day in general, then the poem distinguishes morning from noon. The former's revelry is powerful enough to be called "unspeakable," and it may well thus be considered to disrupt or frustrate the otherwise available verbal categories. However, it has no particular consequences for the speaker and demands no reaction. By contrast the pomps of the gay unknown produce conspicuously conflicting, indeed contradictory responses. The main gap opened in this poem lies between the two sides of the speaker's ambivalent or doubly valent reactions—that noon dowers and deprives—and between the two corresponding qualities or powers possessed by noon, that it both allures and spurns.

If we look closely, the same ambivalence is visible in "A nearness to tremendousness." The sublime is experienced in that poem in the form of pain, often the case in Dickinson, but the sequence of pain and nearness works either way. Depending on how one reads the reversible grammar of the first two lines, nearness to tremendousness is either procured by or procures agony. In the first case, pains that one experiences within the realm of location nevertheless dower by eliciting the nearness to tremendousness and from there the transcendent illocality. In the second, the experience of the sublime is itself an agony, presumably because one is only near tremendousness and not in possession of it. A similar reversibility appears in the second stanza; contentment's quiet suburb either cannot stay affliction, in the sense of warding it off, protecting one from the onslaught of the sublime, or it cannot stay in the sense of remaining in the same place as affliction. Affliction would then exactly mark the line between locality and illocality. It cannot stay in the one; and it ranges the other, both in the intransitive sense of wandering about illocality and in the transitive sense of gauging illocality's unmeasurable boundlessness.

In "Of this is day composed" the affective discontinuity then gives rise to another, the contrast between the speaker's state before and after noon afflicts her. The syntax is characteristically sly here, however, and its effects foreshadow Dickinson's version of the romantic sublime. On the one hand, noon's pomps leave us both without a remedy and in a state of penury, the latter unmistakably a decline from the glory which morning seems to have evoked. On the other hand, although we are still without remedy, the same words can be read as leaving an initial state of penury, perhaps occasioned by morning's revelry, in order to attain a present or incipient glory. Likewise, the absence of pronouns makes it uncertain to whom or for whom the pomps leave the glory: themselves, the speaker, or possibly both. In other words, the poem hesitates about associating sublimity with the desideratum of glory. Of its affective intensity there is no doubt, but of the experience's worth or value there can be much question.

The Sublime and the Beautiful

Up to a point it would be true to say that Dickinson indentifies the poetic or the artistic with the intensity of a specifically qualitative sublime. Her rhetoric regularly seeks to elicit such mighty forces and also to encourage their characteristically disruptive effects. In addition, unlike the inherently agonistic romantic sublime, the qualitative sublimity of some object or experience need not be tainted with mastery. Illocality seeks no particular dominion over Dickinson, nor she over it. Even in "The duties of the wind" no sign of a dyadic struggle for mastery appears until the final line, which is what makes that line so abrupt.

On the other hand, the adjectival sublime does not quite fully or sufficiently define the essence of poetry for Dickinson. For one thing, the distinction between the qualitative and the structural sublime holds only for some of Dickinson's poems, usually the ones that, like "A nearness to tremendousness," objectify the experienced qualities without representing the object in which they are vested. Whenever the dyadic object or alterity appears in the poem, the act of experiencing its sublimity broaches the structure of the romantic sublime and hence of mastery. Furthermore, not all poetic experiences in Dickinson are sublime. Something like the category of the beautiful also has a place in her work, a limited and largely deprecated place but also one that allows us to see more clearly the contrasting function of the sublime.

Enlightenment critics usually distinguish sharply between the beautiful and the sublime. Dickinson does not share their concern to account for the appeal of experiences that are not immediately or entirely pleasing, but traces or echoes of their distinction do appear in her work. Selecting from a congeries of differing accounts only the themes that anticipate Dickinson's work, we can say that the crucial difference between the sublime and the beautiful is between an affect-centered and an object- or form-centered understanding of poetic value. The object-centered esthetics of the beautiful stresses a fusion of material reality with spiritual ideals and hence the manifestation of a harmoniously ordered continuum. The centrally signifying aspect of the beautiful then becomes form, the form primarily of the esthetic object but also of the continuum in which subject and object then find themselves. By contrast, the esthetics of the sublime is predicated on intensely experienced, anguishing forces that rupture normal continuities of habit and belief. As a result the signifying attribute of the sublime is power, initially the power of the object and then also the relations of power between subject and object or within the apprehending subject.

By the middle of the nineteenth century this once warmly contested distinction had lapsed in importance, the attributes of the sublime having largely been assimilated to a more subjectivized understanding of beauty. Poe, for example, in 1850 parenthetically defines beauty as subsuming the category of the sublime: "I make Beauty, therefore—using the term as inclusive of the sublime—I make Beauty the province of the poem."[1] Dickinson also uses "beauty" mainly in this inclusive sense, but the distinction survives for her in such contrasts as that between power on the one hand and the kingdom and the glory on the other. More specifically, her one use of the Burkean phrase "the beautiful" draws centrally and subtly on the older esthetic distinction.

> As imperceptibly as Grief
> The Summer lapsed away—
> Too imperceptible at last
> To seem like Perfidy—
> A Quietness distilled
> As Twilight long begun,
> Or Nature's spending with herself
> Sequestered Afternoon—
> The Dusk drew earlier in—
> The Morning foreign shone—
> A courteous, yet harrowing Grace,
> As Guest, that would be gone—
> And thus, without a Wing
> Or service of a Keel
> Our Summer made her light escape
> Into the Beautiful.
>
> (1540)

This poem about a change of season looks in one direction only, backward upon the season that has gone, and the tone is thus appropriately wistful. The regret would seem to be for the fading of summer's luxuriant splendors. From other poems we know such splendors can be supremely, even sublimely affecting.[2] This poem does not contradict the others, for it is the disappearance of summer rather than its presence that the poem identifies with the beautiful. The passing of the seasons is a frequent theme in Dickinson's work, but here it is handled in an unusual way. We get only the fading and escape, without any language anticipating some changed natural order or signifying some natural mutability. Indeed, the presence of nature itself seems to have lapsed with the summer. Dickinson deleted from the first draft a recognition that autumn had replaced the summer ("gaudy influence / The Maple lent unto the Road"). The change leaves the poem only an absence and a recollecting speaker where the summer had been. Similarly, the comparison to the approach of evening—three slightly different comparisons, actually—functions to make summer's lapse not like the replacement of one thing by another but like the waning of a positivity, the disappearance of the daylight, which leaves only the negative condition of darkness.

Grief would seem the obviously appropriate response to such loss, but Dickinson's initial simile works more subtly than that. Summer's lapse is compared to the fading of grief, suggesting that the regret is as much for something the self no longer can feel as for the object it has lost. The perfidy Dickinson considers but rejects as an accurate name for the event may even suggest she blames the self for having betrayed once strong emotions as much as she blames summer for falsely abandoning the scene.

The beautiful is here thus constituted by absence, especially an absence of affect. Even before the summer fully lapses, it is a remote and self-absorbed presence, one whose lack of relation to the speaker is personified in the figure of the courteous but eager-to-leave guest. When that remoteness has been perfected by actual disappearance, and nature and the speaker have both been entirely sequestered to themselves, then summer fully attains the beautiful. In such a state summer remains available for retrospective contemplation, for that is the stance of the poem we have. Yet the contemplation of absence here does preclude affective intensity; from within the beautiful the summer cannot or can no longer affect the speaker strongly or in some other way manifest a vital relation to her. Separation and loss of affect need not amount to estrangement, of course. One might rashly conclude that the speaker and nature are alienated from one another but only at the cost of lending a speciously melodramatic air to what Dickinson sees as "Quietness distilled" to completion.

Such completion can be a kind of perfection perhaps, but not to Dickinson, who persistently views its stasis, finality, and absence of affective energy with great suspicion. The quietness in this poem is kin to the stillness Dickinson pejoratively identifies with prose, confinement, and oppression in this well-known declaration of personal and poetic exuberance:

> They shut me up in Prose—
> As when a little Girl
> They put me in the Closet—
> Because they liked me "still"—
> (613)

A closer resemblance to the beautiful of "As imperceptibly as grief" is found in Dickinson's occasional characterization of secure religious faith as an estimable but antiquated and unalterable state of mind

that is cut off from experience or otherwise unable to be affected by
its surroundings.

> Safe in their Alabaster Chambers—
> Untouched by Morning
> And untouched by Noon—
> Sleep the meek members of the Resurrection—
> Rafter of satin
> And Roof of stone.
>
> Light laughs the breeze
> In her Castle above them—
> Babbles the Bee in a stolid Ear,
> Pipe the Sweet Birds in ignorant cadence—
> Ah, what sagacity perished here!
>
> (216)

The poem is grandly mean-spirited to the extent that it takes the dead
to task for not being alive to experience nature. On the other hand,
the alabaster chambers are churches as well as tombs, so its point
is similar to the one made in the following poem.

> Through the strait pass of suffering—
> The Martyrs—even—trod.
> Their feet—upon Temptation—
> Their faces—upon God—
>
> A stately—shriven—Company—
> Convulsion—playing round—
> Harmless—as streaks of Meteor—
> Upon a Planet's Bond—
>
> Their faith—the everlasting troth—
> Their Expectation—fair—
> The Needle—to the North Degree—
> Wades—so— 'thro polar Air!
>
> (792)

Whether nobly or absurdly, faith in a fixed and securely nonempiri-
cal order immunizes the martyrs against even the most convulsive
experiences.

The heaven toward which the martyrs' faces are directed is not
the same as the transcendent zone made available by the sublime,
even though the two are often called by the same name. (Dickinson
does sometimes verbally distinguish eternity and immortality, as we
shall see later.) When apprehended through the static category of

beauty, heaven is often as unappealing as it is to the little girl who tells us in "I never felt at home below" that "I don't like Paradise— / Because it's Sunday—all the time— / and Recess—never comes—" (413). It is the same "Heaven to us, if true" that somewhat more winningly "beguiles the tired" in "As watchers hang upon the east" (121).

By contrast to the ideal but static, absent finality of the beautiful, Dickinson consistently prefers the directly affecting intensities of the sublime, even when they are painful.

> There's a certain Slant of light,
> Winter Afternoons—
> That oppresses, like the Heft
> Of Cathedral Tunes—
>
> Heavenly Hurt, it gives us—
> We can find no scar,
> But internal difference,
> Where the Meanings, are—
>
> (258)

Such an experience leaves marks within the self, and these marks persist even when the immediate object or occasion has withdrawn. Moreover, "None may teach it—Any." The experience must be undergone rather than learned of secondhand or merely anticipated.

Although the affecting power is regularly attributed to the object—the light itself here oppresses and gives hurt—the difference in consequences arises not from different kinds of objects or experiences but from the self's differing relation to them. This means that the difference between the qualitative and the romantic or structural sublime is for Dickinson ultimately only a difference in perspective upon a single kind of experience. For example, the presence of summer can be sublime, as we noticed with reference to "As imperceptibly as grief," whereas its passage into absence is explicitly named as an escape into the beautiful. Yet at other times and in other moods even the passing of summer can elicit sublime effects. Consider a poem written about ten years after the first draft and six years before the last version of "As imperceptibly as grief."

> The last of Summer is Delight—
> Deterred by Retrospect.
> 'Tis Ectasy's revealed Review—
> Enchantment's Syndicate.

To meet it—nameless as it is—
Without celestial Mail—
Audacious as without a Knock
To walk within the Vail.

(1353)

An unselected alternative for "revealed" in line 3 is "sublime." Even as quoted, the concentrated intensity of the delighting and deterring prospect is clear enough, the phrase "Enchantment's Syndicate" particularly indicating a combination of forces specifically designated to transact business with any who encounter it. Although the poem considers the possibility of being armored against the forces by "celestial Mail," an option comparable to the protective faith of the martyrs in "Through the strait pass of suffering," the rhetoric is stacked heavily in favor of undergoing the experience audaciously and to the full.

Sublime Heroics

As long as the object remains a spectacle one might safely observe or ponder, its sublimity remains on the side of the qualitative. Once the apprehending subject is constitutively involved, however, we pass from the qualitative sublime to the structural and hence to a poetry of potentially heroic subjectivity. By contrast to "A nearness to tremendousness," where the discontinuity of locality and illocality is agonizing but not especially personal, the dowerings and deprivations of "Of this is day composed" aim at the experiencing self. So, more dramatically, do the triumphs of the wind in "The duties of the wind." And because the experiencing self is the poet's deputed or enacted subjectivity in such poems, the poet's stature is always at stake in the structural sublime.

More specifically, as soon as the subject feels compelled to respond to the object, audaciously or otherwise, the sublime begins to take on the characteristics of a discipline, even sometimes a test or a challenge the poet must undergo. In "The last of summer," for example, Dickinson imagines the challenge as knightly combat, a notably stylized or ritualized form of the dyadic struggle that defines the romantic sublime. Actually the struggle is never quite so rule-governed, else it would lack the sublime's necessarily disruptive and discomfiting power, but it is nonetheless a kind of regimen one must undergo in order to experience sublimity at all.

Knightly combat legendarily originates when one party has some-how insulted the other; the compulsion to respond to the sublime likewise usually originates at least partly in the injury it does to one's pride. This can be true even when the poet starts out by denying pride and humbly submitting herself to external authority.

> A solemn thing—it was—I said—
> A Woman—white—to be—
> And wear—if God should count me fit—
> Her blameless mystery—
>
> A timid thing—to drop a life
> Into the mystic well—
> Too plummetless—that it come back—
> Eternity—until—
>
> I pondered how the bliss would look—
> And would it feel as big—
> When I could take it in my hand—
> As hovering—seen—through fog—
>
> And then—the size of this "small" life—
> The Sages—call it small—
> Swelled—like Horizons—in my breast—
> And I sneered—softly—"small"!
>
> (271)

With one exception the poem is typical of an encounter with the ro-mantic sublime and thus illustrates the usual three-phase pattern de-scribed in an earlier chapter. Normalcy here is the state of mind represented in the first stanza, when submission can be contemplated as a merely solemn act. The act becomes traumatic and thus sublime when Dickinson acknowledges that it would be "plummetless," that is, both unfathomable and endless, and when she recognizes also that it would elicit and confirm the sages' belittling judgment of her cur-rent state. Then comes the explicit reaction; Dickinson announces the triumphant swelling of her own powers, doing so as if it were the recovery of what had all along been their proper magnitude.

The one unusual feature of this relatively early poem is that it allows us to observe how the spectacle of the qualitative sublime can become the trauma of the romantic sublime. The usually elusive tran-sition from qualitative to structural sublimity becomes visible here because the object or alterity is imagined by the speaker rather than actually encountered. (Indeed, from a perspective other than the poem's, a state of blissful submission would not be an object at all.

Dickinson, however, twice carefully calls it a thing, thereby deemphasizing as much as possible its subjective and also hypothetical character.) The transition occurs when the initial image of the self's wearing white is replaced by that of its plunging into the plummetless well. The second trope is less a concrete image than a figure for the absence of such an image; what the trope depicts is that the speaker will have lost the capacity to imagine her life once it has been submitted to God. Such loss is at once an effect and a cause of the traumatic phase, which opens a discontinuity between finitude ("this 'small' life") and infinity (both the spatial infinity of "plummetless" and the temporal of "Eternity—until"). At that point the authority of the external object, somewhat displaced onto the sage's version of an otherwise still possibly pristine holiness, is overcome by the reactive invigoration of native resources, according to the orthodox legerdemain of sublimation.

Unlike an admirer of the beautiful or the picturesque, a connoisseur of the sublime almost invariably plays a heroic role. Indeed, he or she may be obliged to exhibit several heroic virtues and to play the heroic role in more than one form. It can require an admirable boldness to meet without celestial mail the tremendousness of the sublime object, for example, and it can require additional fortitude to withstand the devastations of the traumatic phase. Furthermore, the reactive phase provides opportunity for heroism in a more specifically masterly sense. As we have seen at several points, to attain the elevation or empowerment characterizing the third phase is often to have vanquished a foe or established superiority over the alterity with which one has struggled. The end of "A solemn thing" is thus a triumphant defeat of the sages, and the conclusion of "An ignorance a sunset" confirms one party's victory over another. In addition, the exultation experienced in the reactive phase specifically enhances, restores, or reaffirms the self in its power and glory.

Within the representational world of the romantic sublime the self thus assumes (or believes it has assumed) the master's role vis-à-vis the initially tremendous alterity. This mastery can then be redoubled or reduplicated on another plane, in the relationship solicited by the text between the heroic self and the reader. To the extent that the sublimity of the poet's self is convincing or effective and he or she has heroically overcome the represented object's tremendousness, the poet's heroic self becomes in turn the sublime object for the reader. The triumphant self incarnates the dreadful majesty it has faced, taking on all its power and glory.

Dickinson is far more uneasy about such heroism than other

romantic poets. Her reluctance appears variously motivated, but all the reasons are related to her deep ambivalence about mastery. Although she regularly entertains the possibility of sublimely triumphant mastery and also its opposite, devoted submission to the other, she is far more than normally conscious that mastery always has its costs. A minor example is the diminishment of the object visible in "A solemn thing." The poem traces a progressive diminution of the bliss it begins by taking as inherently worthy. Not only does the magnitude of bliss become uncertain by the third stanza, the speaker now emphasizes its remoteness and she also defensively insinuates that the originally apparent size might have been an illusion of distance and fog. In other words, achieving superiority apparently requires belittling the originally sublime object. That in turn retroactively lessens or cheapens the experiential intensity that it is always part of Dickinson's intention to cultivate.

A more significant cost is that for all its vaunting triumph the masterly self can remain beholden to or dependent upon the object it claims to have conquered, particularly if its majesty directly imitates the object's original majesty. In "A solemn thing," for example, the reactive image of self-assertion is modeled upon or borrowed from the original superiority, the initially mighty bliss that had first to be encountered before the self's horizons could swell. Size counters size; the speaker's newly internal breadth counters the external depth of plummetlessness. "The duties of the wind" offers a starker, more dramatic example of the same dependency. In proclaiming, perhaps somewhat petulantly and certainly with great abruptness, that I do not know whether the wind is too wise for wakelessness, I model my assertive strength directly on the attribute of the wind that has most defeated me.

It might be remembered from an earlier chapter that, according to Mary Arensberg's redaction of the sublime, such a mimesis of the object is explicitly one of the defenses by which the subject appropriates the object's tremendousness. Moreover, as a psychic and indeed specifically psychoanalytic defense, imitation requires repression of the object's authority. Or, if one balks at the language of psychoanalytic theory, the same operation can be described in terms of Girardian anthropology as a mimesis of appropriation, in which one overcomes an alterity who plays the specific role of the subject's rival.[3] According to either description, one must forget or deny the other's power in order to have the experience of acquiring it. The inevitable dissimulation can be seen in "A solemn thing" in the way Dickinson somewhat covertly splits the sanction for holy bliss into two sources.

In addition to the original and still presumably legitimate mystery of God, the poem adduces a bad sanction represented by the sages and their presumably imperfect or erroneous conceptions of mystery. The prideful assertion at the end then triumphs over a substitute alterity only, whose authority the poem is at pains to deny. Meanwhile the poem dissimulates any awareness that the speaker still has not been counted fit by God or undergone the experience of precisely such election.

The claim about repression in Arensberg's account derives from Harold Bloom, for whom the poems we have been examining (and indeed all American poetry) exemplify the countersublime, that most explicitly and overtly reactive mode in Bloom's calculus of poetic stances. As intially propounded, for example, the countersublime presupposes the daemonization of the precursor, that is to say, the apprehension of the other as invested with sublime tremendousness.[4] Bloom has also proclaimed that the sublime is unthinkable without repression, meaning presumably that only repression is a powerful and flexible enough psychic mechanism to lull us into the sublime, where we not only believe we have overcome the other's authority but actually and even somatically experience the exultation of such triumph. Whether repression is a general necessity of the sublime, it is certainly common in Dickinson's ken. However, she can never finally convince herself that it is worth the cost. On the other hand, like Bloom, she sees no other means of gaining experiential access to the transcendent. As a result, the Dickinson sublime often proposes that we should *decide* whether to adopt the inherently unconscious, involuntary strategy of repression.

One word more should be said about the relation of Bloom's theories and Dickinson's practice. He construes defensiveness about authority as an anxiety of influence. The notion may accurately reflect the overt and widespread concern with poetic originality among the English romantics and their immediate predecessors, and it certainly plays a major role in nineteenth-century American literary nationalism. To the Bloomian poet, bliss and glory belong wholly to a mighty precursor (possibly composite), in whom the ephebe first recognizes the nature of literary greatness and against whom he must struggle in order not to lapse into slavish imitation. Dickinson agrees that the recognition of greatness normally entails a discovery of one's own comparative incapacities: "Your riches taught me poverty" (299). Unlike the ephebe's, however, Dickinson's primary concern is not originality but authority.

Thus Dickinson appears to identify herself at a fundamental level as "the only Kangaroo among the Beauty," someone for whom uniqueness or at least considerable difference from others is a given condition, even a sort of affliction (*Letters*, 412). She is a good bit less confident that the distinctiveness of her being possesses authority or potency, however. Although she can indeed model herself upon the anterior presence of the other, as both "A solemn thing" and "The duties of the wind" demonstrate abundantly, the deprivations of the Dickinson sublime are less likely to threaten secondariness or the absence of autonomy than to postulate weakness and illegitimacy.

Authority and potency are Dickinson's primary concerns, in other words, and both are for her preeminently theological matters. Religious transcendence is by no means the only theme of the Dickinson sublime, but it tends to subsume other struggles or at least to supply the primary language in which artistic, perceptual, epistemological, familial, and erotic conflicts get represented. Just as Bloom's ephebe acknowledges and is first instructed in glory by recognizing the authority of a precursor, so the youthful Emily Dickinson appears clearly and unalterably to have acknowledged the legitimacy of Calvinistic Christianity as preached in the Connecticut Valley during one of that region's most intense periods of religious awakening. The letters that survive from her adolescence are dominated by confused reflections on whether she can or will accept Christianity. Although she never finally wavers in locating her destiny outside the church, she also never fails to acknowledge the legitimacy of orthodox piety.

I have a perfect confidence in God & his promises & yet I know not why, I feel the world holds a predominant place in my affection. I do not feel that I could give up all for Christ, were I called to die. (*Letters*, 38)

Elsewhere Dickinson often rejects piety more defiantly but never in terms that deny the authority of the divine. "To the faithful Absence is condensed presence. To others—but there *are* no others" (*Letters*, 632).

The orthodox romantic sublime has one further cost I have not yet explored. It can necessitate a poetics of mastery, in which the reader is dominated as by a Carlylean poet whose authority is intrinsic and unquestionable. When the figure undergoing the sublime is also the poetic subject, as is commonly the case in romantic poetry, then its acquisition of sublime tremendousness is also the acquisition of a specifically literary authority. Not only is the poetic subject potentially a sublime alterity vis-à-vis the reader, he or she must be such a one if the poem is at all to be accepted as effective. The reason is that the authority of such poetry regularly depends upon the poet's achieving sublime stature, sometimes within the poem at hand. An example from a more eagerly heroic poet should make this clearer. In "Out of the Cradle Endlessly Rocking" Whitman explicitly links his authority as a poet—his capacity as a "chanter of pains and joys, uniter of here and hereafter"—to the sublime appropriation of both bird and sea he experienced once on Paumanok. In other words, this poem and Whitman's poetry in general are expressly based upon the sublimely transfigured stature attained by Whitman at the end of the poem. (That this poem is both a reminiscence and a deliberate attempt to restore now eroded powers only slightly complicates the situation, by transposing the experiential sublimity the poem recounts into the stylistic sublimity it manifests. It worked once for Whitman to experience sublimity, in other words, and it is supposed to work now for him to represent the same sublimity.)

It may be inaccurate to speak of necessities when discussing the reader's role, since a wary, obtuse, or unfriendly reader is always free to do whatever he or she pleases. About the sympathetic reader willing to rehearse the part prepared by the text, however, things can be said about the different roles prepared by structurally different texts. Compare first-person accounts of the romantic sublime with third-person accounts such as "A little madness." A sublime clown in that poem can always be apprehended as a spectacle, an object with which we as readers have no obligatory relation, but our involvement with the poetic subject is necessarily more intimate. However else our parts may vary, that relation is what constitutes us as readers. In "A solemn thing" or "The duties of the wind," for example, we are certainly invited to share in the speaker's triumph. And to the extent that we accept that invitation we at least entertain Dickinson's glorious mastery and thus take a step along the path Longinus described: experiencing ourselves as having produced what we have only heard or read. Likewise, within romantic poetry generally the frequent idealization of the poetic imagination invites us to participate in the poet's venture and often frankly to aspire to his estate. To do so is to practice the countersublime, a weaker and inevitably derivative form of whatever sublimity the romantic poet has attained.

The Dickinson Sublime

Dickinson balks at the costs of sublimity I have been describing and demurs from the pattern of the romantic sublime which incurs such costs. The organization of the sublime in her poetry typically differs from the orthodox three-phase pattern in finding some way to hesitate on the threshold of the reactive phase. In other words, she accepts and even enthusiastically endorses the romantic sublime up to the point at which the self appropriates the power of alterity and thereby proclaims its own glorious or heroic mastery.

Dickinson occasionally goes to unusual lengths to avoid this critical moment, as in "The tint I cannot take is best." Rather than admit defeat by nature's "Graspless manners" and rather than confess her failure to appropriate the power she has discerned in nature's mysteries, the speaker in the final stanza suddenly counters the momentum of the whole poem by unexpectedly changing the subject, like a child abruptly breaking off a game it has been losing. The strategy is both different from and more desperate than the similarly abrupt conclusion of "The duties of the wind," because it is not modeled upon the elusive power with which she has been grappling. Without warning the speaker's "Cheated Eye" perversely or petulantly "Shuts arrogantly—in the Grave— / Another way—to see—" (627). That is to say, it opts for death over defeat because it can then proclaim its own mortality as something that is genuinely—even "arrogantly"—its own and therefore a capacity that triumphs over nature's secrets.

The strategy moves the poem entirely out of the orbit of the sublime, in which it has recognizably moved for the first five stanzas. The capacity Dickinson calls upon is truly unprepared for in the poem, unlike the situation in "The duties of the wind." It is justifiable only by the desperation of Dickinson's failure and the cold ideological comfort of her unusually dogmatic faith in the afterlife's superiority. Elsewhere, Dickinson finds more convincing and potent ways of lingering at the moment of transition between the traumatic and reactive phases. These others are the poems of the distinctively Dickinsonian sublime.

This moment between the second and third phases is obviously a crucial one in the romantic sublime, for that is when confusion and dread are transformed into some kind of exaltation or transcendence. This change is normally predicated on the self's appropriating the initially alien power to itself in some way or, less frequently, on its suddenly discovering that it has all along possessed latent powers that allow it to overcome the otherness that has threatened it. Most accounts of the sublime, including Bloom's, suggest that the mechanism of transformation is some form of imitative identification. The subject first sees the other as wholly alien but then in reaction to the other's disconcerting powers gives up its initial sense of identity in order to identify with the other's power. A specifically literary version of identification is central to Longinus, for instance, although he is otherwise more concerned with the rhetorical and thus ultimately social properties of the object than with any psychic mechanism in the subject. Readers' feelings that they have become what they have beheld exemplify what we mean colloquially whenever we talk of identifying with characters.

Kant provided the first convincing explanation of how the subject moves from terror to exaltation, and in so doing he initiated the specifically romantic understanding of the sublime, in which the experience is primarily intrasubjective rather than rhetorical. According to Kant's analysis the object merely occasions a purely psychic drama; identification occurs entirely within the orbit of mental faculties. Yet to the initially balked imagination an identification with reason's triumphant powers must also feel like submission to something external. In the mathematical sublime, for instance, the mind is overwhelmed by the endlessness of some positive phenomenon or by a vast and incomprehensible emptiness in the world. However, what the imagination cannot measure, enumerate, or otherwise represent, the previously inactive reason suddenly discovers it can conceptualize as the supersensible idea of infinity. The imagination then identifies itself and the entirety of the subject with reason, which Kant in turn deems a universal rather than a merely individual faculty.

Reason's advent, Kant insists, is the curiously bracing revelation that one is subject to a universal law. The invigoration presumably comes from the mind's identification with one of its own faculties. This requires, however, the chastening and then the obeisance of our other, henceforth inferior faculties. Furthermore, reason's heroism is perhaps something less than an a priori universal. Kant explicitly distinguishes sublime access to reason's kingdom from what is properly feminine. His example is the ennobling experience of civilized warfare.[5]

With certain changes of emphasis, notably stemming from psychoanalysis, subsequent theories have usually followed Kant's lead. According to most accounts influenced by Freud, for instance, the sublime object is neither a power in itself nor a figure for some transhuman realm but a symbol of forces arising from primal fantasies. Identification with such forces normally resembles what Freud himself meant by the term; the process parallels or recapitulates an oedipal struggle. Crudely put, a man dispels the threat of castration by identifying himself with the father's phallic power. This can variously involve becoming, becoming one with, or overcoming the father.[6]

Dickinson might imaginably object as much to the masculinism that saturates these identificatory theories as to their willingness to accept the costs of mastery. Her distinctive version of the sublime, by contrast, usually works to defer the moment of identification. The complexities of identification in the Dickinson sublime and the difference between Dickinson's version and the orthodox romantic structure can be observed most fully and impressively in "At half past three, a single bird." The poem is one of several Dickinson wrote that belong to a recognizable romantic tradition, in which the poet's relation to a songbird figures his or her relation to poetic glory. Shelley's "To a Skylark," Keats's "Ode to a Nightingale," and Whitman's already mentioned "Out of the Cradle Endlessly Rocking" are the most eminent counterparts; each of them similarly imagines a bird as incarnating some transcendent power the poet comes to claim for his own. Like Whitman, Dickinson structures her claim according to a sublime appropriation of the bird's alterity.

> At Half past Three, a single Bird
> Unto a silent Sky
> Propounded but a single term
> Of Cautious melody.
>
> At Half past Four, Experiment
> Had subjugated test
> And lo, Her silver Principle
> Supplanted all the rest.
>
> At Half past Seven, Element
> Nor Implement, be seen —
> And Place was where the Presence was
> Circumference between.
>
> (1084)

We have in the poem two versions of the sublime encounter, one between the bird and the sky and the other between the speaker and the bird; shadowing those two but never becoming explicitly thematized is the reader's relation to poem and poet.

The poem offers a notably austere version of the romantic sublime, which by virtue of its starkness and brevity can also supply us with Dickinson's particular lexicon for each of the three stages. "Place" here signifies the ordinary world, as it is apprehended by normal modes of understanding or perception; this would be the world disrupted by the onset of the sublime, and it is also the one that here afterward resumes its dominion. "Presence" schematically designates the dazzling and also intimidating power of the sublime bird, a force that in Shelley, Keats, or Whitman might itself directly be the object of appropriation. Dickinson, however, interposes "Circumference" between place and presence, reserving to that geometric term her careful claim about the sublimity achieved by the poem in its encounter with the bird.

Understanding what Dickinson means here by circumference requires a digression, for the poem's complexity is precisely mirrored by that term's semantic complexity. In "The poets light but lamps," "circumference" designates the light transmitted by dissemination. As described in that poem, however, dissemination is alien to the sublime encounter; no rivalry exists among the successive ages, for example, and likewise no threat that a previous age's light can blind our own.

The circle is of course a traditional symbol of perfection and completeness. "On the earth the broken arcs; in the heaven, a perfect round," as Robert Browning's Abt Vogler puts it. So computing circumferences may for Dickinson also constitute a specifically earthly way of measuring and gaining such ideals. Such would be the implication of her proclaiming on the one hand that "My Business is Circumference" and on the other that "The Bible dealt with the Centre, not with the Circumference" (*Letters*, 412, 850). In addition, mathematics is traditionally both an ideal, objective realm—the queen of the sciences—and also a skill or activity Dickinson regards as fully within her own power.

Mathematics occupies a distinctive place in Dickinson's work. Roughly two hundred of Dickinson's poems include some reference to mathematical terms and ideas, often in a precise and pointed way, and a number of others implicitly depend on counting, measuring, and quantitatively assessing. Throughout Dickinson's work mathematical terms and operations represent a means by which the self constructs, controls, organizes, and takes possession of experience. More specifically, calculation works to ensure that objects and experiences do not elude our mental grasp, and circumference usually represents the highest form such control can humanly achieve. In other words, "circumference" honorifically names the poetic or more precisely the mathetic idea as such, that which through its native powers the mind has been able to grasp and hold.

In addition to "circumference," the other most important mathematical terms are "ratio" and "sum." Each designates the appropriation of an otherwise alien and elusive phenomenon.[7] Thus in poems 88, 125, and 257 Dickinson uses "ratio," the geometric quotient of two quantities, to describe setting an experience she possesses in relation to one that is absent. According to a later descredited etymology in her dictionary, the word derives from the Latin *reor*, meaning to set in the mind and also to speak.[8] Computing ratios thus means positing and articulating the absent or unknown quanity. Almost every poem in which she counts, measures, reckons, or estimates implies the operation, even when the word is absent. For instance, her frequent typological scrutiny of earthly moments as prefigurations of what lies beyond presupposes the calculation of a ratio between life and afterlife or time and eternity.[9]

> As by the dead we love to sit,
> Become so wondrous dear—
> As for the lost we grapple
> Tho all the rest are here—
>
> In broken mathematics
> We estimate our prize
> Vast—in it's fading ratio
> To our penurious eyes!
>
> (88)

A ratio can be direct, as of joy to joy in the celebratory nature poems or in love lyrics such as "There came a day at summer's full." Dickinson as often computes a negative or inverse ratio, one that counts secular blessings at religion's expense or measures earthly misery as an index of heavenly bliss. Such calculation is implicit in poems that advocate cultivating the "White Sustenance— / Despair—" (640), for pain and despair inversely prefigure a glory to come. Negative ratios also appear in poems praising distance or absence as guarantees of value. "Delight is as the flight— / Or in the Ratio of it" (257).

A typical instance of a successfully calculated ratio would be

> that Etherial Gain
> One earns by measuring the Grave—
> Then—measuring the Sun.
>
> (574)

The ratio falters, however, whenever a near term can no longer be grasped. "We let go all of—Time without / Arithmetic of him" (1184). The same failure occurs in the fading ratio of "As by the dead we love to sit." Success requires imaginative possession of at least one term; only then can one calculate the forces beyond one's reach.

Imaginative possession is the direct aim of "sum," Dickinson's other crucial mathematical trope. The term appears in nineteen poems, usually as a synonym for bounty or possession. It often implies that taking possession is an especially vigorous act, even an aggression the object of the summing may resist. Moreover, in contrast to casual experiences or objects, a counted sum in inalienable, like the "Two" of love in "Sweet, you forgot but I remembered" (523). Such a "Sum [will] be never hindered," in spite of the lover's forgetfulness or the more foreboding "Decay of You," which includes both the waning of the beloved's affection and the beloved's death. The idea of sum thus acquires its special force from the implication that it entails true and lasting appropriation.

Unlike many romantic artists, who are fascinated by the indefinite, Dickinson usually prefers an accurate count to a wild surmise. Infinity can even be an object of reproach in her work when it contrasts with some countable quantity. In one poem the reason is clearly that Dickinson equates the precisely counted with the securely and genuinely owned.

> Their Hight in Heaven comforts not—
> Their Glory—nought to me—
> 'Twas best imperfect—as it was—
> I'm finite—I cant see
>
> The House of Supposition—
> The Glimmering Frontier that
> skirts the Acres of Perhaps
> To me—shows insecure—
>
> The Wealth I had—contented me—
> If 'twas a meaner size—
> Then I had counted it until
> It pleased my narrow Eyes—
>
> (696)

Similarly, if one can "Bound—a trouble," then "lives can bear it." One should thus "Deal with the soul / As with Algebra," quantifying pain in order to bear it, tame it, and thus master it (269). Mathematics provides Dickinson with a means of taking effective control of even the most agonizing experiences.

This is how Dickinson uses "circumference" in "She staked her feather," where it signifies a bird's triumphant attainment of an ideality or transcendence that is fully its own. Circumference is specifically as much the bird's birthright as the nest in which it was born.

She staked her Feather—Gained an Arc—
Debated—Rose again—
This time—beyond the estimate
Of Envy, or of Men—

And now, among Circumference—
Her steady Boat be seen—
At home—among the Billows—As
The Bough where she was born—

(798)

Seen against an agonistic notion of the sublime, this may be the most impressively idealizing poem Dickinson ever wrote. The bird is able to trade the partial bliss of the arc for the soaring paradise of circumference, and it does so without needing to acknowledge any authority or power outside itself. That the achievement is beyond our estimate seems likely, but the truly optimistic claim is that it is beyond envy. Dickinson apparently identifies with the bird; certainly it is difficult not to associate the bird's glory with her own or the poem's. One might even take writing the poem as an imitation of the bird's triumph and thus a defense against it. To the extent that such identification or defensive imitation takes place, however, and regardless of whatever generosity or lack thereof may be attributed to the bird, achieving circumference means achieving superiority and perhaps even gaining the superlative glory of the sublime.

One meaning of "circumference" in "At half past three" would thus be that Dickinson's own sublime achievement at the end has replaced the previously dazzling presence of the bird. To the extent that circumference imitates the bird's power—in other words, that Dickinson's poem imitates or otherwise directly counters the bird's song—then Dickinson has identified with the bird's sublime power and appropriated it as her own. To the extent that circumference originates in or as some power wholly different from the bird's—in other words, that the poem is of a different order than the song—then Dickinson has supplanted presence rather than appropriated it. Either reading is possible, but in either case Dickinson and the poem achieve the sublimity of circumference. We readers are accordingly solicited to identify with or otherwise admire the mastery she and it have achieved.

These possibilities are less hypothetical than they might be for other poems. In an earlier poem that otherwise reads as if it were a draft of "At half past three," Dickinson seems to disavow the sublime rather than succumb to a pending identification with the earlier, plural equivalent of the birdsong's presence.

The Birds begun at Four o'clock—
Their period for Dawn—
A Music numerous as space—
But neighboring as Noon—

I could not count their Force—
Their Voices did expend
As Brook by Brook bestows itself
To multiply the Pond.

Their Witnesses were not—
Except occasional man—
In homely industry arrayed—
To overtake the Morn—

Nor was it for applause—
That I could ascertain—
But independent Extasy
Of Deity and Men—

By Six, the Flood had done—
No Tumult there had been
Of Dressing, or Departure—
And yet the Band was gone—

The Sun engrossed the East—
The Day controlled the World—
The Miracle that introduced
Forgotten, as fulfilled.

(783)

The bird's chorus represents a majestic and self-sufficient natural presence that might be expected to precipitate the sublime. Dickinson is present in the poem as a first-person speaker, and her response begins with the sense of being overwhelmed that normally inaugurates the sublime. She even names the experience a flood, one of the commonplace images of the mode. The speaker's involvement largely ends with the inaugural moment, however, and with a recognition of the birds' independence. "I could not count their Force." The line mainly functions to indicate the birdsong's intensity. According to what we have noticed about counting and summation, however, the line also acknowledges that the singing is beyond Dickinson's power to appropriate. In other words, the poem refuses the sublimity it discerns in the birds, admitting that their glory is beyond it.

The poem also defends itself against sublimity by noting its impermanence. The higher but also more predictable and thus less threatening power of the sun wholly replaces the birds' miracle, and the miracle is thus retroactively demeaned in the poem's last line. The song can now be forgotten, because it now can get taken as fulfilling some anticipation of it. In other words, by contrast to the sudden and incomprehensible force initially apprehended in the song, the miracle is now only one more humanly predictable power, like the sun.

"The birds begun at four o'clock" is not likely to satisfy those for whom the sublime is the highest order of art, and it may not have satisfied Dickinson either. "At half past three," which Johnson dates as being written three years later, seems directly to revise the earlier poem. If so, several changes are noteworthy. First, the uncounted flock that bursts into full song has been replaced by a single bird, who, like the one in "She staked her feather," begins cautiously. Second, the bird's actions are described in the language of aggressive intellectual activity rather than that of natural force; the bird propounds a term until it becomes a principle that subjugates and supplants. Third, the leisurely narrative of a morning's event has been replaced by a maniacally precise but oddly uninformative timekeeping. The sun—Dickinson's most common image for nature's dominion—has disappeared, replaced in effect by an abstract chronology that no longer even distinguishes morning from evening. The chronology itself is an instance of Dickinsonian computation, in that it takes over from or appropriates an otherwise given, natural interval. Furthermore, the rather copiously detailed scene of the earlier poem has been so emptied out that bird, sky, and poetic voice can truly be said to have supplanted all the rest. We have nearly arrived at Wallace Stevens' American sublime, "The empty spirit / In vacant space."

There is still the bird, however. Dickinson's first response to it is to observe, as poem 783 also did, that the song accomplishes nothing. Where presence, the transfiguring power of the song's silver principle, for a brief time flourished is now mere place, nature in all its mute and empty thereness. In contrast to the bird of 798, which never lands, this one and its predecessors are obliged to stop signing, leaving the silent sky much as it had been.

So far, except for the greater austerity of scene and voice, the poet's orientation toward the bird only echoes and perhaps more begrudgingly amplifies the situation in "She staked her feather," where the poet self-effacingly celebrated the bird's triumph. Dickinson's bolder response is to assert that circumference remains between. Her poetic or mathetic idea, in other words, although less potent than birdsong, surpasses the normal forces of nature. It also seems to triumph over the birdsong's impermanence, perhaps abandoning natural temporality altogether. If one respects the tmesis marked by the line ending, then—alone among the poem's events—circumference gets no time signature. Even if one reads less ingeniously and assumes that the poem has merely elided a "was" or that "Half past Seven" controls the entire stanza, circumference still remains in at least two senses. First, the numerical chronology is already a function of circumference's dominion, and second, circumference is by the stipulation of Dickinson's characteristic uses the realm of the poem itself. Where place and presence were, poem is.

To the extent that this is so we can conclude that in declaring that her business is circumference Dickinson announces her business as the countersublime. Poetic circumferences interpose themselves against naturally sublime presences, thereby presenting themselves to us perhaps defenseless readers as instances of a sublimity with which we are solicited to identify in our turn. Or, to put this in terms used earlier, "At half past three" would be Dickinson at her most Carlylean, authoritatively disclosing meaning and directing the reader's response in such a way as to beggar it. Our place in the politics of the poem would be "place" in all its unredeemed dreariness, unless we accepted the authority of the poet and the poem.

For a Carlylean reading of this poem it is necessary that circumference describe not merely an appropriation of some glory to the self but one that also deprives others of the same glory, at least unless they struggle for it according to the agonistics of the sublime. Such a reading fits with many of Dickinson's other uses of circumference and more generally with how she often regards mathematics. On the other hand, it is not compatible with the disseminative circumference of "The poets light but lamps," and it also goes against one mathematical theme we have yet to notice. Not counting a few references to mathematics as a tiresome course one must undergo in school, Dickinson wrote only one poem seriously treating how the self acquires mathematical skill and knowledge. She represents it there as exactly analogous to reason in Kant's analytic, an individual faculty which is also inherently universal and thus never the property of some masterly other.

> 'Tis One by One—the Father counts—
> And then a Tract between
> Set Cypherless—to teach the Eye
> The Value of it's Ten—
>
> Until the peevish Student
> Acquire the Quick of Skill—
> The Numerals are dowered back—
> Adorning all the Rule—

'Tis mostly Slate and Pencil—
And Darkness on the School
Distracts the Children's fingers—
Still the Eternal Rule

Regards least Cypherer alike
With Leader of the Band—
And every separate Urchin's Sum—
Is fashioned for his hand—

(545)

This may be the most profoundly democratic poem Dickinson ever wrote; certainly its egalitarian vision stands expressly opposed to the patriarchal authority of the schoolteacher here. The poem insists upon a distinction between mathematical skill itself and the master who teaches it to the peevish students. The rules of mathematics are not the rules of the master, in other words. The master exerts an oppressive, stifling authority wonderfully represented in Dickinson's pun on "tract," both a tiresome religious tract and the conventional, that is to say, arbitrary spacing of decimal notation, which combines zero and one to make "10." According to the master, accepting conventional notation entails accepting authority in general. His magisterial claim is also made by the possessive pronoun in line 4, which attributes the numeral ten to the same generalized authority.

By contrast Dickinson presents mathematics itself as an impersonal, egalitarian rule and hence a realm into which power struggles and claims about superior authority need not enter. Learning mathematics is the discovery, not that one must obey its laws, but that its sums are fashioned for one's hand. No submission to the father is required. The crucial step occurs when numerals are dowered back, which happens after the master has imposed some knowledge on his students. Here again the legal phrase has an important nuance, which distinguishes it from some of Dickinson's other, equally precise uses of legal terms with the same root. To dower back means to return to a man's widow that part of the estate originally belonging to her. Acquiring the quick of skill thus precipitates restoration of the native resources of which one has for a time been dispossessed. The student discovers in learning the apparently alien, unknown rules of mathematics that the numerals have been one's own all along. (A telling pun on digits—both numerals and fingers—lurks in the reference to the urchin's hand. Because it is modeled upon a natural, universal feature of the human body, the decimal system is neither arbitrary nor a distinctive possession of the father who teaches it.)

By this reading of the ontology of mathematics, apprehending circumference entails recognizing it as an aspect of our own native endowments. Rather than something uniquely achieved by the poet which then obliges us to take it as a sublime alterity, circumference is an achievement we can duplicate without imitating. "At half past three" would thus supplant the bird's sublime presence with a distinctively different creation, a circumferentiality that in lying between place and presence perhaps falls short of the latter's glory but certainly redeems the former and also breaks the cycle of mastery.

Which reading of "Half past three" is the right one, this or the earlier Carlylean interpretation? Neither, of course, nor is a synthesis possible. Like other instances of Dickinson's style, the trope does not allow the making of an authoritative choice. On the other hand, nothing prevents each of us from preferring one or the other choice, and the poem may even suggest that selection is necessary or advisable. The choice will be personal, however, in that each reader will be free to select one alternative or the other. The ambiguity is anything but fuzzy or evasive; both possibilities are rich and intricate, and we can see in reconstructing them that Dickinson has thought each one through. But the reader can decide only according to his or her own lights.

In other words, without abandoning the structure of the romantic sublime and indeed by making specific use of its forces and phases, Dickinson defers to the reader the moment of final commitment, sublimation, and identification that the full three-phase pattern would determine. In one way or another the vast majority of Dickinson's poems, especially those that most overtly engage the sublime, employ the same strategy. The quintessential Dickinson sublime is a hesitant sublime, one that lingers upon the transition from trauma to reaction or prolongs the moment at which one phase definitely passes into the other.

Subjectivity and Affectivity

Although it has perhaps been implicit in the discussion so far, one additional corollary of the romantic sublime that I have not mentioned is the distinctive, historically novel emphasis it places on interiority. The initial revival of Longinus in particular and ideas about the sublime in general had taken place under the auspices of neoclassical poetics, but the romantic sublime came distinctively and recognizably into its own when speculations about sublime objects and the rhetorically appropriate ways of depicting them came to seem less important than the individual subject's aptitude for the sublime. Kant took the decisive step here by relegating the external object to a mainly instigatory function, thereby locating the action of the sublime in an intrasubjective contest among various mental faculties. More generally the prestige of the sublime in the latter part of the eighteenth century helped legitimize the representation of private consciousness as a fit activity for art.

Dickinson certainly benefits from and carries forward the general subjectivization of poetry that is such a prominent feature of literary history since the early eighteenth century. This is most evident in poems featuring that volatile and elusive pronoun, the "I" of the romantic lyric, and it as much true of poems such as "I years had been from home" (609), which recounts the I's adventures in an external world, as it is of "I felt a funeral in my brain" (280) or the many others devoted to internal adventures. Moreover, the "I" need not appear or be named as such for the poem primarily to represent an act of mind rather than a more public topic. What may be called the lyric plot of "The duties of the wind," "Tell all the truth," and many other such poems is the movement from one statement or image to another by a consciousness that need not objectify itself formally and need not be manifested as a stable or unitary voice.

The same kind of plotting is visible in the declamatory poems in which the speaker begins by dispensing wisdom or confidently defining objects and concepts. Examples include "This world is not conclusion" (501), and "Experience is the angled road" (910). Likewise and somewhat more obviously, a primary focus of Dickinson's descriptive poems is the describing consciousness. Dickinson sometimes even makes a game of foregrounding the performance of the describing mind. Such conspicuously periphrastic poems as "It sifts from leaden sieves" (311), "I like to see it lap the miles" (585), and "A route of evanescence" (1463) never name the objects they ostensibly describe. Their virtuosity is the stylistically performative counterpart to the assertions proclaimed or acted out in poems more obviously emphasizing the speaker's maneuvers.

Dickinson's evident concern with subjectivity has not been considered especially problematic, partly because it is shared to some degree by virtually all her peers, and also because she is deemed to have inherited the introspective habits of New England religious life.

The latter no doubt has some force in her work, although her poems are remarkably free of the soberly hermeneutic and justificatory scrutiny of daily life that typifies either American Puritanism or its secular descendants in the journals of Emerson and Thoreau. Dickinson's letters, by contrast, are more often introspective in just this way, especially when the fruits of the examination are explicitly offered to the letter's recipient as consolatory or edifying.

The revival of the idea of sublimity played an important and well-documented part in the emergence of interiority as a central poetic subject. It is crucial, for instance, to the transition from an idea of art grounded in rhetoric to one grounded in the new discipline of esthetics.[10] Public, discursive, and arguably rule-governed criteria increasingly give way throughout the eighteenth century to more private, expressive, and arguably singular ones that stress the unique genius of the artist. That shift, combined with the intrinsically psychic drama played out in the structure of the romantic sublime, helped both to legitimize and to further the discovery of the poet's own consciousness as an appropriate topic for art.

The rediscovery of Longinus at the end of the seventeenth century has been for literary historians a convenient starting point from which to trace these developments. The eventual romantic emphasis on poetic subjectivity is faithful enough to the spirit of *Peri hypsos* but notably contrary to its letter, and the discrepancy finds an heir nearly two centuries later in Dickinson's work. On the one hand, Longinus defines the sublime as that which exceeds mere *techne*, the rhetorical protocols of accomplished but lesser writing, and he explicitly lists the author's greatness of soul as one of the prerequisites of the sublime. On the other, Longinus holds a predominantly affective theory of poetry, one which defines sublimity as a distinctive effect on the reader. His treatise is therefore thoroughly rhetorical in a different sense; it emphasizes the worldliness of discourse.

The distinctive change brought about by the romantic poets was the substitution of the poet's affective consciousness for the reader's. Until that time sublimity was likely to be thought the property of certain objects—Alpine peaks, most famously—and of the style appropriate for representing those objects rather than any attribute or attainment of the poet's soul. However, as the initial concern among Longinus' heirs with representing and accounting for distinctively sublime objects gave way to an emphasis on the responsive subject and on the cognitive and emotional processes of response, those processes became in contrast a legitimate topic of representation. What for Longinus had been an experience that took place while reading a great text thus got brought within the representational space of the text and was regularly made its primary focus.

Dickinson's affective poetics bears a kinship to Longinus' while her focus on a first-person consciousness owes more to Kant, Wordsworth, Keats, and Emerson. The characteristic Dickinson sublime thus initiates a drama of subjectivity, in most instances an interiority certainly representing her own, and then she opens the theater out to the diverse and incalculable subjectivities of unknown readers. In one early poem, for instance, rather than hesitating at the threshold of the reactive phase, Dickinson continues on past it and beyond the sublimation of her own consciousness. She then imagines the burden of the elevation she has experienced as resting not with her but with futurity.

> Of Bronze—and Blaze—
> The North—Tonight—
> So adequate—it forms—
> So preconcerted with itself—
> So distant—to alarms—
> An Unconcern so sovreign
> To Universe, or me—
> Infects my simple spirit
> With Taints of Majesty—
> Till I take vaster attitudes—
> And strut upon my stem—
> Disdaining Men, and Oxygen,
> For Arrogance of them—
>
> My Splendors, are Menagerie—
> But their Competeless Show
> Will entertain the Centuries
> When I, am long ago,
> An Island in dishonored Grass—
> Whom none but Daisies, know.
>   (290)

As well as any poem she wrote, this one epitomizes the full Dickinson sublime, from the normalcy of the "simple spirit" in an unredeemed world to the dissemination of that spirit's glory in ages to come. In addition, the poem joins without quite fusing two kinds of sublimity that until now I have been treating as interchangeable. One is astonishment occasioned by nature, the kind most typical of romantic poetry; the other is occasioned by a text or some other instance of human signification. Here the relevant text is primarily the poem at hand, which ensues from the poet's encounter with natural sublimity and bestows upon the centuries a verbal imitation of that encounter. The first stanza follows out the familiar romantic structure: confrontration with an alterity that reveals the subject's comparative poverty but then elevates the mind and enlarges its powers once it has identified with the object. However, the textual adventure works in part by a different process, which only provisionally or prospectively belongs to the sublime.

The remoteness and autonomy of the object (apparently an aurora but possibly a summer sunset) resemble the remoteness of nature in "As imperceptibly as grief." Here, however, before the object can escape fully into the beautiful, the speaker finds herself both challenged and inspired by its lofty perfection. An initial clue that the poem both represents and comments upon the sublime is that the object's chief characteristic is invulnerability to the sublime moment: "So distant—to alarms." Sovereignty appears not as power over others but as "Unconcern," Not only is the aurora affectively indifferent to the otherness of "Universe" or "me," it is perfectly "adequate" to and "preconcerted with itself." In other words, the sublime object is structured as an absolute, self-contained harmony. The aurora is a pure esthetic monad and thus potentially a model for not only the speaker but the poem.

Dickinson responds to the object in familiar fashion. The infection and taint that at first challenge her simple soul are overcome by the defensive step of taking vaster attitudes, identifying with and appropriating to herself the aurora's formidable sublimity. The infection takes hold, in other words, and in the last few lines of the poem's first part she specifically emulates the object's sovereignty. Yet her arrogance and disdain are not quite identical to the aurora's unconcern; they manifest her superiority, but superiority is still a form of relatedness. In one sense the natural sublime is complete by the end of the first section of the poem, for the speaker certainly experiences elevation and empowerment. In another sense, however, it is incomplete or faulty, for she has still failed to measure up to the aurora's absolute majesty. Its autonomy remains purer and surer.

The poem might have ended a this point, as a number of Dickinson's poems do, having represented an ambiguous or doubtful sublimity and then leaving it to us to assess the cost of the achievement. "Of bronze and blaze" goes on, however, to consider the reader's role explicitly. The second part both continues the first in another key and also envisages new, potentially different moments of sublimity when the splendors of Dickinson's arrogance and of her poem entertain the centuries, perhaps then replacing the elusive, fugitive glories of the aurora. As a continuation of the first section, the second falls back from the initial arrogance, a lowering already anticipatorily confessed in the image of the speaker as a flower, earthbound by its stem. Oxygen seems to be needed, after all. The vaunting splendors are now no more than menagerie, a frivolous and probably illusory show. The menagerie further compares poorly with the aurora's heavenly display and the speaker's disdain of men by its humbly feminine domesticity. (The English word derives from a French term for housekeeping.) However, this falling back is a strategic advance as well. Unlike the patently imitative arrogance, the show belongs fully to the speaker: "*My* Splendors." More important, the splendors are "Competeless." The neologism may partly be taken as an expression of pride that, like disdain of men, needs what it spurns; my shows are better than competing shows (but must be compared with them for this to be recognized). However, the word's precise form asserts that Dickinson's shows do not compete. Without concern for rivals and peers, they are of themselves and dwell extent among. In other words, although the speaker's subjectivity has failed to attain the aurora's unconcern, her text has achieved it.

It has done more. As the natural sublime gives way to an imagined textual sublimity, the splendors of the poem exceed those of the aurora, for they are distinctively open to the centuries. The only forms of relatedness imagined so far in the poem have been monadlike sovereignty and a structure of at least mildly rivalrous disdain and emulation. The text is open to futurity, however, in a way that transcends the alternatives of unconcern or competition. The crucial lines refer to the speaker's death. One may read them as a disingenuous expression of modesty, the kind that not so secretly vaunts the author by imagining how honored her works will be when she herself has been forgotten. The image of an island in dishonored grass may particularly suggest such false modesty. The grass is dishonored by this bare spot where once a flower strutted, but flowering daisies normally grow higher than the surrounding grasses, so the absence dishonors a public whose feebler capacities include neither loftiness nor bloom.

"Daisy" is one of Dickinson's coy nicknames for herself, used as such in several poems and letters, and here it echoes and specifies the earlier reference to the speaker's stem. The daisies that, unlike the grass, still know and acknowledge Dickinson after her death are thus selves like her own. Indeed, they are perhaps future poets challenged by her splendors as she was challenged by the aurora. But they are not the only ones on whom the menagerie is bestowed. If anything, daisies would seem the readers most likely to repeat Dickinson's only partly successful emulation and incorporation of auroral unconcern. More important, the poem does not envisage their response as the usual or even the appropriate one. Indeed, in another version their place is taken by lowly "Beetles." The poem is directed toward a wider, inherently unpredictable, and presumably diverse audience. The poem promises to entertain that audience, affecting it but not necessarily dominating it, and certainly not obliging it to undergo in its turn another round of infection by and identification with majesty. Such a response is possible and legitimate but not requisite.

The imagined textual affect thus competelessly supersedes the aurora's natural sublime; it both includes such elevation as a legitimate possibility and goes beyond the necessity of competition presupposed by such sublimity. The poem both emulates the object's unconcern and also moves beyond the object's isolation. Actually, like most sublime operations viewed with some detachment and suspicion, this one requires suppressing an awareness that would otherwise be apparent and presumably painful. The idealizing interpretation I have given conveniently forgets that the aurora also presumably remains open to the earthbound viewers in centuries to come. My reading thus collaborates with the poem, enforcing a suspect distinction between the aurora and the menagerie that works to the latter's advantage.

Even without an idealizing reading, however, the poem extends the structure of the romantic sublime beyond the discrete encounter with the aurora, making the subjectivity of future readers an explicit part of its reach. Against the context of Dickinson's rhetoric of stimulus and her attraction to a sublime poetics, "Of bronze and blaze" articulates as well as any single poem the project of the Dickinson sublime. The guiding purpose of her work is to stimulate the reader's mind without necessarily determining it. More particularly, the poems aim to provoke in the reader a sublime empowerment that need not require submission to the authority of Dickinson's text or identification with her poetic self.

The project distinguishes Dickinson's work as different in degree though not in kind from a sublime more firmly centered in the poet's heroic subjectivity. All texts are by definition open to the diversity of responses and interpretations they engender. Moreover, unlike Dickinson's poems, most romantic poetry was put into public circulation, so materially and socially it requires at least as much as hers does the solicitation of a readerly affect for its completion. On the other hand, their models of ideal subjectivity are more restricted to the heroics of the sublime. The reader is usually invited, as much as he is able, to be like the poet, to emulate his heroic stance or (as explicitly in *Song of Myself*) to do that first before going to some loftier but unspecified greatness. A crucial thing about the affect that would complete Dickinson's poem is that it does not oblige the reader to become a daisy.

6

Skirting Mastery

In order to explore the range of the Dickinson sublime and to see how fully or firmly it shapes her work, we need to reconsider Dickinson's treatment of mastery. Mastery is a pervasive structure in her work, as I hope by now to have demonstrated, and it appears variously as a predicament, a temptation, and a threat. Moreover, the characteristic Dickinson sublime responds directly to her doubts about it; hesitation and the deferral of reactive elevation serve to keep some distance between herself and the rivalrous dyad of domination and submission. Yet Dickinson's representations of mastery and her attitudes toward it are more diverse than I may have allowed. By no means does she consistently spurn domination or keep it at arm's length. Indeed, she wrote a number of poems that suggest nearly opposite sentiments. Few poets can at times voice such fiercely triumphant mastery; few can more impressively proclaim their own imperial selfhood. If discomfort with mastery provides a chief motive for the Dickinson sublime, it does so only in the context of other responses to domination and submission and other ways of imagining exultant intensities.

The link between mastery and the sublime in Dickinson's poetry is rivalry; conflict between self and other is basic to the romantic sublime and a similarly jealous competition produces and sustains the structure of mastery. The crucial question then is the place and value of rivalry. Is some form of rivalrous conflict necessary to the sublime intensities Dickinson prizes? If so, how or to what extent would rivalry compromise cherishing power?

Ultimately the answer to these questions depends upon beliefs about the nature and the sources of power. Hints of a conflictual sublime can be found in Longinus, but he is otherwise quick to acknowledge that a reader's vaunting identification with Homer's Ajax does not abrogate the natural superiority of either Homer or Ajax. In other words, Longinus generally accepts the legitimacy of traditionally established authority; indeed, the concern of his treatise is to explain the effects upon us of beholding authentic greatness. Such piety is one of the obvious victims of Enlightenment criticism and its continuation in romanticism. According to Hegel, all hierarchies of authority or stature or power must be seen as products of spiritual conflict rather than as naturally ordained differences; more specifically, they arise during the first stages of sociality out of the rivalrous conflict between subjectivities otherwise or previously alien to one another. To put this another way, whatever objective differences might exist between the rivals, the one's superiority is never established until the other subjectively recognizes it. And this in turn means that any encounter with an alien phenomenon, especially any in which one senses a potential opponent, can always rekindle such conflict. Sublime objects or alterities are, by definition, such phenomena; they inevitably challenge the encounterer's powers. Virtually all modern accounts of the romantic sublime accordingly presume that agonistic rivalry is the very motor of the sublime.

A poet not a theorist, Dickinson is not obliged to agree or disagree. The main candidate in Dickinson's work for nonrivalrous sublimity would be an object that can fully and persistently maintain "Unconcern," as the aurora does in "Of bronze and blaze." Such beings are rarer in Dickinson's work than in the writings of most romantics, mainly because she construes almost all phenomena as selflike beings, that is, as intentional subjects capable of will, consciousness, and agency. The consequence, as Joanne Feit Diehl has argued, is that to Dickinson "all externality represents threat." More specifically, "because the empowering influx of the sublime finds its source in nature or in other human or god-like persons [rather than in one or the other only], Dickinson does not differentiate, as had Emerson, between persons and things."[1]

Nevertheless, there can be a difference between the occasionally self-sufficient mentality of natural phenomena and the usually jealous intentions of men and gods. Unlike the despotic or vindictive God Dickinson regularly depicts in her poems and unlike her human masters and minions, natural phenomena can sometimes exhibit a saving remoteness or indifference. The sunsets she imagines as rivalrously seeking victory over her are balanced by the natural phenomenon she sees as having achieved a gloriously "intransitive estate." I take the phrase from its opposite number in the following example.

The most triumphant Bird I ever knew or met
Embarked upon a twig today
And till Dominion set
I famish to behold so eminent a sight
And sang for nothing scrutable
But intimate Delight
Retired, and resumed his transitive Estate —
To what delicious Accident
Does finest Glory fit!

(1265)

Like the poems examined in Chapter 5, this one represents achieved sublimity as birdsong. More sharply than the others, however, it proposes that in attaining the sublime the bird reaches, momentarily, a genuinely autonomous state. The bird loses all relation to anything outside itself in singing "for nothing scrutable / But intimate Delight." The somewhat simpler draft version—"And sang for nothing in the World / But competent Delight"—may more clearly delineate the reflexive motive and the auto-affective result of the singing. Both versions specifically exclude awareness or concern on the part of the bird that anyone else may be listening, and both characterize the bird's glory, by contrast to the transitivity it then resumes, as inherently intransitive.

On the other hand, the poet is listening and she is accordingly and enviously famished to behold so eminent a sight. The bird's glory does demean hers, in other words. Furthermore, she describes the bird as "triumphant" and his achievement as "dominion," albeit of a largely impersonal, competeless sort. The poem cannot thus be taken as blithely transcending rivalry, for rivalry is what the speaker explicitly feels. Yet that may be precisely why the speaker must look at the bird from below, because she cannot behold it without comparing her powers and glories with its own and her powers and glories accordingly can never measure up to its at least momentary autonomy. Acknowledging the existence of a rival inevitably compromises sovereignty. Moreover, the poem's crucial reference to the speaker can be construed in a significantly different way, which also supports the poem's disparagement of dominion. Rather than saying that the poet famished to behold the bird's triumph, in the other reading the poem would assert that until the commonplace world of dominion, rivalry, and transitive estates finally and forever sets, that is, disappears, the poet must continue hungering to behold again or behold more lastingly what she momentarily heard in the birdsong.[2] In other words, the poet would have been inspired by the bird's intransitive glory to long for a thoroughly competeless world.

Seeing Comparatively

Dickinson proclaims in one poem that "We see—Comparatively" (534). The truth of that assertion underlies the prevalence of rivalry, for whenever forces, intensities, and values of any kind whatsoever are measured as a contrast between thine and mine, then rivalry is always structurally present. The most forceful claims about an intransitive sublime can thus never appear in nature poems, for the poet's relation to the natural object inevitably introduces a potential comparison of powers. Their more appropriate venue is poems voicing the speaker's most intimate and unalienable powers. The two kinds may be intimately connected, however, for Dickinson tells us in one poem that "Growth of Man—like Growth of Nature— / Gravitates within" and therefore "Transaction is assisted by no Countenance." In other words, only through the "solitary prowess / Of a Silent Life" can one achieve the "difficult Ideal" (750). Moreover, the ideal in each case is autonomous glory.

In the following, seemingly programmatic poem Dickinson sharply distinguishes between interiority and exteriority, and she seeks to link the solitary prowess of the former directly to the achievement of sublimity. What the poem calls exhilaration is inherently such a private, inviolable state that it precludes conflict. Potentially rival capabilities will then merely stimulate a manifestation of one's native resources.

> Exhiliration—is within—
> There can no Outer Wine
> So royally intoxicate
> As that diviner Brand
>
> The Soul achieves—Herself—
> To drink—or set away
> For Visiter—or Sacrament—
> 'Tis not of Holiday
>
> To stimulate a Man
> Who hath the Ample Rhine
> Within his Closet—Best you can
> Exhale in offering.
>
> (383)

The poem is not entirely convincing, partly because the attempt to imagine a competeless source of intoxication breaks down in the last stanza. Breath and intoxication are traditional figures of poetic imagination, used as such elsewhere in Dickinson's work, but here their joining makes for a grotesque image that seriously undermines a mechanism about which Dickinson seems serious. The idea, clearly enough, is that as a wholly private affair exhilaration draws on purely internal resources. And in the first two stanzas inner and outer stimulants simply and credibly enough stand parallel to one another, without interacting in the way an agonistic sublime would require. Dickinson remains committed to the idea of poetry as stimulus, however, and so apparently feels obliged to imagine some response to it. An observable display of your diviner brand ought to do no more than stimulate me to reach for my own stock. To exhale in offering would then stand as one ideal image for a sublime poetry that eschews mastery. Unfortunately, it looks here more like two comic drunkards breathing in each other's faces.

The bathetic conclusion of "Exhilaration is within" seems more like simple clumsiness than deliberate self-deprecation, but the poem is not alone in first advancing a vision of solitary, intransitive sublimity and then undermining it or veering away from it.

> To be alive — is Power —
> Existence — in itself —
> Without a further function —
> Omnipotence — Enough —
>
> (677)

The stanza may be the single most impressive example of a recurring idealization in Dickinson's poetry: power imagined as both inalienable and exuberant. Such power is precarious, however. Like sublime birdsong it must be without further function, that is to say, purposeless and intransitive. Then and only then can it be "Omnipotence — Enough," a pointedly oxymoronic phrase that already subtly introduces a possibility of comparison and thus of conflict. Like the intransitive estate of birdsong, the inward gaze of solitary prowess can apparently never be maintained for long. The second and concluding quatrain of the poem thus introduces both will, which presumes transitivity, and a potentially rival power with whom the self compares itself.

> To be alive — and Will!
> 'Tis able as a God —

The Maker—of Ourselves—be what—
Such being Finitude!

(677)

Without quite silencing the poem's manic voice, the second stanza further compromises omnipotence by obliging us to see it as a comparative value. And once that is the case, mastery and rivalry have been reintroduced to an initially solitary realm.

The Politics of Hesitation

In addition to the handful of poems in which Dickinson attempts to imagine or embody a nonrivalrous sublimity, there are a number of comparably manic poems that accept and indeed sometimes flaunt mastery. "Dare you see a soul at the white heat" (365) thus openly invites the addressee's admiring wonder, and "With pinions of disdain" (1431) represents the soul's proud flight as disdain for matter. "Mine by the right of the white election" (528) celebrates a similarly heightened selfhood, which the reader can presumably only admire and hope to emulate if he or she is to respond at all sympathetically. Unlike the hesitant or equivocal poems examined in previous chapters, in other words, most of Dickinson's avid declarations of her own majesty invite us to identify with her glories. The poems appear to be openly heroic in the Carlylean sense and deliberately representative in the Emersonian sense. They manifest to readers a figure of the poet who bids to be more themselves than they have yet managed to become.

These poems thus seem free from the doubts about mastery Dickinson elsewhere expresses. Perhaps they are then to be categorized as experiments in following the romantic sublime through to completion and hence in providing images of the imperial selfhood that appears when hesitation ceases.

Purple—is fashionable twice—
This season of the year,
And when the soul perceives itself
To be an Emperor.

(980)

On the other hand, some of the most avid poems exhibit a different uneasiness about mastery. Instead of a tyrannical structure Dickinson attempts to circumvent or forestall, mastery appears in these poems as a form of power that is never masterful enough.

According to a paradox at the heart of Hegelian dialectic, the master is ultimately the weaker, less autonomous party for his mastery depends upon recognition by the minion. Because she too identifies supremacy with autonomy, Dickinson understands that mastery is not quite a supreme form of power. The various dukes and queens and emperors in her poems all need recognition by their inferiors. In such poems as "A mien to move a queen" (283) and "Smiling back from coronation" (385), the speaker thus openly lords it over her inferiors or gloatingly imagines their humble fealty.

The difference between mastery and a genuinely intransitive sublimity becomes most pointed in poems expressing and exploring the speaker's solitary prowess. "The Soul's Superior instants" may be said to "Occur to Her—alone," but the poem partly belies that solitude. Such superior instants occur when the soul has "ascended / To too remote a Hight / For lower recognition / Than Her Omnipotent" (306). She may become nothing less than omnipotent, but her stature still apparently requires some recognition by inferiors and is thus not quite as solitary, as independent, or as absolute as the poem initially claims. Likewise, "The Soul selects her own Society" expresses a memorably intense isolation but also one that acquires much of its value from the soul's desire to have its solitude acknowledged by the populace. The soul clearly relishes shutting the door to others or unmovingly noting the emperor kneeling on the mat, and she also does royally choose one, apparently both needing another being and needing to be the one who chooses it.

Even in some of her most avid declarations of imperial selfhood, then, poems that are among the most ferocious in the English language, Dickinson does usually see comparatively. She usually acknowledges the pervasiveness of rivalry and mastery in the sublime, and she measures the master's sublimity according to the minion's fealty. However, there is one further possibility that lies partly outside the hesitant Dickinson sublime. Within the differential and comparative hierarchy of the sublime the emperor's is not the only role.

In a number of her love poems Dickinson openly relishes submission and inferiority. "Forever at His side to walk— / The smaller of the two!" (246). Such poems typically argue or imply, furthermore, that devotion to a master can lift the devotee toward much the same state of exhilaration promised by the romantic sublime. Except to comment upon their biographical significance, Dickinson's best critics often pass over these poems in embarrassed silence, for they are difficult to reconcile with the more attractive, equally frequent poems in which images of noble, fiercely independent selfhood predominate.

They would seem equally difficult to reconcile with the sublime, which I at least have been claiming gives shape to the whole of Dickinson's work.

Can there be a deferential sublime? In one respect the sublime must be deferential, if often secretly or guiltily so, for it depends upon recognizing and responding to the other's authentically overmastering might. Thus in Longinus sublimity always explicitly has about it something of the secondhand and the derivative; the genuine greatness to which a reader responds, thereby experiencing *hypsos,* always retains its superior majesty throughout. Even from the continually jealous perspective of the romantic sublime, some recognition of the other's superiority persists. Thus in Bloom's theory sublime mimesis requires repression specifically in order to banish the self's awareness that it remains inferior to the sublime object. Apprehension of the vaunting affect and the derivative, belated actuality thus gets divided between the conscious and the unconscious realms of the mind. Dickinson recognizes the same contradictory reality, it would appear, but she is less willing to accept the universal necessity of repression or to divide the sublime's vaunting and humbling outcomes. Indeed, this recognition may be one motive for her characteristic hesitation at the cusp of the reactive phase.

Dickinson unmistakably views love as a sublime experience, linking it in one poem both to poetry and to theophany.

> To pile like Thunder to it's close
> Then crumble grand away
> While Everything created hid
> This—would be Poetry—
>
> Or Love—the two coeval come—
> We both and neither prove—
> Experience either and consume—
> For None see God and live—
>
> (1247)

Love and poetry are both equivalent to the quintessential biblical moment of the sublime, seeing the face of God. More specifically, the encounter with either love or poetry is sublime; the lover here is not an author but a reader, astonished by the potent art woven into or wielded by the beloved. The key device in the poem is the grammatical suspension we can see in "consume" and also in "prove," which is this poem's mark of hesitation. Construed as a transitive verb, "consume" presupposes taking love or poetry into the self from the outside. The word cannot fully hold off its participial complement, however, a reversed sense in which experiencing the sublimity of love or poetry entails being consumed. "Prove" has a similarly reversible transitivity, love and poetry putting us to the proof fully as much as we them. In other words, in representing the apocalyptic outcome of the sublime Dickinson leaves the self suspended between its two fates, absolute aggrandizement and absolute abasement. The two are similarly intense, but Dickinson here is either unwilling to distinguish them or uncertain that they can be distinguished.

Other love poems take the possibilities singly. The doubtful grandeur of crumbling away in Dickinson's love poems normally entails that the beloved's majesty be seen as his dominion over the lover's correspondingly abject selfhood.

> He put the Belt around my Life—
> I heard the Buckle snap—
> And turned away, imperial,
> My Lifetime folding up—
> Deliberate, as a Duke would do
> A Kingdom's Title Deed—
> Henceforth, a Dedicated sort
> A Member of the Cloud.
>
> (273)

The speaker clearly cherishes her bondage, imagining in the second half of the same poem that with shy pride she will decline all invitations to any other life.

> Yet not too far to come at call—
> And do the little Toils
> That make the Circuit of the Rest—
> And deal occasional smiles
> To lives that stoop to notice mine—
> And kindly ask it in—
> Whose invitation, know you not
> For Whom I must decline?
>
> (273)

Submission to the imperial lover lifts her above the circuit of the rest, in other words, albeit at the price of bowing before the master's still greater glory, from which hers derives. The contradiction I spoke of earlier between vaunting affect and derivative actuality is overcome here by replacing the usually binary scale of the sublime with a three-step hierarchy: beloved, lover, and the rest.

Other poems likewise imagine a high but still secondary and derivative rank the speaker will enjoy in heaven for having accepted her master's dominion. The following stanza describes an angel judging the speaker.

> And then—he'll turn me round and round—
> To an admiring sky—
> As one that bore her Master's name
> Sufficient Royalty!
>
> (336)

Despite the sufficiency of Dickinson's royalty here, the abasement should not be underestimated. Bearing the master's name surrenders all power of self-definition, and indeed Dickinson often eagerly or even proudly acknowledges her identity is defined by the master.

> You said that I "was Great"—one Day—
> Then "Great" it be—if that please Thee
> Or Small—or any size at all—
> Nay—I'm the size suit Thee
>
> . . .
>
> I'm that—or nought—
> Or other thing—if other thing there be—
> With just this Stipulus—
> I suit Thee—
>
> (738)

Similarly one thirteen-word text from about 1865 attributes the speaker's entire worth to the master.

> 'Twas my one Glory—
> Let it be
> Remembered
> I was owned of Thee—
> (1028)

Glory derives from being owned: recognized, possessed, and determined by the other.[3] The surrender of selfhood entailed by such poems reaches a masochistic peak in "Sang from the heart, sire," in which the pelican-like speaker dips her beak into her own blood in order to sing the master's praises (1059).

In other poems Dickinson openly sacralizes the beloved master, and in one she explicitly names her love a form of idolatry. The term

seems to mean for her not simply falsely worshiping some idol in place
of God but any unconditional devotion.

> You constituted Time —
> I deemed Eternity
> A Revelation of Yourself —
> 'Twas therefore Deity
>
> The Absolute — removed
> The Relative away —
> That I unto Himself adjust
> My slow idolatry —
>
> (765)

Two things are notable about such devotion: that it bears the extreme,
indeed unbounded intensity characteristic of sublime experience and
that this intensity is nonetheless attenuated by the implicit narrative context, in which the beloved is spatially or temporally distant
from the speaker. "You" and "Deity" here represent distinct and hence
competing objects of the speaker's adulation, and the speaker has apparently been separated from the first by the second's jealous, indeed
possibly murderous intervention.[4]

The plot structure implicit in this otherwise highly schematic
poem is a version of the narrative invoked or assumed in dozens of
Dickinson's love poems. The story has always begun at some moment
in the past when the speaker has been struck by love and has usually
also pledged herself to the beloved, consummated the love, or entered
into something like a marriage. Although that commitment persists
and is usually devoutly reaffirmed by the speaker, the initial moment
has long passed and the lovers are now separated. Sometimes the
speaker looks back upon the initial, sublimely intense moment, but
she also always anticipates a reunion, which she imagines will entail
an even more binding commitment and will be experienced as an even
more utterly intense grandeur. Most often the ectasy of reunion is not
expected to come before both have died, in which case it is usually associated with assuming angelic (or, sometimes, counterangelic) rank.[5]

Although the three-part story of separated lovers is not always
point-for-point identical to the three-phase pattern of the romantic
sublime, the characteristically hesitant Dickinson sublime chiefly
enters into and shapes her love poetry through the tripartite plot. The
crucial similarity is temporal stance, for in both cases Dickinson is
located between two extraordinary intensities. Just as in the love story
the speaker looks both back upon the moment of commitment and

ahead toward the reunion, so in the Dickinson sublime the speaker confronts the already experienced moment of trauma and also anticipates a reactive empowerment that has not yet quite taken place. Likewise, just as the hesitant sublime unequivocally affirms the intensity of the trauma while equivocating about the consequences or the speaker's endorsement of them, so the love story affirms the force of the initial experience but maintains a certain reserve about the outcome.[6] The reserve is sometimes expressed through equivocal stylistic details, such as the grammatical suspension of "consume" in "To pile like thunder." And even where no such ambivalence is expressed, as in many of the abject poems, it is there structurally, in the difference between the actual intensity of the past moment and the hypothetical or imagined futurity that may or may not match it.

Separation in the love poems is often represented as an affliction, something visited on the lovers by fate or circumstance. However, its prolongation is often partly within the speaker's control, and in such cases the love poems merge fully with the characteristic patterns of the Dickinson sublime. The fullest example of such merging appears in "I cannot live without you."

> They'd judge Us—How—
> For You—served Heaven—You know
> Or sought to—
> I could not—
>
> Because You saturated Sight—
> And I had no more Eyes
> For sordid excellence
> As Paradise
>
> And were You lost, I would be
> Though My Name
> Range loudest
> On the Heavenly fame—
>
> And were You—saved—
> And I—condemned to be
> Where You were not—
> That self—were Hell to me—
>
> So we must meet apart—
> You there—I—here—
> With just the Door ajar
> That Oceans are—and Prayer—
> And that White Sustenance—
> Despair—
>
> (640)

The speaker here is doubly in thrall, both to her beloved and to a divine authority she accepts but has no feeling for. This is secretly an advantage to her, especially given the lover's allegiance to serving heaven, for divine judgment acts as a counterweight to the lover's otherwise absolute power over her. Though insisting to him, presumably in all honesty, that "Your face / Would put out Jesus'—," and that paradise is sordid excellence compared with his, she employs her double vulnerability as a reason for keeping distant from the beloved. To "meet apart" defines the relation between the lovers on her terms and at her insistence. More important, it almost wholly internalizes the relation, transforming it from the satauration of sight that the lover's presence inevitably causes to the more manageable "sustenance" of despair. Despair is a sustenance in two collaborating senses. First, it can be fed upon, nourishing the lovers while they are apart by its lesser but hardly negligible intensity. Second and more important, it can both sustain itself and be sustained by the lovers. In contrast to a consuming and apocalyptic presence, it can be prolonged without requiring the parties to be consumed.

The postponement Dickinson openly argues for in this poem may not be strategic in the full sense of a policy deliberately and conscientiously pursued. The speaker seems too desperate and anxious to be credited with such calculation. However, in a number of other poems Dickinson's hesitation before a moment of threatening, irrevocable finality is clearly a matter of policy. She becomes in many of these poems a connoisseur of crisis, exploring some unconditional intensity from a minimal distance that is never entirely safe and never entirely exposed. Thus in "Crisis is a hair" she warns that

> Let an instant push
> Or an Atom press
> Or a Circle hesitate
> In Circumference
>
> It—may jolt the Hand
> That adjusts the Hair
> That secures Eternity
> From presenting—Here—
> (889)

This image appears also in another poem from about the same time that even more closely links risk and boldness with the infinitesimal but momentous cusp of a hair.

> Staking our entire Possession
> On a Hair's result—

> Then — Seesawing — cooly — on it —
> Trying if it split —
>
> (971)

The image of seesawing on the hair of crisis is a brilliant example of Dickinson's verbal inventiveness. Part of its force derives from a subtle reanimation of cliché, here the image of splitting hairs in the usual sense of multiplying distinctions or inflating minute differences as a lawyerly delaying tactic.

Dickinson always insists on the finality and irreversiblity of the moment she holds in prospect. Just as there could be no reversing of eternity's presenting itself, so the third phase of the sublime and the third stage of the love story will entail absolutely binding commitments. Moreover Dickinson's allegiance to the departed lover is unbreakable, as she avows in a number of poems. On the other hand, the terms of that commitment and the conditions to be met with in the future reunion are neither firm nor clearly known. To borrow imagery from a scene that appears in a number of her works, the situation in which Dickinson finds herself in the love poems, recollecting the sublime moment of commitment and anxiously anticipating the coming, perhaps transcendent reunion, is that of a prospective bride who has accepted the lover's proposal but lingers in negotiation over the terms of the dowry and other articles of the marriage settlement. Abject endorsement of the master's dominion remains always a possibility, but Dickinson is by no means above splitting hairs in prospect. Her doubts are most emphatic in poems that explicitly contemplate marriage or a wifely estate, as in the rather panicked "I'm 'wife' I've finished that" (199) or in the following calmer, third-person poem.

> She rose to His Requirement — dropt
> The Playthings of Her Life
> To take the honorable Work
> Of Woman, and of Wife —
>
> If ought She missed in Her new Day
> Of Amplitude, or Awe —
> Or first Prospective — Or the Gold
> In using, wear away,
>
> It lay unmentioned — as the Sea
> Develope Pearl, and Weed,
> But only to Himself — be known
> The Fathoms they abide —
>
> (732)

The poem is unusual in imagining that the sublimity of marriage may be a cheat, marital awe and amplitude threatening to prove illusory or impermanent. The poem is also unusual in not imagining the marriage as final; the wife still retains a private sense of selfhood in which some majesty may yet otherwise be achieved. It is typical, however, in leaving possibilities open rather than either affirming or denying them.

More commonly and with considerably more pronounced ambiguity, Dickinson writes from within sight of the critical third phase, raising questions for the reader that the poem conspicuously fails to resolve. Such an unanswered question is expressly the conclusion of this better known poem on the same topic.

> Title divine, is mine.
> The Wife without the Sign—
> Acute Degree conferred on me—
> Empress of Calvary—
> Royal, all but the Crown—
> Betrothed, without the Swoon
> God gives us Women—
> When You hold Garnet to Garnet—
> Gold—to Gold—
> Born—Bridalled—Shrouded—
> In a Day—
> Tri Victory—
> "My Husband"—Women say
> Stroking the Melody—
> Is this the Way—
>
> (1072)

(I quote the later variant, which adds "Tri Victory," removes exclamation points from the first two lines, and deletes both a question mark and an underlining of "this" from the last line.) The poem is sometimes read, in the context of the separated-lovers plot, as referring to a secret and platonic betrothal that has left the speaker spiritually wedded but without any public sign of her estate and without the sexual swoon of earthly nuptials. The title being divine, it will be recognized only in heaven, when the lovers meet again. Whether we adduce such context or not, the speaker's committed but uncertainly determined state allows her to question wifehood without quite being fully bridaled and shrouded but also without merely anticipating it as prospect. The stakes are triumph and status, as the imagery of titles, degrees, crowns, and victories makes clear, but no clear answer is forthcoming to the question in the last line.

The poems in the marriage group lend themselves especially well to a strategic deferral, for a moment of deliberation is built into the plot. Whatever empowerment she (or more rarely he) envisions in the marital state, she must commit herself to that state irrevocably. Moreover, thanks mainly to feminism, we have recently had little difficulty appreciating Dickinson's reluctance to commit herself to the Master's care. Indeed, contemporary prejudices make it difficult to understand the lure of embridalment, about which Dickinson is equally emphatic. Perhaps more fully than we, she accepts in these poems the most baleful premise of the romantic sublime, namely that empowerment requires emulating another's majesty.

Prolonging the Sublime

Other poems also practice a rich policy of anticipation and hesitation. Chief among these are Dickinson's many poems of baffled or thwarted quest. That Dickinson's poetry can often best be understood as belonging to the romantic quest for cognitive or spiritual advance is one assumption uniting her most ardent defenders—notably Robert Weisbuch, Suzanne Juhasz, and Greg Johnson—with such doubters as Porter. They point to the numerous poems literally representing some journey and the great many others in which the speaker embarks on a metaphorical journey in search of epistemological, perceptual, or existential breakthrough. These commentators understandably also measure Dickinson's stature partly according to her persistence in pursuing the quest and her success in achieving its goals or attaining some definitive perspective upon it. In *Perception and the Poet's Quest*, for instance, Johnson updates and significantly bulwarks Robert Sherwood's argument that one can in spite of appearances chart stages of thematic progress in Dickinson's poetic ventures.[7]

However, at least on the question of whether Dickinson achieves a perspective on her main thematic concerns or progressively enhances her understanding of them, the doubters clearly have the better case. Defending Dickinson's victories of consciousness, perception, or understanding requires selectively deafening oneself to her repeated cries of bewilderment and uncertainty. And in a number of poems, as Porter has insisted, the situation seems much worse. Such poems either falter in confusion or openly confess failure to resolve the very matters they insist are crucial.

Consider "A loss of something," one of Dickinson's few clearly programmatic statements about the theme of the quest, here specifically a Byronic search for lost or usurped majesty.

A loss of something ever felt I—
The first that I could recollect
Bereft I was—of what I knew not
Too young that any should suspect

A Mourner walked among the children
I notwithstanding went about
As one bemoaning a Dominion
Itself the only Prince cast out—

Elder, Today, a session wiser
And fainter, too, as Wiseness is—
I find myself still softly searching
For my Delinquent Palaces

And a suspicion, like a Finger
Touches my forehead now and then
That I am looking oppositely
For the site of the Kingdom of Heaven—

(959)

Arguably this is one of the worst poems of Dickinson's maturity. (It dates from about 1864.) In all apparent solemnity the poem begins with a worryingly conventional and self-congratulatory portrait of the self as a cast-out prince. As always when Dickinson seeks instant pathos she gives us a pitiable child. However, the prince cannot even take his own situation seriously, and the poem declines from virile if sentimental youthfulness into middle-aged befuddlement. The sinking is marked or consummated by the last line, which abandons the earlier iambics for an anapestic rhythm, this new meter being far more suited to comic than heroic effects. The poem pointedly collapses, in other words, going from the potentially sublime to the flatly ridiculous as it undermines the initial venture of questing. Worse, the collapse verifies the initial predicament of loss but leaves the speaker helpless to deal with it.

On the other hand, perhaps the poem's shift from pathos to bathos is its deeper point. Our attention is drawn away from the content of the poem and toward the esthetic mode in which this content is apprehended, making the poem as much our search for an appropriate attitude to Byronic postures as the prince's for a response to loss. Such a reading might seem fancifully apologetic if it were not corroborated by the same shift in the prince's attitude. He also becomes concerned with how he appears to an audience, exhibiting in the last stanza a sheepishly theatrical awareness that seems thoroughly incompatible with the solitary pride of the Byronic hero.

Both poem and prince sink when they introduce the bizarre image of suspicion as a monitory finger. Until then the poem voices a sincere if jejune heroism, and our attention should correspondingly be held by the predicament and by the prince's subjectivity. His stature, moreover, like that of Byron's Cain and Manfred, the poet in Shelley's *Alastor*, Goethe's Werther, or Milton's Satan, depends upon his alienation. It is not only that he is unlike the other children and rightly proud of the fact, it is that his true rank is conferred by his own judgment of himself. No one else recognizes his stature but him, a fact that actually guarantees or possibly even constitutes its authenticity. To depend upon another's endorsement or recognition would be to lack self-trust, the romantic hero's cardinal virtue.

Yet depend he does once the grotesque finger appears. The gesture of touching the forehead delivers an inherently public, even theatrical message and thus necessarily plays to an audience (an internalized one possibly). Rather than proudly cherishing his aloofness, the prince signals to the other persons he imagines watching and judging. This allows a face-saving exaggeration of the act of recognizing one's own folly, but it also makes his stature depend upon the opinions of others and thus no longer qualify for the heroism of romantic solitude.

"A loss of something" is unusual in mocking the idea of the quest but typical in both affirming a primordial experience of loss and declining to provide positive knowledge as a compensation for that loss. The question of the quest's outcome and of the possibility of gaining spiritual, perceptual, or cognitive insight from it is most pointed in poems organizing the quest according to the romantic sublime. The goal of the search is imagined as sublime elevation and hence as a state or phase requiring irrevocable commitment. More specifically, Dickinson's poems of cognitive or spiritual quest usually demand of the searcher unconditional belief in the particular revelation the quest vouchsafes. Rather than ever definitively avowing or disavowing any belief, however, Dickinson typically hesitates at the moment of commitment and often expresses intense anguish about her uncertainty.

Such poems of bafflement would represent a failure of the poet's enterprise if the enterprise were construed primarily as the successful or at least relentless pursuit of knowledge. As important to Dickinson, however, is the affect of the sublime. And the quintessentially sublime feeling of "Wonder" normally requires "not precisely Knowing / And not precisely knowing not —"(1331). That is, wonder is poised at the transition between trauma and sublimation, after habitual forms of understanding have been breached but before some heightened state has brought a new cognitive equilibrium. Rather than herself or her persona fully undergoing the experience of the sublime and thus either dispelling the wonder or installing the poem's protagonist as a new object of wonder, Dickinson defers such finality beyond the poem. She reserves it for the responses of a reader she declines to influence further.

At her most sentimental Dickinson comes close to opposing certainty and sublimity. "If Summer were *an Axiom* — / What sorcery had *Snow*?" we have already noticed her asking (191). More often, however, preceptions, beliefs, inferences, interpretations, and other forms of reliably authorized understanding serve as a means toward some further affect. The strategy is most conspicuous in poems that attempt to establish some enlarged comprehension and then bemoan their failure. At the extreme such poems may seem to repudiate the poem's apparent thematic quest, converting it into a coy or frivolous exercise.

The bathetic ending of "A loss of something" does this to an extent, and it is typical in locating the deflation at the end of the poem rather than as part of an ironic perspective visible from the beginning. Dickinson has rarely been celebrated for the brilliance of her poetic closure, and in several other poems over the course of her career she compounds a concluding confession of ignorance with what seems a flagrant arbitrariness of structure. Poems of apparently serious meditation or speculation end with an abrupt, tone-shifting statement that the poet cannot or will not conclude the meditation satisfactorily. We have already analyzed one such poem, "The duties of the wind" (1137), which peremptorily answers its own rhetorical question with "However, know not I." "One blessing had I than the rest" (756) similarly abandons its topic with "I speculate no more," and "I should have been too glad I see" (313) concludes plaintively with "Faith bleats to understand."

Slightly less abrupt but equally peculiar for its unprepared shift to the first-person singular and its redundant insistence on an already fully established uncertainty is the last stanza of "The frost was never seen."

> The Frost was never seen —
> If met, too rapid passed,
> Or in too unsubstantial Team —
> The Flowers notice first
>
> A Stranger hovering round
> A Symptom of alarm

In Villages remotely set
But search effaces him

Till some retrieveless Night
Our vigilance at waste
The Garden gets the only shot
That never could be traced.

Unproved is much we know—
Unknown the worst we fear—
Of Strangers is the Earth the Inn
Of Secrets is the Air—

To analyze perhaps
A Philip would prefer
But labor vaster than myself
I find it to infer.

(1202)

The poem belongs to a familiar lyric genre, meditation on the meaning of an image from nature. As such it would seem internally complete at the penultimate stanza. The mystery of frost is recounted through the first three stanzas, after which we get one of Dickinson's rare uses of an internal full stop. The punctuation apparently signals a shift to the broader, summary level of generality in the next stanza, in which the poet concludes from the failure to locate one stranger that earth and air are widely populated by spiritual agencies recognizable only by their effects. The poem seems finished at this point and indeed is arguably stronger in theme than the actual text. The undiluted theme of a four-stanza version would be that "search effaces him," in other words, that the elusiveness of frost and of similar strangers not only frustrates our efforts to track them down but is actually caused or enhanced by the search.

In a modest way the poem courts the sublime, for it confronts an alarming but also enticing otherness that obliges us to recognize both the presence of unseen forces and a blockage of our own powers. That the frost obscurely symbolizes some transnatural power is perhaps clear early on, and the signification is made certain by the reference to Philip. In John 14 Jesus replies to Philip's questioning by saying, "He that hath seen me hath seen the Father." The analogy is that the visible effects of the frost—ice crystals and blasted gardens—stand to the invisible stranger engendering them as the corporeal Jesus does to the transcendent Father.

All this makes the poem's admitted failure to locate the frost a peculiarly triumphant one. Although the poem says that our vigilance is to no avail and that we cannot trace, analyze, or infer from the effects any specific, comprehensible cause, the failure itself is converted into a higher form of knowing. The fear and perplexity we feel at our failure become the reliable signs that supervening powers attend our earthly existence.

The compensatory pattern here is a familiar manifestation of the romantic sublime. An empirical loss or bafflement is recuperated by the gain in transcendent understanding, the poem and more specifically the poet's imagination thus serving heroically to give us access to the heightened awareness. Note that it is the poet's subjective fear, rather than some property of the frost, which indicates transcendence. Elusiveness per se need not represent the sublime, but the uncanny feeling caused by elusiveness does certify the presence of higher powers.

On the other hand, the more aware we may be that the poem deploys a well-established literary strategy, the more awkward the final stanza seems. Even granting the value of the scriptural allusion in making a theophanic context more explicit, two things amplify the oddity of tacking on another stanza after such an impressively conclusive one. The first is that in a redundant and also backsliding fashion the failure gets reemphasized, as if the grand apprehension of the penultimate stanza had been forgotten or ignored. The second is that the sudden reference to the speaker as "I" dilutes the previously collective "we." Either the plural or the singular would be innocuous if maintained consistently, but changing from one to another calls attention to the pronouns. What had first been represented as general or even necessary failure is now perhaps restricted to the speaker. A mystery first represented as intrinsic to the frost is compromised by the possibility that the speaker suffers from local, circumstantial failings. At the very least, the speaker's apparently exemplary powers of interpretation and imagination are directly disparaged.

I do not want to claim that, contrary to this preliminary reading, the last stanza is unquestionably necessary or that the poem is incontrovertibly better for including it. However, the last stanza does add a characteristically Dickinsonian level to the poem. It bursts open an apparently determined finality, minimizes the achieved stature of the poet, and defers any ultimate conclusion to the mind of the reader. Without the last four lines the poet meditates in a relatively traditional fashion on an image that proves successfully revelatory. With the final stanza included the relation between alarming uncertainties and sublimely compensatory interpretations becomes far more problematic. The more conventional poem this one would be if truncated negotiates an easy and largely comforting passage from the moment of perplexity to the delaration that earth is an inn full of strangers. Compare here the similarly rapid and also comforting passage made by the clown in "A little madness." If not quite a power we can claim for our own, as nature proves to be for the clown, the frost's invisibility does turn out to be reassuring. The "worst we fear" would deliciously populate the air with secrets and happily redeem the "waste" our vigilance first appears to be.

Dickinson takes such reassurance seriously, but she does not quite endorse its sufficiency. Maybe, she suggests, the portentous inferences of the next-to-last stanza have confused the limitations of my finitude with a proof of the infinite. Something like sublime awe might then still be felt, but it would be indistinguishable from prospective weariness at a "labor vaster than myself."

Such labor differs significantly from the fruitless search for a visible agency which the collective "we" have already undertaken. The contrast depends ultimately on the double denotation of "frost." The word signifies both visible hoarfrost, the shot one finds in a chilly garden, and also the genuinely invisible condition precipitating hoarfrost. In folklore the latter is Jack Frost and the former his work. To announce that the frost was never seen (then punningly refer to its "too *unsubstantial* Team") is to select the second meaning, thereby nicely also preparing for the personification of that condition as a marauding stranger whom search effaces. It will then be true that no vigilance can avail and Dickinson's imagery need brook no embarrassing reminders, such as the fact that visible pellets of shot can in fact sometimes be traced to the guns that fired them or the men who aimed the guns.

In the final stanza the speaker's labor is called inference and Philip's questioning analysis. (The latter is pointedly contrary to Scripture, where only being *shown* the father will satisfy Philip.) Inferring from the evidence of hoarfrost that the dew point has fallen below 32 degrees Fahrenheit is an act of cognition readily available to nineteenth-century meteorology. One can indeed sometimes analyze visible effects for their invisible causes. Does the last stanza then abandon verisimilitude for the sake of a dubious epistemological pessimism? It would do just that if analysis and inference were merely additional names for the initial search. However, they refer more directly to two distinguishable cognitive acts following from and depending upon the failure of the search for frost.

Inferring and analyzing first describe kinds of mental labor by which one may reason from natural facts to supernatural explanations.

They resemble but are perhaps not quite identical to the cognitive process enacted in the penultimate stanza, which the last stanza accordingly invites us to query. The penultimate stanza's vaster, more dubious, but not discredited labor is one proper to a particular version of sublime cognition. Weiskel calls it the hermeneutic or reader's sublime.[8] I have already described this labor briefly. After an initial failure to understand some phenomenon has given rise to wonder and dread, those feelings (rather than the initial phenomenon) are taken as signs of a transcendent realm. In this case the poem moves from "unknown" and "unproved" to an unequivocal declaration about strangers and secrets. The final stanza, by comparing this move with the more reputable labors of inference and analysis, calls into question the reliability of the declaration. Like the equivocal "God be with the Clown" and the pointed "as if it were his own," in "A little madness," the maneuver acknowledges the experience of such apprehension without affirming the truth of it.

Analysis and inference also refer to a second mental activity. This one operates on the outcome of the hermeneutic sublime rather than reflecting on the process. The nearest, likeliest complement of "to analyze" in the final stanza is "Secrets" in the previous line. The genuinely vast (rather than, say, lofty, deep, or dubious) labor of inference here is occasioned not by the frost's singular appearance but by the multiplicity of strangers and secrets that its mystery has called forth. In other words, the further task faced by Philip and the speaker is comprehending the otherness produced by a now completed hermeneutic sublime.

Broached here is a different literary and cognitive pattern, which Weiskel distinguishes as the poet's sublime. In this pattern one does not encounter an object that eludes habitual forms of comprehension or disrupts normal orders of meaning, one confronts a superfluity of intense meaning that dwarfs, disorients, or intimidates the mind's native powers. The typical situation is of being faced by more than one can grasp, as when Wordsworth enters Bartholomew Fair in *The Prelude* or Whitman is overwhelmed by anguish in section 37 of *Song of Myself*. Because such challenges are inherently directed to one person's powers, Dickinson downshifts from "we" to "I," relocating the center of attention in a particular self's dismay rather than in an object all must find elusive. The failure is not in our habitual categories of understanding, which like language are always partly a collective capacity, but in the being of a singular self, whose authority or majesty the sublime leaves in the dust.

In completed versions of the poet's sublime the moment of traumatic devastation usually gives way to some reassertion of the self's powers, one that often marks an enlarging or a replenishing of them. Thus Whitman abruptly and insouciantly declares: "I troop forth replenish'd with supreme power, one of an average unending procession." Here, however, Dickinson goes no further than the traumatic phase, apparently because she invokes the poet's sublime only as a way of delimiting the reader's sublime. Rather than an entirely satisfactory conclusion, the poem thus suggests, the otherwise triumphantly chilly intimations in the penultimate stanza represent the onset of still another task. The multiplicity of strangers may be an advance on the initial mystery of frost, but it does not yet provide a power she will freely cherish.

Both referents of analysis and inference work to hinder closure. The first does so by questioning the validity of an otherwise triumphant apprehension, and the second by reformulating that apprehension as the opening of new endeavors. In neither case does the poet's understanding simply falter or fail to advance, but in neither case does it attain any stable end. If measured by the results of the search it initiates, the poem indeed represents a failure. The more appropriate measure, however, is the poem's capacity to engage us both fully and reflectively in the search and perhaps stimulate us to some decisive continuation. Nothing in the poem suggests that the endeavors cannot or should not be prolonged, and indeed it is organized to carry us from the local mystery of the frost, past a promising but incomplete resolution, and on to the apprehension of a grander, more challenging task. Rather than an exemplary response to this apprehension, the speaker's confession of personal weakness further ennobles the task and perhaps invites us to surpass her efforts.

Like a great many of Dickinson's poems, then, "The frost was never seen" places beyond the representational limits of the text a finality it otherwise eagerly solicits. By her usual standards, this is a remarkably calm poem, and its wary postponement of closure is correspondingly studied. More often, her poems are urgently proleptic. "A wife at daybreak I shall be" (642), "Our journey had advanced" (615,) and "My life had stood a loaded gun" (754) differ importantly from one another in subject, stance, and situation, for instance, but each depicts an impending crisis it stops abruptly short of resolving. And in each poem we are invited to decide the crisis for ourselves, an invitation whose force and openness can be measured by a glance at the diverse commentary each poem has attracted. Even poems that do not so sharply break off before the resolution they contemplate often curiously attenuate seemingly conclusive positions. For instance, so joyously declarative a poem as "There is a zone" compromises the timeless, seemingly absolute presence it affirms, by anticipating an oddly subsequent and superior moment of full internalization.

> There is a Zone whose even Years
> No Solstice interrupt—
> Whose Sun constructs perpetual Noon
> Whose perfect Seasons wait—
>
> Whose Summer set in Summer, till
> The Centuries of June
> And Centuries of August cease
> And Consciousness—is Noon.
>
> (1056)

Clearly modeled on a familiar hymn pattern in which paradisal realms are lovingly depicted, the poem unconditionally posits a perfect, timeless permanence in the opening lines. The poem's rhetoric trades impressively on depicting the zone in calendrical terms whose temporality is canceled or suspended. The cleverest line additionally puns on "set" in order to fuse temporal process (as in the setting of the sun) and spatial fixity (as in the setting of a jewel). Yet the zone's lasting and perfect present eerily precedes the time when consciousness is noon. Indeed, it must cease before the subsequent moment when consciousness will be what the sun now constructs.

Closer to "The frost was never seen" are the traumatic poems in which some previous belief or reliable form of understanding is suddenly shattered and the speaker thus left in anguish. Examples include some of Dickinson's best-known poems: "I heard a fly buzz when I died" (465), which ends with "I could not see to see," "I felt a funeral in my brain" (280), which concludes "And Finished knowing—then—" and others such as "It was not death for I stood up" (510), in which the moment of blockage persists throughout the poem. "I felt a cleaving in my mind" compactly depicts the cognitive rupture all these poems have in common, representing it as the decomposition of sequential thought.

> The thought behind, I strove to join
> Unto the thought before—
> But Sequence ravelled out of Sound
> Like Balls—upon a Floor.
>
> (937)

"The frost was never seen" gives a much fuller context than most such poems. For example, the rupture between normal understanding and the sublimely traumatized consciousness follows there from the deliberate venture of the search; it may even be caused by the search. In "I felt a cleaving," however, the break arises as an inexplicable affliction. More important, the poem is anecdotally complete; no further labor is named beyond the catastrophe.

Understood as self-contained representations, all such poems of mental breakdown are all amenable to a variety of local readings, and few have lacked for able explication. As a group of roughly similar poems, however, they pose some problems. Each seems motivated by the desire to express an occasion of great suffering and also by the need to gain some control over this suffering. Dickinson succeeds in bringing impressive analytical, even clinical resources to bear on articulating the precise stages of anguish. Yet as annotations of crisis endured, however vivid and acute these poems are, they seem to lead to little more than further annotations of further crisis. Why did Dickinson write so many such poems, and what part do they play in the business of her poetry? We have no more thorough answer than a vague, somewhat embarrassing psychobiographical explanation. She must have experienced such moments frequently or at least attached an enormous significance to them. Never far from such speculations is her own question in one of the poems: "Could it be Madness—this?" (410).

Yet whatever evidence these poems offer about Dickinson's mental stability and however much they should be taken as expressing the fate of a real or fictive soul, they also depict the kinds of intensities by which Dickinson elsewhere regularly undertakes the sublime. Each isolates the traumatic moment of rupture and discontinuity. Their business is thus at least in part the business of the Dickinson sublime. But the promise of that sublime, access to an unequivocally conclusive power, repeatedly lies beyond the space of the poem, its grandeur marked by the intensity of the crisis but its nature still fundamentally undetermined and the possibility of attaining it left to an unrepresented and hence open reponse to the crisis. The poems of mental breakdown do not exactly seesaw coolly on the hair of crisis, but they serve similar ends.

The most strongly proleptic force in Dickinson's otherwise conclusive poems of interior crisis comes from the gap between the poetic enunciation and the enunciated scene. Some of this is normal to romantic first-person lyric. In addition, the feature that most unites these poems and gives them a distinctive uncanniness is that they are all narrated in the past tense. Moreover, most of them are spoken from some ghostly space either explicitly after death or eerily beyond some comparably definitive boundary. In contrast to the apocalyptic "Here," which in "Crisis is a hair" is barely kept from presenting itself, "I felt a funeral in my brain" halts at what seems an equally apocalyptic "then," which the enunciation has nonetheless already passed beyond.

As an epitome of such prolepsis consider the following brief poem that borrows its climactic lines and images from one already quoted.

> The Dust behind I strove to join
> Unto the Disk before—
> But Sequence ravelled out of Sound
> Like Balls upon a floor—
>
> (992)

The poem is too brief and too dependent upon a private code to measure up to more celebrated examples, but it has the advantage of placing the breakdown in the context of an explicit if cryptic project, and of even more sharply contrasting the enunciated catastrophe from the proleptic scene of enunciation.

The code's abstractions can be unpacked with some confidence. Here and elsewhere "disk" seems to be Dickinson's shorthand for a perceptible image of transcendent wholeness: the face of God, the glory of the sun, the circle of totality. It would thus signify the supersensible content that "circumference" proposes to bind and claim. Like "asterisk," Dickinson's term for a minimally legible character, one that can be recognized as a sign but not further construed or determined, "disk" is a minimal image, a barely concrete percept otherwise lacking additional features or properties. The moment of rupture is thus depicted as a stage in the attempt to link empirically given materiality ("Dust," also a liturgical image of mortal corporeality) to a dimly descried image of transcendence. In other words, the moment is explicitly the consequence of a visionary quest, and it can further be identified as the moment of blockage in the romantic sublime, the negative moment that precedes any elevation or empowerment.

No such reactive phase gets depicted in the poem. Yet the text's formal and phonological orderliness sharply belies the catastrophic unraveling it does represent. Neither sequence nor sound unravels, and indeed the quatrain's iambic fours and threes are unusually regular. The poem's form thus presupposes a renewed capacity precisely counter to the immediate effects of the crisis. Moreover, the dire intensity of the crisis is apparently the necessary prelude to the strength of the recovery. As Dickinson says flatly in "I lived on dread,"

> To Those who Know
> The Stimulus there is
> In Danger—Other impetus
> Is numb—and Vitalless—
>
> (770)

Dread, anguish, and catastrophe thus get cultivated in Dickinson's poetry as the impetus to new or increased vitality.

Impetus is not attainment, however. Dust and disk remain unjoined. Such poems as "The dust behind" anticipate the reactive phase of the sublime, but they do not represent it or give it any determinate content. Several of the poems examined earlier portray a moment of breakthrough, as when the speaker takes on the power of wind or aurora. But even the most determinate of these moments, the clown's incorporation of nature's experiment, is bracketed with an "as if" rather than affirmed as a definite achievement. Though Dickinson persistently avows the feeling of elevation and empowerment provoked by confrontation with the sublime, she almost always stops short of giving it any positive content.[9] In this the Dickinson sublime differs both from that of Emerson, for whom it validates the high hopes entertained of man, and more strikingly from that of Wordsworth, for whom it authorizes the great visionary passages of *The Prelude.*

The Dickinson sublime only rarely provides access to any specific content, belief, or vision. To be sure, she will occasionally make declarations such as the following.

> Paradise is of the option.
> Whosoever will
> Own in Eden notwithstanding
> Adam and Repeal.
>
> (1069)

The text exists as verse on a worksheet draft and as something more like prose at the end of a letter to Higginson, in which she separately enclosed other texts unmistakably meant as poems. The resulting, possibly accidental borderline mode is an apt emblem for the simultaneously brazen and equivocal claim it makes. In light of Dickinson's disparagement of prose as something in which others try to shut up her freedom, the uncertainty about whether this text declares a great freedom in verse or in prose tells us something about her claims.

The notably formal diction of the text derives mainly from the language of law. Law presupposes a legitimate authority exceeding whatever is uniquely one's own, and of course it regulates claims of ownership through statutes ("Repeal"), contracts ("option"), and other public speech acts. Against such discursive authority the text's literally antinomian claims assert a radically private, inviolable Own-ness. To exercise the power of option it claims would be an act of pure will. However, this power has no language and thus no representable content other than what it can appropriate from the public realm, in defiance of the Judge. Its claims thus depend on isolating Own-ness from lawful ownership, but making such claims in the language of law contradicts them. All poetry must partly be shut up in prose, that is. Hence the possibly more apparent crux in the text's language, that to "Own in Eden" is both the goal of "option" and a precondition of exercising the option.

In other words, even Dickinson's boldest affirmations about embodying or possessing sublime power equivocate somewhat. Elsewhere, her poems more often acknowledge in relatively orthodox fashion that any permanent realization of paradisal hopes waits upon God. The result is the same with respect to any positive content in the attainment of the sublime, for Dickinson consistently represents immortality and heaven as unknowable.

> Adversity if it may be, or
> Wild Prosperity
> The Rumor's Gate was shut so tight
> Before my Mind was sown,
> Not even a Prognostic's Push
> Could make a Dent thereon —
> (1576, also 1584 and 1588)

Insisting always that "Experiment escorts us last" (1770), Dickinson rules out the possibility of any assured knowledge of the transcendental realm to which the experience of the sublime usually points.

In contrast then to the romantic quest aiming to unite knowledge and power, one that in Wordsworth, Hegel, Carlyle, or even Whitman takes on the form of a sustained *Bildungsgeschichte,* Dickinson's venture disassociates the public, objective realm of representable knowledge from the radically private nature of power. That such power exists in and of the self is Dickinson's single most unshakable conviction, and her second-firmest belief may be that is primarily activated by the confrontation with otherness. Beyond that, however, not only does the nature of such power elude investigation but Dickinson seems conscientiously to hold any further determination of it in abeyance.

The major unresolved question is whether death and the possibility of immortality will mark a transforming perfection of the self's power, a direct continuation of it, or some dimunution or termination. Dickinson's hope is clearly that "Expanse cannot be lost" (1584), a claim whose relation to the self's unique powers is made clear in another poem written the year before.

> Obtaining but our own Extent
> In whatsoever Realm—
> 'Twas Christ's own personal Expanse
> That bore him from the Tomb—
>
> (1543)

The claim, however, comprises the first lines of one of the poems containing the already quoted lines about rumor's gate being shut to the living. The question is more interestingly begged in another poem.

> Power is a familiar growth—
> Not distant—not to be—
> Beside us like a bland Abyss
> In every company—
> Escape it—there is but a chance—
> When consciousness and clay
> Lean forward for a final glance—
> Disprove that and you may—
>
> (1238)

In contrast to a heavenly property that is but "distant" and only at some later time "to be," power is said to be available as our own and here and now. More strikingly, the only possibility of escaping such power requires making certain of the afterlife. The poem turns on the pointedly ambiguous referent of "that" in the last line and consequently on the relation of power to two different but equally unavailable proofs. Read as an expression of piety, "that" would refer to immortality, in which the soul attains power freely and joyously. The only escape from such power would come if one could disprove the Christian heaven. Alternatively "that" can refer to the act of eagerly and anxiously leaning forward and thus to a force of human yearning fueled by the unknown. If one could disprove the anxiety we feel at the mystery of death, then one could escape the more exclusively human power that our unfulfilled need for certainty indicates. However, as Dickinson says in a number of ways and one a number of occasions, "Narcotics cannot still the Tooth / That nibbles at the soul." As the cardinal instance of the unknown that is the intellect's largest need, the uncertainty of the afterlife and of whether "This World is not Conclusion" (501) seems itself a source of power or at least the condition that makes room for it. The speculation is corroborated by the inaptitude for the sublime we noticed earlier in Dickinson's resolutely faithful martyrs. In contrast to their belief Dickinson frankly cherishes uncertainty.

> Sweet Skepticism of the Heart—
> That knows—and does not know—
> And tosses like a Fleet of Balm—
> Affronted by the snow—
> Invites and then retards the Truth
> Lest Certainty be sere
> Compared with the delicious throe
> Of transport thrilled with Fear—
>
> (1413)

The delicious throe here is both an anticipation of death, when certainty will doubtless come, and an experience of the distinctively Dickinson sublime, which works by inviting and then retarding knowledge.

Dickinson's separation of knowledge from power may be something of a mystification, if only because it conveniently preserves from inquiry the mystery of power's wildness. On the other hand, it avoids the rival mystification of faith in a divine or utopian realm. Consider here Weiskel's explanation of why Marxism is usually hostile or indifferent to the sublime.

Like all Marxist estheticians [Lucien] Goldmann is thinking in terms of *beauty*, for in the judgment of the beautiful a "final" correspondence between the ideal and the real is subjectively (symbolically) given. . . . The experience of the beautiful enables man to be momentarily and subjectively identified with humanity. . . . But what about the sublime? In Goldmann's esthetic, which is the standard idealist line, the sublime must simply drop out. For the judgment of the sublime comes into play precisely insofar as man cannot attain the totality; the intensity of the sublime experience is a direct function of the impossibility of realizing (in any way) the idea of humanity (or any supersensible idea).[10]

As it happens, identifying with the idea of humanity plays a small but essential role in Dickinson's poetry. By contrast to the notion of immortality, which is obviously more important to her thematically and about which she correspondingly makes no commitments, the idea of humanity is needed to define the playing field of Dickinson's ethics of dissemination. We have seen Dickinson's belief in human solidarity before, in her assertion that "every separate Urchin's Sum— / Is fashioned for his hand" (545). In other words, the mathematics learned "One by One" in the father's classroom proves to be an "Eternal Rule" belonging to all. Faith in such a rule assures Dickinson that, unlike lamps and individual poets, circumference will not go out, thereby guaranteeing the boundaries within which her rhetoric of stimulus can operate. Despite her ultimate faith in an eternal rule about what rightly belongs to all human beings, however, Dickinson never directly represents the rule. To do so would be to risk playing the role of the schoolteacher, a bullying, patriarchal master. Instead the urchins must ideally learn the rule one by one. Indeed, they must apparently learn it through sublime struggles with the Father in order to make it truly their own.

Dickinson's ethics here derive from a distinction Weiskel makes in the context of examining the politics of the sublime. Dickinson consistently avoids what he calls visionary poetry, which requires the representation of some transcendental reality, in favor of an unrelenting poetry of the sublime, which must eschew all such representation to remain itself. Distinguishing between the visionary outcome of the Simplon Pass episode in *The Prelude* and the properly sublime moment that precedes and sanctions it, Weiskel notes that "'greatness' for Wordsworth lies not in man's proper *Bestimmung*, infinitude, but in the 'strength / Of usurpation': this strength preserves and indeed depends upon the resistance of sense to its overcoming." As a result, "in both Kant and Wordsworth the sublime conducts us, as it were, to the frontier of the 'invisible world' but leaves us as soon as that world is consciously represented or given any positive content. The sublime remains negative, dialectical, a movement between two states, an indeterminate relation."[11]

Unlike Wordsworth, then, who moves on to a visionary affirmation, Dickinson lingers with the sublime and with a poetry that hovers between determinate states. Indeed, the theoretically necessary in-between quality of the sublime can be said to be literalized in the usual spatial and temporal siting of Dickinson's poems. Temporally, as we have observed before, the poems prolong the otherwise vague interval between a past traumatic phase and an anticipated reactive phase. Spatially, the notorious scenelessness of many of her poems exemplifies the interderminate relation between those two moments, which would themselves presumably occur in specific and specifiable localities.

Dickinson may even fear that a visionary resolution of the movement between two states will jeopardize her power. The infrequent visionary content in her poems plays much the same role as any more finite form of understanding. Indeed, visionary knowledge can hardly be distinguished from normal understanding, for it is always effectively given to us as a quotation from one of the "sages."

Rather than a conclusion of what the poet has been searching for all along or even a proleptic glimpse of such finality, the visionary apprehensions in Dickinson usually put in question the terms and value of the quest. They give pause to her endeavors and provoke a reconsideration of her commitments. The apprehension of strangers and secrets in "The frost was never seen" provides one example of this doubling back from an apparent finality. A more thorough instance can be found in the urgently apocalyptic "Behind me dips eternity."

> Behind Me—dips Eternity—
> Before Me—Immortality—
> Myself—the Term between—
> Death but the Drift of Eastern Gray,
> Dissolving into Dawn away,
> Before the West begin—
>
> 'Tis Kingdoms—afterward—they say—
> In perfect pauseless Monarchy—
> Whose Prince—is Son of None—
> Himself—His Dateless Dynasty—
> Himself—Himself diversify—
> In Duplicate divine—
>
> 'Tis Miracle before Me—then—
> 'Tis Miracle behind—between—
> A Crescent in the Sea—
> With Midnight to the North of Her—
> And Midnight to the South of Her—
> And Maelstrom—in the Sky—
>
> (721)

The poem is a masterpiece of sublime "Illocality," the nearness to tremendousness that never quite takes place nor has a place at any empirical site. Yet in focusing explicitly on such a nebulous topic as the movement between two states and the indeterminate relation between them, the poem is also one of the more carefully structured that Dickinson ever wrote, structurality being one of its major issues. Dickinson depicts placeless liminality by precisely noting her cartographic and corporeal orientation, a precision which then reveals profound disorientation.

Although she represents herself as launched on a voyage, one that already seems to be leaving death behind, the speaker advances in this poem only by redefining the threshold at which she remains halted. Between the strongly parallel first and third stanzas she reinterprets an initially dread but hopeful journey as a catastrophe from which no ready escape is at hand. The predawn scene of the first stanza locates her on the brink of immortality, which is virtually always a desirable goal in Dickinson and here also one that is pointedly contrasted to eternity. In the third stanza, however, time has either reversed or revealed itself as the darkness of midnight, and the placeless scene has proven to be inverted. A moon is in the water and a whirlpool in the sky. The reconfiguration from an east-west axis to a north-south one is perhaps also relevant. Not only does the former axis track the sun and thus imply progress and purpose, a position on its latitudinal grid is readily calculable. In the 1860s, however, no reliable way of ascertaining longitude had yet been discovered.

The reconfiguration replaces the contrast of immortality and eternity with indistinguishable miracles before and behind. The miracles are thus associated with identically absolute polar midnights, whereas immortality and eternity differ as does a still-darkened western futurity from an eastern horizon in which the first gray light of dawn has already appeared. Eternity can be a positive term in Dickinson's lexicon, as immortality always is, but it can also denote a bad infinity: a blank, appalling endlessness that is devoid of vitality. Digressing for a moment to examine Dickinson's notion of a bad infinity will help us understand why she first poses and then cancels a contrast between immortality and eternity in "Behind me dips eternity."

The baleful infinity Dickinson sometimes distinguishes as eternity always discloses vistas of monotonous endlessness.

> As if the Sea should part
> And show a further Sea—
> And that—a further—and the Three
> But a presumption be—
>
> Of Periods of Seas—
> Unvisited of Shores—
> Themselves the Verge of Seas to be—
> Eternity—is Those—
>
> (695)

Eternity, in other words, can be an infinite regress of desolate sameness. The poem perhaps backs away from the desolation at the last moment is designating eternity as "Those." The demonstrative pronoun phonically reaches for the safety of "Shores." By contrast the expected word, "These," would place eternity closer at hand and effectively capitulate to the insistent long *e* in "Seas" and all of the poem's other rhyme words.

A bad infinity is also kept at a distance in the following poem, which contrasts time and eternity according to the presence and absence of marks of discrimination.

> Forever—is composed of Nows—
> 'Tis not a different time—
> Except for Infiniteness—
> And Latitude of Home—
>
> From this—experienced Here—
> Remove the Dates—to These—
> Let Months dissolve in further Months—
> And Years—exhale in Years—
>
> Without Debate—or Pause—
> Or Celebrated Days—
> No different Our Years would be
> From Anno Dominies—
>
> (624)

The poem can be considered an expansion of the otherwise innocent second line, because rather than being a "different time" forever proves to be the disappearance of the differences marked on calendars. The undifferentiated sameness of forever culminates in the punning reference to "Anno Dominies," which sardonically links divine and clerical authority to the most celebrated year of all, that in which Christ was born. (The reference to clerical authority comes via the Scottish "dominie," a word which Dickinson uses straightforwardly elsewhere.) Forever belongs with the infiniteness of the deity, in other words, but it obliterates the most distinct, discrete, and hopeful moment in sacred history.

The bad infinity is the one that "Behind me dips eternity" initially appears to contrast to the more promising permanence of immortality. In the course of the poem, however, the invocation of visionary knowledge suspends the contrast and removes the poem's most hopeful prospect. In a colloquial sense, both the first and third stanzas are certainly visionary; both are fantastic and vividly imaginative. Strictly speaking, however, neither one represents the contents of a transcendental realm. The poem's properly visionary content is reserved for the intervening stanza, a representation of heaven that the poet carefully distinguishes ("they say") from anything for which she herself can or will vouch. The signal characteristic of the vision of "perfect pauseless Monarchy" is its excessively ordered unity. Perfection is the absence of pauses, dates, generation, or diversity of any kind. Differentiation is limited to divine duplication, but that apparently proliferates. Rather than a single heaven there are multiple kingdoms that seem to repeat one another identically, like the infinite regress of seas in "As if the sea should part." This multiplication of identical entites is best caught in Dickinson's language by the stammering repetition of "Himself" and perhaps also by the concentration of internal rhymes and alliterations (also prevalent in the other two stanzas).

The infinite repetitions in this vision of heaven do not strictly or unmistakably appall the speaker, but the vision does precipitate the altered scene of liminality in the third stanza. The newly interpreted liminal scene now stands in sharp contrast to the vision of heaven, for the former is recognized as a state of utter disorder. Yet it is not at all clear that such chaotic inversions of the natural world are any worse a fate than the repetitiously regimented order of heaven. Heaven's immortality proves no different from eternity, but the threshold state between them is equally a "miracle" of doubtful appeal.

What can one do in such a fix? Unlike Dickinson's many playful or flatly satirical contrasts between heaven and earth, this poem does not suppose that one can choose between the vision and the scene, and it also provides no grounds for expressing a preference. The dubious vision certainly does put in question the value of the initially somewhat hopeful or at least open-minded journey, but at the apparent cost of leaving no alternatives. As in "Our journey had advanced," an otherwise similar poem that stops short of this one's detailed proleptic vision, the initial "Fork in Being's Road" gives way to a one-way street.

> Retreat—was out of Hope—
> Behind—a Sealed Route—
> Eternity's White Flag—Before—
> And God—at every Gate—
>
> (615)

Although retreat is impossible and no opportunity for an alternative vision is at hand, the poem does subtly disengage from the scene in which the speaker is otherwise firmly placed. The disengagement works through small verbal discriminations, on the order of the contrast between the expected but avoided "these" and the uttered "those" in "As if the sea should part." To see the withdrawal, we must examine the speaker's relation to what she sees or apprehends and also the degree to which her selfhood is constituted by what she sees and where she is located. In the first stanza not only is she irrevocably embarked on the voyage, her selfhood is wholly and unprotestingly defined by her position at the threshold between eternity and immortality. Moreover, in the phrase naming the self ("Myself—the Term between"), "Term" refers equally to a linguistic and a positional designation.

The final stanza opens by reiterating the same situation but then begins to suggest a poetic self that would no longer be identical to the voice speaking in the poem. If, according to a strict parallelism, the "Crescent in the Sea" is a new designation of "Myself—the Term between," then the "me" has already begun an attenuation that culminates in the two references to itself as "Her." And if the crescent is on the one hand a sliver of moon (or its reflection) in the sea, hence a helpless frailty with no radiance of its own and as astronomically likely to be waning as waxing, the word "crescent" on the other hand etymologically also suggests a being that is growing or increasing on its own. Neither possibility is certain: "Her" could be the sea or also the crescent, which itself is not unchallengeably to be identified with "me." Moreover, the self's predicament has by the end of the poem hardly been salvaged. Yet both readings of crescent point to a reassertion of the self's powers and the exercise of an at least partial independence from the apocalyptic voyage. A precarious hesitation before the finality of this particular vision of immortality thus remains possible.

Dickinson's disengagement from the catastrophe manifests two features that help define the distinctiveness of her literary project. The first is that, unlike the potency arising from identificatory or emulative responses to the sublime, the power she exercises in disengaging is not simply a mirroring countersublime, one that would play by the same rules as the perfect pauseless monarchy. It is defined not only by its difference from the monarchical powers she apprehends but by a countering affirmation of difference or diversity as such. The second is that the power is entirely linguistic or discursive—that is to say, poetic—as distinct in this poem from her more helpless positionality.

The perfect pauseless monarchy is a kingdom of sameness, and as such it cannot be contested directly, for a struggle with and for its power would affirm the blankly infinite lifelessness central to such power. Likewise, submission would also perpetuate the bad infinity.

To the extent that confrontation with such sublime majesty requires either abjection or masterly appropriation, there is no escape. Even an unresolved, perpetual struggle would be no solution, as the following remarkable poem makes clear.

> Like Eyes that looked on Wastes—
> Incredulous of Ought
> But Blank—and steady Wilderness—
> Diversified by Night—
>
> Just Infinites of Nought
> As far as it could see—
> So looked the face I looked upon
> So looked itself—on Me—
>
> I offered it no Help—
> Because the Cause was Mine—
> The Misery a Compact
> As hopeless—as divine—
>
> Neither—would be absolved—
> Neither would be a Queen
> Without the Other—Therefore
> We perish—tho' We reign—
>
> (458)

Except for the reference to misery being as hopeless as divine, the poem has nothing directly to do with an apprehension of heaven as a drear infinity. It articulates instead a confrontation with otherness balked by its being mutual and reciprocal. The "face I looked upon" may be understood as a rival's. It may also be an aspect of the self seen literally in a double mirror and thus dissolving into an endless regress of reflecting images. Both alterities are common to the Dickinson sublime. Until now there has been no reason to single out sublime conflicts within the self, but it can be no surprise that her poetry frequently depicts otherness as some interior faculty or aspect of the self. "Me from myself to banish" (642) is a clear example. The result is the same as what looms in "Behind me dips eternity," although here the bad infinity is if anything more explicitly a lifeless void: "Wastes," "Blank—and steady Wilderness / Diversified by Night," and "Infinites of Nought." As in the Girardian mimesis of appropriation mentioned earlier, a mutual rivalry necessarily issues in the rivals becoming doubles of one another. The duplication arises out of the very intensity of each one's fury to triumph over and thus distinguish himself from the other. Neither can, for instance, be a queen without the other accepting the role of handmaiden.

As this poem may help make clear, "Behind me dips eternity" tells us as much about the operation of the Dickinson sublime as about how she envisions heaven. As more happily anticipated in other poems, immortality for Dickinson often perpetuates earthly variety and degree, this being a characterization she shares with and takes from the sentimental religiosity of her day.[12] Even those poems do not necessarily resolve the question of the deity as a sublime otherness; in fact, they tend to set the stage for Dickinson's satirical comparisons of earth's joys and heaven's decrees. In other words, the dangers of mastery arise whenever self and other vie for power. But that means dangers arise whenever the sublime does, for in Dickinson even natural objects are sometimes depicted as actively struggling against the self.

In "Behind me dips eternity," however, instead of either submitting to the "Prince" or competitively seeking to emulate and outdo his deadening power, Dickinson withdraws from the scene by dividing herself from her previously integral identity and by transforming the earlier definition of self as the term between eternity and immortality. Split between "Me" and "Her" and also perhaps distinct from the unnamed "I" that speaks the poem, her diversity avoids emulating the "Duplicate divine" of heaven and presumably encourages the reader to do so also. Proliferation is thus the mark of her crescency and of the Dickinson sublime in general, for it draws upon nonimitative, nonidentificatory resources wholly alien to the pauseless monarchy. The affirmation of difference is not a simple victory, of course, and its power is not necessarily a match for the Prince's or an answer to the plight of the speaker. But it does exemplify the activation of a power that is occasioned by the sublime yet that escapes the snares of identificatory appropriation.

7

Beautification and Consequence

Although Emily Dickinson was far keener on consequences than conclusions, both are needed to round off the views developed in this
study. Let me accordingly first summarize the claim that Dickinson
is a poet of the hesitant sublime. I will then suggest a little of what
follows from such a claim, particularly the implications for Dickinson's place in American literature.

A poetry of postponed or deferred sublimity leaves considerable
room for the finlessness some critics have objected to. Yet it does so
in a way that makes Dickinson less idiosyncratic a poet than many
have claimed. Furthermore, whatever disorder, uncertainty, and darkness may be found at the level of theme, such finlessness is under-
written by a poetics of admirable integrity and consistency.

The difference between these levels may be visible in the reading of "Behind me dips eternity" offered in the preceding chapter. One
might initially be tempted to say of the poem what Emily Dickinson
said about Alexander Smith's *Life-Drama:* it contains some wonderful figures, but are they coherent? Although the language exhibits remarkable powers of positing and troping, the poem ends in deliberate
confusion. The legerdemain of the pronouns throws up a thematic
smokescreen, for example, behind which the speaker ducks in order
to avoid an apparently certain fate.

Yet confusion has an unmistakable strategic function in this poem
and others as well. Indeed, Dickinson maintained with great consistency and not infrequent glee that "Experiment escorts us last—" (1770).
Not only does death mark an ontological and epistemological divide
putting every belief at risk, the same uncertainty attends all we do
or say in life. The maxim would itself justify a poetics of hesitation,
for it makes openness and even indecision a mark of wisdom. At face

value, furthermore, the maxim might rationalize incoherence or encourage the malign influence Dickinson's poetry has been said to represent in American literature.[1]

Can a thematics of uncertainty support major poetry? My argument all along has been that under the auspices of the romantic sublime it can and does. Regulating the uncertainties and hesitations of Dickinson's poetry is an unwavering commitment to the sublime. Moreover, Dickinson's is arguably a purer or more loyal version of the enterprise than most, because it most strenuously resists any conversion of the sublime's volatile power into the stable and pleasing forms of the beautiful.

Among the consequences of Dickinson's commitment, two stand out as indicating the distinctive unity of her work. The first is that above all else Dickinson values the intensity characterizing sublime experience. Second, both her poems and her understanding of literary experience are organized according to the three-phase structure of the romantic sublime. Few poems represent all three moments, but the entire structure is regularly adumbrated whenever she addresses one phase or another.

Dickinson's commitment to the romantic sublime means also that she subscribes to its basic ontological premises. Beneath her diverse experiments of belief, gesture, voice, and thematic positioning lie several constants. First, she imagines the world according to a phenomenological divide between self and other, or to be more precise, between subjectivity and alterity. Second, she experiences her own selfhood as inwardness and as will, offering thereby one additional voice to a nearly unanimous chorus of major American writers. Such inwardness can be threatened, but for Dickinson it always remains finally inviolate. It is not the creature of some other agency, in other words, and it never quite loses its phenomenological priority.

Third, the otherness standing against or confronting inwardness is usually met with as an alien subjectivity, not a neutral object. We have accordingly seen on numerous occasions that nature is suffused with the same intentionality and agency as man or God. Whether this animation is intrinsic or only symbolic (of God as nature's creator, for example), Dickinson does not say and only rarely stops to ask. Put another way, Dickinson attends to the character and properties of otherness less often and less vividly than to the shock of meeting it. Recall "Of bronze and blaze." The poem is far clearer and more emphatic about how she encounters the heavenly alterity than about what in this instance it happens to be. Although Dickinson is an impressively philosophical poet, her interest in phenomena has only partly to do with whether or how they can be known. The fourth constant is accordingly that for Dickinson epistemological issues take second place to ones having to do with authority or sovereignty. Questions of knowledge are raised with some frequency in Dickinson's poetry, but they usually derive from or serve as approaches to the more central questions of power and mastery.

Fifth and last, Dickinson sees the relatedness of subjectivity and alterity as principally agonistic. The intersubjective field that joins self and other is structured by a rivalrous struggle for domination. The struggle may even be, she sometimes fears, obligatory. If immortality is her flood subject, mastery is the watershed.

All five conditions or convictions belong within the mainstream of the romantic sublime. On the other hand, Dickinson's version departs from normal practice in continually seesawing coolly on the hair of crisis. The peculiarly hesitant sublime that results is designed to cherish power. Cultivating the force of the sublime while withholding sublimation fosters wildness, which Dickinson singles out in her note to Susan as the identifying attribute of power. The strategy thus helps maintain power's saving difference from the centralizing regimes of the kingdom and the glory.

Dickinson keeps sublimation at bay in at least two respects. First, her poems never represent an irrevocable passing over into the reactive phase. "None see God and live" (1247). Second, they do not rhetorically enact such passage or posit of their own discursive stature some achieved sublimity. Several voice a remarkably manic enthusiasm, to be sure, but overall Dickinson refrains from speaking with sublime authority or claiming any comparable form of mastery. Her poetry instead is given over to the unpredictability of dissemination.

To the extent that Dickinson sustains the rhetoric and the ethics of dissemination throughout her work, she is at once less private and more remote a poet than she is usually deemed. The poems are inherently public in their deliberate openness to completion by the reader. Whatever their origins in private experience, as poems they are precisely the letters to the world Dickinson said they were. Yet the always potentially Carlylean selfhood of the poet remains diffracted or dispersed amid the textual coils. The astounding intimacy the poems sometimes promise is always ultimately withheld in the withholding of sublimation. That in turn makes possible the competeless elation which Dickinson learned from Browning and which she proposes as the ideal consequence of dissemination.

How unusual is a poetics of sublime dissemination? The broader category of the romantic sublime is now frequently regarded as a characteristic mode of literary modernism, which American romanticism in general and Emily Dickinson in particular are often said to anticipate.[2] Enlisting Dickinson as a poet of the sublime thus says nothing new about her place in the pantheon. Within the elastic confines of sublime esthetics, however, what counts is how a writer adapts the mode. This in turn can largely be reduced to the question of how a writer textualizes the fundamentally phenomenological or ontological category of sublimity.

Such textualizing Ronald Paulson has somewhat sourly called the humanizing of the sublime and also its beautification. Invoking John Dennis' understanding of the sublime as man's encounter with God, Paulson suggests that any artistic representation ultimately travesties the force and solemnity of such a moment.[3] Indeed if the third phase of the sublime entails mimesis, then sublimation itself constitutes a betrayal of sublimity. Thematically, such an act of taming or trivializing would humanize the intrinsically nonhuman; esthetically, it would beautify the inherently formless. The romantic sublime in this view thus concludes with the revenge of the beautiful. Measured forms of various sorts reassert their prestige or even increase it by taking on the experiential alibi of the sublime.

Emerson offered the most influential beautification of Dickinson's time in his prophecy of the central man. As described a century later by Wallace Stevens, the figure is explicitly an avatar of the hero and also a Carlylean discloser of meaning.

> The philosophers' man alone still walks in dew,
> Still by the sea-side mutters milky lines
> Concerning an immaculate imagery.
> If you say on the hautboy man is not enough,
> Can never stand as god, is ever wrong
> In the end, however naked, tall, there is still
> The impossible possible philosophers' man,
> The man who has had the time to think enough,
> The central man, the human globe, responsive
> As a mirror with a voice, the man of glass,
> Who in a million diamonds sums us up.[4]

That Dickinson had reservations about such a figure can by now go without saying. Less obvious may be the central man's link to the romantic sublime, which Stevens indicates here by allusion to Walt Whitman pacing the shore at Paumanok and voicing the words of the mother. The primary source is "Out of the Cradle Endlessly Rocking," in other words. As noted earlier, the intensity of Whitman's dae monic encounters in that poem engenders and legitimizes his vocation as "chanter of pains and joys, united of here and hereafter." Successful sublimation can thus constitute the central man's authority; it can give him the power to sum us up or disclose our meaning. Furthermore, in claiming or wielding such power literarily the central man becomes a master of signs and meanings. He is thus a practitioner of symbolism in the sense that Charles Feidelson has definitively established it as a characteristically American literary mode.[5]

Sublimation generates mastery, in other words, primarily although not exclusively the cognitive and semiotic mastery of the symbolist. The result has often troubled American writers. In "The Poet" Emerson notes with some puzzlement that young men revere the man of genius because he is uncannily more themselves than they are. Whitman embraces such mastery more fully and flexibly in *Song of Myself*. Among other images for his role in relation to the audience, late in the poem Whitman settles happily for an analogy from sport.

> I am the teacher of athletes,
> He that by me spreads a wider breast than my own proves
>   the width of my own,
> He most honors my style who learns under it to destroy
>   the teacher.[6]

The sentiment is gracious and perhaps somewhat yielding, but the imagery presupposes a contest for supremacy, even a notion that democratic poetry must be a zero-sum game.

Dickinson balks at such mastery, even as she acknowledges the agonistic sublime from which it emerges. More specifically, she postpones beyond the representational space of the text any central man's appropriation of authority, just as she does any other determinate sublimation. Yet in saying this of Dickinson we may also notice that it is widely true of Emersonianism as well. If the central man is a beautification he is normally so only proleptically. The image is hardly more often realized or proclaimed in American literature than immortality, its exact structural equivalent in Dickinson's texts.

More is at stake here than degrees of literary ambition or vainglory. According to a dominant myth of American literary culture, the great writer is an isolato, who retreats from the uncaring or impure realm of public discourse in order to create a world elsewhere, the artistic sanctuary in which he is the lord of meaning and form. Dickinson herself is more easily assimilated to this myth than to most of the ones we tell in and of American literature. That is why Porter's and Blackmur's charges cannot be dismissed lightly. They deny—for the most part correctly, I would say—that Dickinson achieves the formal closure and the thematic coherence required for symbolist mastery.

One can of course doubt that symbolist mastery is the true measure of American literature. The formal and thematic openness licensed by the Dickinson sublime is arguably more typical of American romanticism than not. And although American writers have generally endorsed ideals of organic form and artistic unity, their most telling writings have been fragmentary, incomplete, or disjunctive.[7]

More important, Dickinson's reader-centered practices are perhaps also not so idiosyncratic. Identifying Dickinson's disseminative model of literary exchange may even allow us to see other writers in a different and clearer light. Consider Robert Frost and more specifically his "Mending Wall." Frost is on record as endorsing a moderate version of symbolist mastery. Poetry, he says in "The Figure a Poem Makes," is a "momentary stay against confusion."[8] He makes it clear elsewhere, in programmatic or doctrinal poems such as "West-Running Brook," that nature and even being itself present a cataract of confusion. Against this torrent art and imagination can briefly send up local countercurrents, reversing or annulling in the symbolic space of the poem an entropic flow that is otherwise irreversible. The charming modesty of Frost's claims should not disguise the presumption of mastery. Art may be brief and life long, but momentary victories over confusion are victories nonetheless.

"Mending Wall" lends itself to a triumphalist reading of the sort that Frost's critical prose celebrates; moreover, it specifically thematizes victory as the speaker's mastery over his less imaginative neighbor. The annual rite of repairing the wall nicely exemplifies the serious playfulness involved in art's battle against nature's disordering forces; indeed, Frost explicitly calls the labor a game as he prepares to mock his presumably practical neighbor about the inutility of the wall. More important, through such mockery he also openly glorifies his role in the art and play, bidding for mastery less through the deft balancing of stones than the juggling of words and ideas.

Frost's ascendancy derives directly from his greater command of language and meaning. Moreover, he explicitly seeks the neighbor's obedience to this command. As they work together with the wall between them, presumably both equal partners in the physical labor, Frost is impelled to "wonder / If I could put a notion in his head." Such an authoritative dictation of meaning would obviously defy any disseminative ethic. Furthermore, referring to the silent pun on his own name as the "something there is that does not love a wall," Frost insists that "I'd rather / He said it himself." Like a good Hegelian *Knecht*, the neighbor would thereby recognize and thus establish Frost's superiority.

However, the neighbor never does acknowledge Frost, and the example of Dickinson can help us see that his recalcitrance has its own inalienable force. Frost suggests that the neighbor is too stupid to appreciate elflike quickness of mind and tongue; indeed, in frustration Frost nearly calls the neighbor a troglodyte for so contentedly and solemnly mouthing words he has not himself even originated.

> He moves in darkness as it seems to me,
> Not of woods only and the shade of trees.
> He will not go behind his father's saying,
> And he likes having thought of it so well
> He says again, "Good fences make good neighbors."[9]

Yet the father's proverb has a truth to it which the poem and the activity of mending walls both confirm. The neighbor's recalcitrance and even his very dullness point up the limits of Frost's solitary mastery. Thus the pun that certifies Frost's greater cleverness also indicates the perversity of walling himself into his own art. As natural force *frost* spills the stones; as masterly artist *Frost* reorganizes them once more. But if triumphing over one's own name is in part a symbolically effective stay against the confusion of the stones, it also bespeaks an uncanny impotence. Either the pun is a mere verbalism (the more likely course), or the triumph is somehow also a self-wounding. Moreover, the name is itself a patronymic, so Frost in a sense also will not go behind his father's words. No one can ever fully go behind such words, the poem hints, for they always predate us and probably also predefine us. Nevertheless, one can certainly respond to them with a certain freedom and then disseminate the ensuing circumference once more out into the world.

The difference between Frost's saying and the neighbor's is thus finally not decisive; it counts for less than the difference between symbolist mastery and an elfin rhetoric that makes provocative mischief without commanding assent. Defending his reliance on traditional forms and meters, Frost is once famously said to have likened writing free verse to playing tennis without a net. "Mending Wall" would seem more apprehensive about playing without an opponent or a partner, at least in the context of Dickinson's countering of mastery with dissemination. Good fences make good neighbors because the wall-mending ritual gives the pair an excuse to reestablish neighborly communication. The two then mutually submit to an exchange neither fully controls. That is why Frost eagerly initiates the game each year and also why he does not triumphantly disclose or masterfully dictate its meaning, at least not to the neighbor.

Frost is not Dickinson, to be sure. For one thing his version of nonmastery regularly deploys more than one character and hence more than one voice, as in "Mending Wall," whereas Dickinson usually writes with monological equivocality. But the disseminatory practices of each share a marked family resemblance, one that can perhaps also be discerned in a wide range of American authors.

As Emily Dickinson understands and practices it, dissemination cannot be regarded as a beautification of the sublime. Certainly it limns no recuperative form, and it always refuses the private sublimations and the visionary or ideological determination of content that entail beautification. Yet dissemination is clearly a humanization, for it proposes that out of the sacred tremendousness of sublime experience specifically human and secular benefits can come. Such a rhetorical humanization of mastery is one whose significance Emily Dickinson can perhaps help us rediscover, both in American literature and in modernity more generally.

Notes
Index of Poems
Index

Notes

Chapter 1. A Poet without a Project?

1 I refer in each case to the most recent two-volume edition of these widely used college anthologies: *The Norton Anthology of American Literature*, 3d ed. (New York, 1989); *Anthology of American Literature*, 4th ed. (New York: Macmillan, 1989); and *The Harper American Literature* (New York, 1987).

2 *Harper American Literature*, 187.

3 Lawrence Lipking, *The Life of the Poet: Beginning and Ending Poetic Careers* (Chicago: Univ. of Chicago Press, 1981), xiii, 131.

4 Richard P. Blackmur, "Emily Dickinson: Notes on Prejudice and Fact," in *The Recognition of Emily Dickinson: Selected Criticism since 1890*, ed. Caesar R. Blake and Carlton F. Wells (Ann Arbor: Univ. of Michigan Press, 1964), 223.

5 *Selected Prose Works of Arthur Hugh Clough*, ed. Buckner B. Trawick (University: Univ. of Alabama Press, 1964), 165.

6 Dickinson's letters will be cited parenthetically by page number from *The Letters of Emily Dickinson*, ed. Thomas H. Johnson, 3 vols. (Cambridge: Harvard Univ. Press, 1958).

7 That Higginson also specifically understands the force of Dickinson's language as divergent from the coherence and purpose of her poems is clearer in the article he wrote for the *Christian Union* after her death. It is reprinted as "An Open Portfolio" in *Critical Essays on Emily Dickinson*, ed. Paul Ferlazzo (Boston: G. K. Hall, 1984), 20–26.

8 J. V. Cunningham, "Sorting Out: The Case of Dickinson," *Southern Review*, 5 (1969), 455.

9 David Porter, *Dickinson: The Modern Idiom* (Cambridge: Harvard Univ. Press, 1981), 140.

10 The presence of this questioning has sometimes been confused with a commitment to the values in question. A cardinal example of the confusion has been the interpretation of "This was a poet," which I discuss later in this chapter. Until 1976, when Nina Baym pointed out that the speaker clearly identifies herself with the poet's audience rather than with the poet, most readings of the poem took its figure of the poet as representing

Dickinson's own literary ideals and aspirations. See Baym's untitled review article in *JEGP,* 75 (1976), 301–7.

11 The phrases quoted are from Porter, *Modern Idiom,* 152, 181, 160. The litany of neglect is primarily developed in chapters 5–7.

12 Porter, *Modern Idiom,* 294, 296.

13 Dickinson's poems will be cited parenthetically by the numbers they are given in *The Poems of Emily Dickinson,* ed. Thomas H. Johnson, 3 vols. (Cambridge: Harvard Univ. Press, 1955). When a poem is referred to in the text as if the first line or some part of it were a title, idiosyncrasies of punctuation, capitalization, and spelling will generally not be retained.

14 Among the many studies that interpret Dickinson's poetry in terms of questing, see especially Inder Nath Kher, *The Landscape of Absence: Emily Dickinson's Poetry* (New Haven: Yale Univ. Press, 1974); Suzanne Juhasz, *The Undiscovered Continent: Emily Dickinson and the Space of the Mind* (Bloomington: Indiana Univ. Press, 1983); and Greg Johnson, *Emily Dickinson: Perception and the Poet's Quest* (University: Univ. of Alabama Press, 1985).

15 Thomas Carlyle, *On Heroes, Hero-Worship, and the Heroic in History* (New York: Wiley and Putnam, 1846), 94.

16 The poem has become something of a litmus test. Porter, stressing the poem's bleakness and its epistemological and teleological skepticism, regards it as one of Dickinson's many allegories of ignorance (*Modern Idiom,* 163–75). Christopher Benfrey specifically contests both Porter's reading and his general conclusions about Dickinson's mind, finding radical acceptance rather than radical skepticism. *Emily Dickinson and the Problem of Others,* (Amherst: Univ. of Massachussetts Press, 1984), 113–17.

17 Let me state explicitly here that I rely on an idealist or metaphysical notion of mastery in this study, primarily on the grounds that it explains and correlates the widest range of Dickinson's writings. The two main rivals to a Hegelian reading would be Harold Bloom's theory of the anxiety of influence and any feminism that considers mastery a derivative of patriarchy rather than the other way around. In the work of Juhasz, Homans, Barker, Pollak, Mossberg, and Diehl, both alternatives have been put to good use, so the necessity of choosing between them is not paramount. See, in addition to studies of Dickinson cited elsewhere, Wendy Barker, *Lunacy of Light: Emily Dickinson and the Experience of Metaphor* (Carbondale: Southern Illinois Univ. Press, 1987); Margaret Homans, *Women Writers and Poetic Identity: Dorothy Wordsworth, Emily Brontë, and Emily Dickinson* (Princeton: Princeton Univ. Press, 1980); Vivian Pollak, *Dickinson: The Anxiety of Gender* (Ithaca: Cornell Univ. Press, 1984); Barbara Clarke Mossberg, *Emily Dickinson: When a Writer Is a Daughter* (Bloomington: Indiana Univ. Press, 1982); and Joanne Feit Diehl, "Dickinson and Bloom: An Antithetical Reading of Romanticism," *Texas Studies in Language and Literature,* 23 (1981), 572–87.

One difficulty with patriarchy as an explanatory principle is that in Dickinson's poems mastery is not always gendered. When it is, it is not always gendered according to conventional masculine and feminine roles or their direct inversions. The difficulty with understanding Dickinson according to the anxiety of influence is nearly the opposite; as Diehl especially has argued and contrary to Bloom's theorizing, gender does make a difference in Dickinson's responses to other poets. Not all influences must be struggled with. If nothing else, an advantage here of the Hegelian model, which logically and historically underlies the model of struggle in the other two, is that it is far more general. G. W. F. Hegel, *The Phenomenology of Mind*, trans. J. B. Baillie (New York: Harper, 1967), especially 229–40.

Chapter 2. Style and Sensation

1 Except where noted, I follow Johnson's dating of the poems. It must be kept in mind that many of the dates are approximations and that they often represent the year a poem is believed to have been transcribed. Almost any poem thus could have been composed earlier than the earliest manuscript that has survived, the rare exceptions being those that make some unmistakable reference to datable, contemporary events.

2 Porter, *Modern Idiom*, 145–49.

3 Johnson transcribes it "silent West," without a capital *S*, but the facsimile of the manuscripts shows this to be a clearer, more emphatic capitalization than that of "Sails" in the following line. Compare the phrase "So Sailors say" from poem 30, which appears in the same fascicle. See R. W. Franklin, *The Manuscript Books of Emily Dickinson*, 2 vols. (Cambridge: Harvard Univ. Press, 1981), 15, 17.

4 Porter, *Modern Idiom*, 95–97.

5 The most recent and thorough study of Dickinson's style is Cristanne Miller's *Emily Dickinson: A Poet's Grammar* (Cambridge: Harvard Univ. Press, 1987). Other important studies include Brita Lindberg-Seyersted, *The Voice of the Poet: Aspects of Style in the Poetry of Emily Dickinson* (Cambridge: Harvard Univ. Press, 1968), and Roland Hagenbuchle, "Precision and Indeterminacy in the Poetry of Emily Dickinson," *ESQ* (1974), 33–56.

6 Miller, *A Poet's Grammar*, 20–112.

7 For an argument that the resulting avoidance of iambic pentameter constitutes a deliberate rejection of established norms, see A. R. C. Finch, "Dickinson and Patriarchal Meter: A Theory of Metrical Codes," *PMLA*, 102 (1987), 166–76.

8 Robert Weisbuch, *Emily Dickinson's Poetry* (Chicago: Univ. of Chicago Press, 1975).

9 Jay Leyda, *The Years and Hours of Emily Dickinson* (New Haven: Yale Univ. Press, 1960), 1:xxi.

10 Miller, *A Poet's Grammar*, 20.

11 The line to which she refers has not been identified, so far as I know, but it is presumably to be found in the poems enclosed with this letter ("Before I got my eye put out" and "I cannot dance upon my toes") or the

previous one ("Of tribulation these are they," "Your riches taught me poverty," "Some keep the Sabbath going to church," and "Success is counted sweetest"). Most of the letter seems to be a point-by-point response to Higginson's comments on the four poems sent the month before.

12 The remark to Higginson also confirms how fiercely she identified style as her exclusive property: "because it is mine" (*Letters*, 271). Subjects and themes, in contrast, evoked no such worries about originality. In 1879, for instance, she wrote a poem about the oriole at the specific suggestion of Helen Hunt Jackson.

13 Jay Hubbell, *Who Are the Major American Writers: A Study of the Changing Literary Canon* (Durham: Duke Univ. Press, 1972).

14 In addition to Finch and Miller, see Homans' *Women Writers and Poetic Identity* and the same author's "'Oh, Vision of Language!': Dickinson's Poems of Love and Death," in *Feminist Critics Read Emily Dickinson*, ed. Suzanne Juhasz (Bloomington: Indiana Univ. Press, 1983), 114–33. Homans' arguments are by far the most theoretically sophisticated investigations of Dickinson's language that exist, but this is also their drawback as accounts of how and why Dickinson's style appears. The arguments depend, that is, on a theory of language which derives largely from Lacanian psychoanalysis and which thus lacks historical rooting in Dickinson's times or her cultural inheritance.

15 One exception is the poem "I cannot dance upon my toes" (326), which can plausibly be read as a woman's vindication of her native artistic resources against male cultural hegemony.

16 On the influence of popular verse, see Barton Levi St. Armand, *Emily Dickinson and Her Culture: The Soul's Society* (Cambridge: Cambridge Univ. Press, 1984). For an overview and a bibliography of the many discussions about the relation of Emerson's and Dickinson's poetics, see Paul Ferlazzo, "Emily Dickinson," in *The Transcendentalists: A Review of Research and Criticism*, ed. Joel Myerson (New York: Modern Language Assn., 1984), 321–27.

17 For a valuable polemic on this topic, see William Spengemen, "American Writers and English Literature," *ELH*, 52 (1985), 209–38.

18 One possible reason for singling out Browning would be that she was a fellow poet. On the other hand, Dickinson never mentions Christina Rossetti, who was her exact contemporary and who might be expected to have recommended herself to Dickinson for her relatively spare style and her fusion of religious and erotic feeling. (The parallels between Dickinson and Rossetti have recently been recounted in Sharon Leder and Andrea Abbott's *The Language of Exclusion: The Poetry of Emily Dickinson and Christina Rossetti* [New York: Greenwood, 1987].) Cristanne Miller has proposed another reason for singling out Browning, that she wrote "on Record," that is, under her own name rather than a male pseudonym. *A Poet's Grammar*, 164.

19 Jerome Buckley, *The Victorian Temper* (New York: Vintage, 1964), 61–63.

20 Dickinson was enough of a Latin scholar that her reference to silver may

suggest that Browning was a silver age poet. The era concluded with Browning's death would then have only weakly furthered a first or golden age of English romanticism.

21 Arthur Henry Hallam, "On Some of the Characteristics of Modern Poetry," reprinted as "A. H. Hallam on *Poems, Chiefly Lyrical*" in *Tennyson: The Critical Heritage*, ed. John D. Jump (London: Routledge and Kegan Paul, 1967), 34–49.

22 Quoted by Cora Holden in the introduction to Elizabeth Barrett Browning, *Aurora Leigh and other Poems* (London: Woman's Press, 1978), 12.

23 Jack Capps also notes that Emily Dickinson owned an 1863 edition of the play. *Emily Dickinson's Reading* (Cambridge: Harvard Univ. Press, 1966), 91.

24 *The Works of Sir Henry Taylor*, Vol. 1 (London: Kegan Paul, Trench, 1883), v–viii.

25 "Author's Preface, 1853," *Poetical Works of Matthew Arnold*, ed. C. B. Tinker and H. F. Lowry (London: Oxford Univ. Press, 1950), xxiii–xxvi.

26 The memorial poems can be dated somewhat more confidently than others, partly because of Franklin's reconstruction of the fascicles. Poem 312, "Her 'last poems,'" appears in the earliest fascicle, number 26. Because the volume of Browning's poetry with that title did not appear until 1862 Dickinson's poem could not have been written earlier. "Ourselves were wed one summer" appears in the same fascicle, its considerably greater ambivalence about Browning possibly reflecting how recently she had died. Poems 593 and 363 appear in later fascicles, numbers 29 and 31 respectively, which seem to have been put together later that same year, 1862.

27 Ellen Moers, *Literary Women* (Garden City, N.J.: Doubleday, 1976), 56–57.

28 William Butler Yeats, "Arts and Ideas," in *Essays and Introductions* (New York: Collier, 1968), 347–49.

29 The facsimile of the torn fascicle sheet clearly shows commas ending both of the visible lines. The rest of the poem is known only from a transcript made by Mabel Loomis Todd, who apparently missed the second comma.

30 Jane Donahue Eberwein, *Dickinson: Strategies of Limitation* (Amherst: Univ. of Massachusetts Press, 1985), 76.

31 The major voice here is Paul de Man's. See his *Allegories of Reading* (New Haven: Yale Univ. Press, 1979), especially 3–19, and the late essays reprinted in *The Rhetoric of Romanticism* (New York: Columbia Univ. Press, 1984) and *The Resistance to Theory* (Minneapolis: Univ. of Minnesota Press, 1986).

32 Ralph Waldo Emerson, "The Poet," *Essays and Lectures* (New York: Library of America, 1983), 462.

33 Susan Howe, *My Emily Dickinson* (Berkeley: North Atlantic, 1985).

Chapter 3. Cherishing Power

1 Foucault's understanding of power and of the wider power/knowledge couple is itself elusive and perhaps variable. The core of his thinking about the topic is most conveniently available in a 1978 interview. Michel Fou-

cault, "On Power," *Politics Philosophy Culture: Interviews and Other Writings, 1977–1984* (New York: Routledge, 1988), 96–109.

2 Juhasz, *Undiscovered Continent,* 98.

3 For a summary of the earlier textual and exegetical scholarship and the definitive modern commentary, see Ernest Lohmeyer, *The Lord's Prayer,* trans. John Bowden (London: Collins, 1965). Lohmeyer notes, for instance, that *basileus,* kingdom, presupposes and comprehends the terms translated as power and glory, which are themselves nearly synonymous in both the Greek text and its most likely Hebrew sources.

4 Perhaps the starkest instances of such double operations occur on a larger scale than Dickinson ever employs. The quixotic novel, as practiced by Cervantes, Flaubert, and many others, depends upon promoting what it ostensibly contests: chivalry, romance, and so on. Such novels must in some way actively and positively glamorize the very objects and ideas whose false glamour they at the same time work to expose.

5 One of the charges Porter makes in *Dickinson: The Modern Idiom* is that Dickinson's poetry detaches itself from nonverbal realities by succumbing to a vaguely poststructuralist free play of language.

6 In addition to Lord Kames's *Elements of Criticism,* used at Amherst Academy and owned by Susan, Samuel Newman's *Practical System of Rhetoric,* also a textbook at Amherst Academy, Richard Whately's *Elements of Rhetoric,* which Edward Dickinson owned, and certain other compendia available to Emily Dickinson, her main source of information about criticism and esthetics would have been contemporary periodicals, especially *Harper's, Scribner's,* and the *Atlantic Monthly.* On Dickinson's reading in this and other areas see Jack Capps, *Emily Dickinson's Reading, 1836–1886* (Cambridge: Harvard Univ. Press, 1966), and Carlton Lowenberg, *Emily Dickinson's Textbooks* (Lafayette, Ca.: privately published, 1986).

7 Thomas Weiskel, *The Romantic Sublime: Studies in the Structure and Psychology of Transcendence* (Baltimore: Johns Hopkins Univ. Press, 1976). See also, in addition to works on the romantic sublime more specifically cited elsewhere, Marjorie Nicolson, *Mountain Gloom and Mountain Glory: The Development of the Aesthetics of the Infinite* (New York: Norton, 1959); Stuart Ende, *Keats and the Sublime* (New Haven: Yale Univ. Press, 1976); Jerome C. Christensen, "The Sublime and the Romance of the Other," *Diacritics,* 8 (1978), 10–23; Bryan Jay Wolf, *Romantic Re-Vision: Culture and Consciousness in Nineteenth-Century American Painting and Literature* (Chicago: Univ. of Chicago Press, 1982); Paul Fry, *The Reach of Criticism: Method and Perception in Literary Theory* (New Haven: Yale Univ. Press, 1983); and Louis W. Marvick, *Mallarmé and the Sublime* (Albany: SUNY Press, 1986).

8 *Longinus on the Sublime,* trans. W. Rhys Roberts (Cambridge: Cambridge Univ. Press, 1899), 55.

9 See Neil Hertz, "The Notion of Blockage in the Literature of the Sublime," *The End of the Line: Essays on Psychoanalysis and the Sublime* (New York: Columbia Univ. Press, 1985), 40–60.

10 Emerson, *Essays and Lectures*, 385.

11 Porter, *Modern Idiom*, 9–24, which largely reproduces a justly celebrated article from 1974.

12 As Helen Regueiro Elam points out, romantic poetry is obsessed with the traumatic phase: "The expectation [of attaining wholeness] is consistently thwarted in post-Enlightenment poetry, and the sublime appears instead as an experience of doubling and negativity—an abysmal experience of self-loss." "Dickinson and the Haunting of the Self," in *The American Sublime*, ed. Mary Arensberg (Albany: SUNY Press, 1986), 83.

13 Dickinson quotes the scriptural passage accurately in "A little east of Jordan" (59).

14 Mary Arensberg, Introduction, *The American Sublime* (Albany: SUNY Press, 1986), 3–4.

15 Weiskel, *Romantic Sublime*, 77. As Stuart Ende has argued, the sublime has historically been a compensatory genre. Like Milton writing *Paradise Lost* after his political hopes had been eclipsed and he had been overtaken by blindness, the one who seeks sublimity in one realm has usually suffered great losses in another.

Chapter 4. The Rhetoric of Stimulus

1 As Shira Wolosky has argued in correction of earlier beliefs that Dickinson simply ignored the war, both the fact of its unprecedented violence and the discourse of apocalyptic glory within which it was articulated at the time exert a distinct pressure on Dickinson's poems and letters. See *Emily Dickinson: A Voice of War* (New Haven: Yale Univ. Press, 1984).

2 On Dickinson and Husserl, see Hagenbuchle, "Precision and Indeterminacy," 34, 38. On the idea and experience of presence, see Sharon Cameron, *Lyric Time: Dickinson and the Limits of Genre* (Baltimore: Johns Hopkins Univ. Press, 1979), esp. 88–90, 142–45, and 185–200.

3 Hagenbuchle, "Precision and Indeterminacy."

4 Ibid., 36–37.

5 Emerson, *Nature*, in *Essays and Lectures*, 20.

6 E. Miller Budick argues that point at length in chapters 1, 2, 5, and 6 of *Emily Dickinson and the Life of Lanuage: A Study in Symbolic Poetry* (Baton Rouge; Louisiana State Univ. Press, 1985). However, she views Dickinson's critique of symbolism as a process of purifying it until "a true and reformed symbol can emerge" (43).

7 One of the fine ironies of modern intellectual history is that Saussure, the father of scientific linguistics, is also the century's main exhibit of the madness of anagram hunting and of the chaos it makes of language understood as a system.

8 On Dickinson's familiarity with flower symbolism see St. Armand, *Emily Dickinson and Her Culture*, 75, 327n.

9 The second stanza, which dwells on the vitality of the word as a power of breath, that is, of spirit, also at least partly takes the recipient's view.

The advent of the living Word can credibly be taken as the moment of inspired composition, of course, but the second stanza clearly refers to an already living word, not to one that is just being uttered or fleshed. We have already noticed Dickinson's doctrine about language and life, that words live in their dissemination rather than in their origination, and to the extent that this poem accords with that doctrine it must then refer to a scene of reading.

10 As Cristanne Miller notes, this text also exists in a version that changes every "him" to a "her." *A Poet's Grammar*, 6–18. My discussion of epistolary contexts owes much to hers.

11 Jerome Loving notes that, especially after about 1861, Dickinson increasingly sought out responses from the world outside her family but kept all such relations with other persons at a carefully controlled distance. *The Poet on the Second Story* (Cambridge: Cambridge Univ. Press, 1986).

12 Cameron, *Lyric Time*, especially chap. 4. See also Homans, "'Oh, Vision of Language!'"

13 Jacques Derrida, *Of Grammatology*, trans. Gayatri Spivak (Baltimore: Johns Hopkins Univ. Press, 1976), 44–73.

14 Part of Jerome Loving's argument is that about 1862 Dickinson began a "secret career," moving beyond the audience of family and friends she had had until that time. *Poet on the Second Story*, 59–62.

15 As always, one cannot confidently take the sentiments of a single poem to represent Dickinson's considered opinions. On the subject of art in relation to economic exchange, she expresses nearly the opposite opinion in poem 880:

> The Bird must sing to earn the Crumb
> What merit have the Tune
> No breakfast if it guaranty

16 Charles Anderson, *Emily Dickinson's Poetry: Stairway of Surprise* (New York: Holt, Rinehart, and Winston, 1960), esp. 3–29.

17 *The Lyman Letters*, ed. Richard B. Sewall (Amherst: Univ. of Massachusetts Press, 1965), 62.

Chapter 5. The Dickinson Sublime

1 Edgar Allan Poe, "The Poetic Principle," *Essays and Reviews* (New York: Library of America, 1984), 78.

2 Poems in which summer embodies a sublime affectivity include "A something in a summer's day" (122) and "The trees like tassels hit and swung" (606).

3 René Girard, *Violence and the Sacred*, trans. Patrick Gregory (Baltimore: Johns Hopkins Univ. Press, 1972), especially 143–92.

4 Harold Bloom, *The Anxiety of Influence* (New York: Oxford Univ. Press, 1973), 99–112. Later formulations of Bloom's thinking on sublimation and repression can be found scattered throughout *Poetry and Repression* (New

Haven: Yale Univ. Press, 1976) and *Agon: Towards a Theory of Revisionism* (New York: Oxford Univ. Press, 1982).

5 Immanuel Kant, *The Critique of Judgment*, trans. James C. Meredith (New York: Oxford Univ. Press, 1952), 90–204.

6 Both Neil Hertz and Thomas Weiskel also emphasize the importance of pre-oedipal fantasies. Hertz, *End of the Line*, 49–53, 230–33, and Weiskel, *Romantic Sublime*, 99–106.

7 See also Johnson's discussion of "ratio" in *Perception and the Poet's Quest*, 81–101.

8 By "her dictionary" I refer to the 1844 issue of the 1841 edition of Noah Webster's *An American Dictionary of the English Language*, published by J. S. Adams and C. Adams. Edward Dickinson owned a copy of this, though his daughter may also or at other times have used other editions. The *reor* etymology appears in all the editions of Webster from the 1840s and 1850s that I have been able to consult. On the vexed issue of what dictionary Emily Dickinson used, Carlton Lowenberg's discussion is the most temperate and cites the other important arguments. *Emily Dickinson's Textbooks*, 104–6.

9 On typology in Dickinson see Weisbuch, *Emily Dickinson's Poetry*.

10 See Samuel Monk, *The Sublime: A Study of Critical Theories in Eighteenth-Century England* (New York: Modern Language Assn., 1935).

Chapter 6. Skirting Mastery

1 Joanne Feit Diehl, "Woman Poets and the American Sublime," in *The American Sublime*, ed. Mary Arensberg (Albany: SUNY Press, 1986), 184.

2 The syntax of this second reading is corroborated by the draft: "And till Dominion set / I perish to behold / *Another* such a might" (my emphasis).

3 The poem also nicely exemplifies the equivocality of some of Dickinson's abject poems. Contrary to the otherwise remarkably confessional intimacy of this poem, it may well have been written to accompany the gift of a flower (as so many of her verses did), in which case the words would represent the speech of the flower and the poem would be an elaborately polite compliment to the recipient. This alternative reading of the pronouns makes an almost shocking difference in the poem's effect. The shock may in turn suggest that, however much the abject poems are taken as expressing the poet's state of mind, they need also to be understood as designating, in an eerily dispassionate manner, the structure of a particular kind of relation. Likewise, fierce or manic poems such as "Mine by the right of the white election" may primarily designate the same structure viewed from the other side.

4 The syntax of "You constituted time" allows for another reading, in which the two stanzas represent discrete stages of the same idolatrous moment. According to that reading, the fourth line refers not to God's jealous intervention but to what the speaker had taken "Eternity" and "Yourself" to be a revelation of, i.e., the lover's divinity.

5 The separated-lovers plot has widely been taken as autobiographical, most recently and in greatest detail by William H. Schurr in *The Marriage of Emily Dickinson* (Lexington: Univ. Press of Kentucky, 1983). By contrast Barton Levi St. Armand persuasively demonstrates that the plot was commonplace in American popular culture of the time. *Emily Dickinson and Her Culture,* 79–151.

6 The same temporal structure organizes most of Dickinson's typological poems; the poem is spoken from a point between the recollected earthly moment and its anticipated fulfillment or counterpart in the afterlife. Dickinson explicitly describes and endorses this structure in "The admirations and contemps of time" (906).

7 Robert Sherwood's arguments appear in *Circumference and Circumstance: Stages in the Mind and Art of Emily Dickinson* (New York: Columbia Univ. Press, 1968).

8 Weiskel, *Romantic Sublime,* 28–29.

9 From this practice arises what has often rightly been taken as the elusively allegorical quality of Dickinson's poems. Weisbuch, who confusingly calls it anti-allegory, describes the practice most succinctly and accurately. *Emily Dickinson's Poetry,* 40–58.

10 Weiskel, *Romantic Sublime,* 45. For a less dismissive examination of the sublime in modern political theory see Gary Shapiro, "From the Sublime to the Political: Some Historical Notes," *New Literary History,* 16 (Winter 1985), 213–35. At a more rarefied level it has been claimed that the sublime plays a crucial role in esthetic ideology, which in turn is said to have an important but obscure political efficacy. See Paul de Man, "Hegel on the Sublime," in *Displacements: Derrida and Beyond,* ed. Mark Krupnick (Bloomington: Indiana Univ. Press, 1983), 139–53, and Jacques Derrida, "Parergon," *The Truth in Painting* (Chicago: Univ. of Chicago Press, 1987), 15–147.

11 Weiskel, *Romantic Sublime,* 43.

12 St. Armand, *Emily Dickinson and Her Culture,* 117–51.

Chapter 7. Beautification and Consequence

1 Porter, *Modern Idiom,* 245–96.

2 For an examination of the "strain of modernist poetics and esthetics which exalts the sublime at the expense of the beautiful," see Gary Shapiro's "From the Sublime to the Political," 213. Also of interest in this regard are the other contributions to the Winter 1985 issue of *New Literary History,* which is devoted wholly to post-Weiskelian reconsiderations of the sublime and the beautiful.

3 Ronald Paulson, "Versions of a Human Sublime," *New Literary History,* 16 (1985), 427–37. A similar point is made by David Simpson in a similar situation: responding to the contributions to a postmodern symposium on the sublime. "Commentary: Updating the Sublime," *Studies in Romanticism,* 26 (1987), 245–58. In supposing that representation is incom-

patible with sublimity, especially sublime enthusiasm, both critics reproduce without naming Nietzsche's polarity of Dionysus and Apollo.

4 "Asides on the Oboe," *The Collected Poems of Wallace Stevens* (New York: Knopf, 1955), 250–51.

5 Charles Feidelson, *Symbolism and American Literature* (Chicago: Univ. of Chicago Press, 1953).

6 Walt Whitman, *Leaves of Grass*, ed. Sculley Bradley and Harold W. Blodgett (New York: Norton, 1973). The text is the deathbed edition of 1891–92.

7 "American writers in this period seem especially dissatisfied with their own creative output; James's sense of the 'deviations and differences' in his own work as in themselves the eccentric center for his own canon may be said to apply as well to the work of Emerson, Thoreau, Hawthorne, Melville, Whitman, and Twain." John Carlos Rowe, *Through the Custom-House: Nineteenth-Century American Fiction and Modern Theory* (Baltimore: Johns Hopkins Univ. Press, 1982), 24.

For one image of the discrepancy between ideal and practice notice the title of the Wallace Stevens poem in which he proclaims the central man's powers: "*Asides* on the Oboe." For another consider the revealingly mechanical titles of the books in which Emerson proclaims organic doctrine: *Essays: First Series* and *Essays: Second Series*.

8 *Robert Frost on Writing*, ed. Elaine Barry (New Brunswick, N.J.: Rutgers Univ. Press, 1973), 126.

9 From *The Poetry of Robert Frost*, ed. Edward Connery Lathen (New York: Holt, Rinehart, and Winston, 1969).

Index of Poems

Poems are listed alphabetically by first line. In parenthesis is the poem number. No attempt has been made to reproduce Dickinson's distinctive spelling, punctuation, and capitalization.

Index

Abbott, Andrea, 202n18
"Abt Vogler" (Robert Browning), 133
act of mind, poetry of the, 113–14, 142
affect, 10, 38–39, 43–46, 50, 90, 106, 116–17, 119–20, 167
affective understanding of poetry: Dickinson's, 10–11, 23, 46, 48–50, 97; Longinus's, 143–44; Poe's, 50; the Victorians', 38–39, 48
aftermath of experience, 73, 159. *See also* retrospective stance
Ajax, 150
Alastor (Shelley), 166
allegory, 60–61, 208n9
alterity. *See* other; self and other
American literature: anthologies of, 3–4; characteristic modes of, 127, 192–93, 195, 209n7; institutionalized study of, 32
American literary nationalism, 33–34, 127
Amherst Academy, 204n6
Anderson, Charles, 105, 206n16
anticipation, 159, 161, 174–87, 208n6
anti-Victorianism, 32
anxiety of influence, 127
Apollonian, 39, 209n3
Arensberg, Mary, 77, 126–27, 205n14
Arnold, Matthew, 36, 37, 39, 203n25
"Asides on the Oboe" (Stevens), 191
Augustine, St., 54
Aurora Leigh. See Browning, Elizabeth Barrett
author-centered criticism, 7–10, 192–93
authorship, Emily Dickinson on, 10–15
autonomy: of art, 9; of the self, 112–14, 128, 145–46, 151, 155

Barker, Wendy, 200n17
bathos, 153, 165–67
Baym, Nina, 199–200n10
beautification, 191–92, 195
beauty and the beautiful: esthetics of, 16–17, 118, 179, 191; Emily Dickinson on, 118–22
Beddoes, Thomas Lovell, 36
Benfrey, Christopher, 200n16
bird imagery, 87–89, 132–33, 135–39, 151–52
Blackmur, Richard P., 5–6, 9, 39, 56, 66, 193, 199n4
Blake, Caesar R., 199n4
Blake, William, 5, 80
blockage, moment of, 115–17, 125. *See also* traumatic phase of the sublime
Bloom, Harold, 76, 127–28, 130, 156, 200–201n17, 206–7n4
Bowles, Mr. and Mrs. Samuel, 24
Bowles, Samuel, 24–28, 41, 103
Brontë, Charlotte, 34, 35, 40
Brontë, Emily, 34–35
Browne, Sir Thomas, 37
Browning, Elizabeth Barrett: "A Vision of Poets," 45; *Aurora Leigh*, 35, 36, 37, 45; Emily Dickinson and, 34–37, 39–46, 49, 190, 203n26; *Last Poems*, 46, 203n26; memorial poems for, 39–45, 82; place in English poetry of, ix, 34, 35–37; poetry of, 35
Browning, Robert, 37, 40–42, 76, 114, 133
Buckley, Jerome, 202n19
Budick, E. Miller, 205n6
Burke, Edmund, 69, 119

heroism: act of, 81–82; and romantic solitude, 165; and the sublime, 122–27, 148; artistic, 9–10, 13–14, 16–17, 22, 76, 154

Hertz, Neil, 204n9, 207n6

hesitation, 82–84, 129–30, 141, 149, 154–87, 188, 190

Higginson, Thomas W., 6–7, 10, 27, 31, 35, 37, 40, 49, 60, 103–4, 106, 177, 199n7, 202n11,12

Holden, Cora, 203n22

Holland, Dr. and Mrs. Josiah, 10, 24, 103

Holmes, Oliver Wendell, 32

Homans, Margaret, 200n17, 202n14

Homer, 36, 150

Hopkins, Gerard Manley, 5

Howe, Susan, 51–52, 203n33

Hubbell, Jay, 202n13

humanity, 139–41, 179–80

Hunt, Leigh, 36

Husserl, Edmund, 89, 205n2

hymns and hymnology, 25, 30, 173

Hyperion, 114

identification, 130–33, 136–41, 145, 187

idolatry, 14, 18, 46, 150, 207n4

imagination, 10, 48, 131, 169

imitation. *See* mimesis

immortality, 39, 79, 121, 177–79, 182–85, 192

infinity, 25, 79, 135, 182–84

intention, 49–50, 81, 85–87, 89, 90, 98–99, 102, 112

intoxication, 58, 152–53

Isabella (Keats), 39

Jackson, Helen Hunt, 202n12

Jacob, 76

James, Henry, 209n7

John, Gospel of, 168, 170

Johnson, Greg, 164, 200n14, 207n7

Johnson, Samuel, 104

Johnson, Thomas, 25, 199n6, 201n1

Juhasz, Suzanne, 57, 164, 200n14, 204n2

Kafka, Franz, 5

Kant, Immanuel, 69–71, 89, 131, 139, 142, 144, 180, 207n5

Keats, John, 34, 35–37, 39, 45, 55, 56, 132, 144

Keble, John, 37

Kher, Inder Nath, 200n14

Kimball, Benjamin, 103

kingdom, 53, 59–61, 119, 190. *See also* monarch imagery

Kingsley, Charles, 37

knowledge, 16–17, 38, 166–69, 177–87. *See also* epistemology

Lacan, Jacques, 202n14

lake poets, 36

landscape, 15–18, 20, 71, 75–76, 138–39, 150

Last Poems. See Browning, Elizabeth Barrett

Leder, Sharon, 202n18

"Letter to a Young Contributor" (Higginson), 37

letters, Emily Dickinson on, 81, 97–100, 190, 206n9

Leyda, Jay, 31, 201n9

Life-Drama (Alexander Smith), 6, 188

Lindberg-Seyersted, Brita, 201n5

Lipking, Lawrence, 199n3

Lohmeyer, Ernest, 204n3

Lord, Judge Otis, 18

Lord's Prayer. *See* doxology

Longfellow, Henry Wadsworth, 32, 36

Longinus, 69, 70, 77, 114, 131, 143–44, 149, 156, 204n8

Loomis, Eben, 103

love poems, 20, 97–98, 156–61

lovers, plot of the separated, 159–61, 208n5

Loving, Jerome, 206n14

Lowell, James Russell, 32, 36

Lowenberg, Carlton, 204n6, 207n8

"Lycidas" (Milton), 24

Lyman, Joseph, 105–6

Manfred (Byron), 166

manic poems, 11, 153–54, 207n3

marriage poems, 162–64

Marwick, Louis, 204n7

Marxist esthetics, 179

master-slave relation, 15, 18–21, 84

mastery: 141, 149, 154–56, 157–59, 164, 190; authorial, 9, 12–15, 18–21, 54, 59–60, 84, 100–102, 128–29, 192–93, 200–201n17; and the sublime, 68, 75–76, 110, 117–18, 125–27, 149–50, 155–56

Index

uncertainty, 8, 16–17, 38–39, 51, 67, 164–84, 178, 188–89. *See also* coherence, problem of; epistemology

unknown, need of the, 38–39, 51, 177. *See also* knowledge

Vanderbilt, Gertrude, 103

Victorian literary debates, 34–39, 48–49

visionary poetry, 176, 179–84

volcano imagery, 19–20

Webster, Noah, 207*n8*

Weisbuch, Robert, 30–31, 164, 201*n8*, 207*n9*, 208*n9*

Weiskel, Thomas, 53, 68–70, 79–80, 171, 179–80, 204*n7*, 205*n15*, 207*n6*, 208*nn8*, *10,11,2*

Wells, Carlton F., 199*n4*

Whately, Richard, 204*n6*

Whitman, Walt, 4, 9, 129, 132, 148, 171–72, 177, 191–92, 209*nn6,7*

Wolf, Bryan Jay, 204*n7*

Wolosky, Shira, 205*n1*

women writers, Emily Dickinson's interest in, 32, 25, 202*n18*. *See also* Browning, Elizabeth Barrett

Wordsworth, William, 36, 69, 144, 171, 176, 177, 180. *See also* sublime, Wordsworthian

Yeats, William B., 48, 203*n28*

The Wisconsin Project on American Writers

A series edited by Frank Lentricchia

F. O. Matthiessen and the Politics of Criticism
William E. Cain

In Defense of Winters: The Poetry and Prose of Yvor Winters
Terry Comito

A Poetry of Presence: The Writing of William Carlos Williams
Bernard Duffey

Selves at Risk: Patterns of Quest in Contemporary American Letters
Ihab Hassan

Reading Faulkner
Wesley Morris with Barbara Alverson Morris

*Repression and Recovery: Modern American Poetry and the
Politics of Cultural Memory, 1910–1945*
Cary Nelson

Lionel Trilling: The Work of Liberation
Daniel T. O'Hara

*Visionary Compacts: American Renaissance Writings
in Cultural Context*
Donald E. Pease

"A White Heron" and the Question of Minor Literature
Louis A. Renza

The Theoretical Dimensions of Henry James
John Carlos Rowe

Chicano Narrative: The Dialectics of Difference
Ramón Saldívar

The Dickinson Sublime
Gary Lee Stonum

The American Evasion of Philosophy: A Genealogy of Pragmatism
Cornel West

Specifying: Black Women Writing the American Experience
Susan Willis